SAINSBURY'S
REGIONAL WINE GUIDES

FRENCH
WHITE
WINES

Oz Clarke

Published in the UK exclusively for
J Sainsbury plc, Stamford House, Stamford Street,
London SE1 9LL by Webster's Wine Guides,
Axe and Bottle Court, 70 Newcomen Street, London SE1 1YT

First published 1989

ISBN 1 870604 02 4

Typeset by Black Bear Press Limited, Cambridge, England
Colour separations by Spectrum Reproductions, Colchester, England
Printed and bound in Italy by Arnoldo Mondadori, Vicenza

Conceived, edited and designed by Webster's Wine Guides

CONTENTS

THE WHITE WINE REGIONS OF FRANCE

Y ou can make out a case of sorts for other countries excelling in the red wine stakes. Italy, Spain, Portugal, even Australia and the United States all have their devotees although, keen as I am on their wines, I would still back the French reds when the chips were down. But there just isn't any doubt at all that when it comes to endless variety, and superb quality in every sort of *white* – from wispy pale and dry to big, round and alcoholic, from tart and tangy to luscious, from reserved to exotic, from sparkling to still – France has far more to offer than any other wine-producing nation.

Above all, it is France's geographical position which allows such ascendancy. At 50 degrees of latitude north the vine struggles to ripen at all, but can produce light, yet intensely flavoured wines. At 40 degrees it is getting so torrid that delicacy in white wine is all but impossible, yet the superripeness makes it possible to create wonderfully rich, heady Muscats. Between these two extremes every kind of white wine *is* possible, and *is* created by the genius of French winemakers.

Champagne, in the far north, is cold and uninviting for most of the year, but in the folds of the Marne valley and on the neighbouring slopes near Reims and Épernay, the chalky soil produces the thin acid white which is the perfect base for sparkling wine. Champagne! The name says it all: the world's greatest fizz, and it only comes from this single area of France.

The eastern frontiers of France are a series of mountain ranges and all of these produce highly individual wines. The Vosges mountains in Alsace slope into the Rhine valley opposite Germany's Baden, and the east-facing vineyards, warm and dry long into the golden days of autumn, produce fabulously spicy, perfumed wines, unlike any other. In the Jura mountains further south they make strange, unforgettably flavoured wines and from Savoie – the old alpine kingdom on the Italian border – come whites which are sharp, tasty and mouthwateringly good.

Inland from these mountainous redoubts is the great swathe of land which used to make up the Duchy of Burgundy. It has been famous for wine and food since Roman times and it is still the birthplace for some of the most irresistible white wine flavours in the world. And the reason? It has the ideal growing conditions for the world's greatest white wine grape, the Chardonnay.

Chablis, between Dijon and Paris, is an ordinary little town, yet the name it has given to its stone-dry wine is as celebrated as any in France. South of Dijon runs the Côte d'Or, a lean sliver of vineyard slope encompassing more famous wine names than any other area. The Côte de Nuits is mainly red wine land, but the Côte de Beaune, with its great wine villages of Aloxe-Corton, Meursault, Puligny-Montrachet and Chassagne-Montrachet, produces the most sought-after, most memorable of white wines to be found anywhere.

The Côte Chalonnaise to the south doesn't have the famous names but it does have delicious wine; and the Mâconnais is one vast expanse of vineyard, mostly planted with Chardonnay grapes, making wines from the ghastly to the great, with each year demonstrating a few more greats and a few less of the gruesomes.

The Rhône valley is basically a paradise for red wine drinkers, but the little white produced can be very exciting. The Viognier grape is one of the world's rarest and it makes startlingly good wine at Condrieu. And Châteauneuf-du-Pape may be famous as a red, but the tiny amount of white from the same vineyard area is quite unlike any other with its tangy lime-and-liquorice flavours.

In the Loire valley the Sauvignon, Chenin and Muscadet grapes dominate the viticultural landscape, and produce some of France's most distinct wine styles. In the Upper Loire, Sauvignon creates world classics in the tangy, dry, white stakes with Sancerre and Pouilly-Blanc-Fumé. The ultra-dry, almost smoky green flavour has spawned imitators the world over, and made the Sauvignon Blanc a superstar. The Sauvignon also thrives in Touraine, the Loire's centre, but the Chenin now takes over, both at Vouvray, and further west in Anjou. Although difficult to ripen, Chenin can produce tip-top

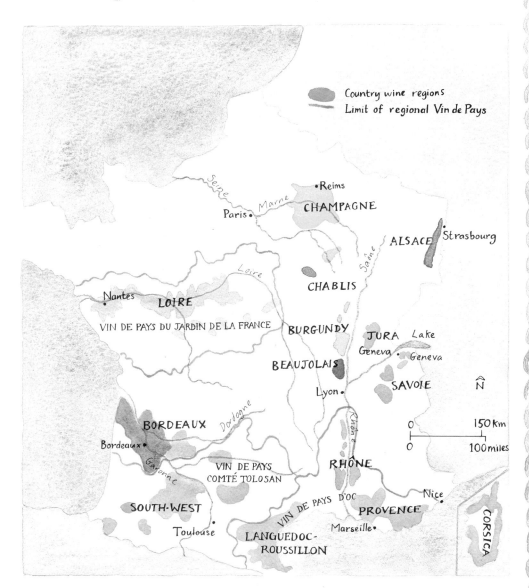

Country wine regions
Limit of regional Vin de Pays

•Reims
CHAMPAGNE
Paris•
Seine
Marne
ALSACE •Strasbourg
Saône
CHABLIS
Loire
Nantes•
LOIRE
VIN DE PAYS DU JARDIN DE LA FRANCE
BURGUNDY
JURA Lake
Geneva
Geneva•
BEAUJOLAIS
Lyon•
SAVOIE
Ñ
BORDEAUX
Dordogne
Bordeaux•
Garonne
VIN DE PAYS
COMTÉ TOLOSAN
RHÔNE
Rhône
0   150 km
0   100 miles
Nice•
SOUTH-WEST
VIN DE PAYS D'OC
PROVENCE
CORSICA
Toulouse•
Marseille•
LANGUEDOC-
ROUSSILLON

sparkling wines as well as dry, medium and sweet whites, all depending on the weather and the whim of the winemaker. And the Muscadet grape makes – Muscadet, the perfect easy-going light, soft, fresh dry white. If ever there was an all-purpose white, this has to be it.

It's possible to forget Bordeaux's white wine's achievements amid all the razzamatazz which greets the red wine vintage every year. But Bordeaux also makes *great* whites. Using the Sémillon and Sauvignon Blanc grapes, Entre-Deux-Mers is increasingly providing easy-to-drink, fruity but dry whites at a decent price, while Graves is set to

recover its position as one of the white wine world's classics. Sauternes and Barsac have been the sweet white wine classics for as long as sweet wine has been made. Rich, unctuous, oozing with sweetness, they set the standard for sweet wines worldwide.

These are the classic areas of France, but everywhere you look, there are lesser names producing wines of style and flavour, not famous yet, but who knows how soon the winds of fashion might scoop them up and plant them centre stage? Great or small, they've all provided me with so much pleasure, and I hope this book will help you enjoy some of the magic of France's white wines.

MAKING WHITE WINES

The creation of any wine begins in the vineyard, but the wine-making process proper starts with the annual grape harvest. When it comes to white wines, this involves choices: pick early and make a snappily fresh wine for quick-drinking, or pursue ripeness until the grapes fill with sugar or, in certain parts of Bordeaux and the Loire, leave the grapes to overripen and hope for an attack of the sweetness-intensifying noble rot.

When the grapes arrive at the winery, choices continue. Traditionally the bunches are immediately pressed and the juice run off into tanks or barrels to settle – any bits of gunge fall naturally to the bottom. Alternatively, crush the grapes lightly and leave the juice and pulp to steep together for between 12 and 48 hours *before* fermentation. This dramatically increases the fruit flavour in a young white wine.

Once the juice has cleared itself of solids, or been filtered or centrifuged to quicken the process (although filtration will invariably remove some potential flavour as well), it is pumped into a tank – generally of stainless steel, if the objective is to make a young fresh white. A suitable yeast culture will normally be added to ensure the fermentation is both efficient and controlled. (There are wild yeasts on the grape skins, but – especially when the grapes are pressed on arrival at the winery – they may not have a strong enough presence to ensure the ordered progression of fermentation.) If the sugar level of the grapes is low, addition of sugar is allowed in most areas except in the Rhône and far south. This happens at the onset of fermentation, as does any necessary and permitted adjustment of acidity – upwards for overripe southern grapes, and downwards for acidic northern ones.

The advantage of fermenting in a stainless steel tank is that this is the easiest material to keep sterile-clean, and the easiest in which to control temperature. Either through inserting heat-exchange coils into the tank, or by wrapping the tank in insulation jackets full of coolant, maintained temperatures of about 64–68°F (18–20°C) give a fruitier, fresher style of white. For the fullest white styles, the juice is fermented in a wooden barrel which imparts a rich, mellow flavour even to a dry wine. All the great white Burgundies and Pessac-Léognans use this method.

After the primary alcoholic fermentation, there is a second fermentation, called the malolactic in which green, appley, malic acid is turned into soft, creamy, lactic acid. Most classic whites undergo the malolactic, but as it reduces fresh-fruit character and tangy acidity, it is generally prevented – by filtration – in modern quick-drinking whites.

A wine for drinking young is generally stored in a stainless steel tank for a short time, racked off its lees, if necessary, fined, filtered to produce a star-bright, stable liquid and then bottled – often at only six months old – to maximize its fresh, fruity character. However, the best wines of Burgundy and Bordeaux, as well as some in Alsace, the Loire, the Rhône and the south, will usually have a period of maturation in 225–litre *barriques* (barrels). If the barrels are new or fairly new, they give a strong, buttery or spicy character to the wine. Older barrels merely soften and round out the wine due to the slight contact with oxygen – rather than impart any particular flavour. This maturation can take up to 18 months but, in general, six are quite long enough for a white wine; during this time the wine is racked at least once, with the exception of some Muscadets which are kept purposely on their lees to pick up flavour from the yeast deposits.

Finally, the bottling. The objective is to have a totally clean product, but intensity of filtering varies. Ideally, the very best wines are hardly filtered at all, since any filtration also removes a little of the flavour. Sterile conditions are crucial to avoid bacterial spoilage and a little sulphur dioxide is generally added as necessary anti-oxidant.

SWEET French wines achieve a measure of sweetness in three different ways. Firstly, there are lots of wines which are medium in style – fruity, vaguely sweet; these demand the retention of *some* sugar. So fermentation needs to be stopped while there is still some sugar left unconverted to alcohol. Traditionally, this was done by pumping in sulphur dioxide to kill the yeasts, but nowadays it is much more common to remove the yeasts either by chilling the wine right down or by centrifuging it, which eliminates all the solids, including yeasts, and leaves a stable wine, sweetness and all. It is also possible to add back a little sterilized grape juice after the wine has fermented to dryness.

Secondly, the wine can be fortified. The rich Muscats of the south use this method. The sugar-rich juice is partially fermented and then high-strength neutral spirit is added which raises the alcohol level to between 17 and 24 per cent. Yeasts cannot operate at more than about 15–16 per cent alcohol, so fermentation stops and the remaining sugar stays in the wine as sweetness.

However, the great sweet wines of Sauternes and the Loire valley do not rely on anything being added to the fermenting juice. The grapes are left on the vine well into the autumn when they are attacked by a horrid-looking fungus called 'noble rot' (*Botrytis cinerea*). This sucks out the water from already overripe grapes, concentrating the sugar. During the fermentation, the sugar is converted by yeasts into alcohol and the more sugar in the grape juice, the higher the alcoholic strength. But yeasts can only work in alcohol levels of up to about 15 per cent (and frequently the winemaker will add a little sulphur dioxide to stop fermentation at around 12–13 per cent). So when the yeasts stop, *all* the rest of that grape sugar remains in the wine as sweetness – full of potential lusciousness.

SPARKLING The secret to making sparkling wine is the fact that carbon dioxide is a very soluble gas. Carbon dioxide is given off during fermentation and if the fermenting wine is kept in a pressurized container – either a bottle or tank – the gas is absorbed by the wine – for as long as the pressure remains. That explains why as soon as you open a bottle of sparkling wine there is a whoosh of froth and bubbles as the pressure is released.

That sounds simple enough, but there is one major problem – the dead yeast cells form a deposit after they've finished fermenting out the sugar, leaving a nasty sludge in the container. So let's look at ways of getting the bubbles into the wine, then at how to get the sludge out.

The most basic method is simply to carbonate the wine by pumping gas into it. I've never had a decent example of 'carbonated' fizz yet, and a slug of sparkling lemonade would considerably improve most of them.

The tank method involves putting wine into a pressurized tank and then adding sugar and yeast to start a second fermentation. The carbon dioxide dissolves in the wine, which is then filtered and bottled under pressure. Most cheap fizz is made this way and the only reason so much of it tastes nasty is that the base wine was foul in the first place. The Italians make delicious Asti Spumante wine using the tank method, so it *can* be done.

▲ These noble-rot-affected grapes will be used to make Monbazillac, a sweet white wine from the Bergerac region in the south-west.

All the greatest sparklers are made by inducing a second fermentation in the actual bottle from which the wine will be served. This is called the Champagne method. The wine is initially fermented in tanks or barrels in the usual way. It is then bottled with the addition of sugar and yeast, corked up, and stored in a cool cellar for anything from a few months to several years. The second fermentation slowly takes place, creating carbon dioxide which is trapped in the wine. It also leaves a yeasty sludge which has such an attractive creamy taste that the best sparkling wines will spend a couple of years on their yeast, becoming softer and richer.

So the wine is sparkling – but what about the sludge? Well, in the tank method it is quite simply filtered out before the wine is bottled under pressure. The Champagne method calls for more care. Firstly, the sludge must be dislodged from the side of the bottle. So the bottles go through a process called *remuage*: they are gradually transferred from the horizontal to the vertical – but upside down – as well as being regularly turned and tapped, causing the deposit to collect on the cork. *Remuage* used to be done by hand – a tedious, time-consuming process – but is now generally mechanized.

The next stage – removing the sediment – is called *dégorgement*. The neck of the upturned bottle is frozen in brine. The bottle is then turned upright, the cork is whipped out, and a small pellet of frozen sludge is ejected. If done properly there is almost no loss of wine.

So now you top up the bottle with varying amounts of sugar and wine, depending on how sweet you want the final taste to be. You bang in a cork, secure it with wire, finish it off with foil – and there it is – a lovely inviting bottle of sparkling wine.

CLASSIFICATIONS

France has the most complex and yet the most workable system in the world for controlling the quality and authenticity of its wines. First and foremost it is based on the belief that the soil a vine grows in, and the type of grape variety employed, are crucial to the character and quality of the wine.

There are three levels of specific quality control for French wines above the basic *Vin de Table* – table wine – level. At the top is *Appellation d'Origine Contrôlée* (Controlled Appellation of Origin) usually abbreviated to AOC or AC. All the great classics and most other top wines belong in this group.

The second level is *Vin Délimité de Qualité Supérieure* (Delimited Wine of Superior Quality), usually abbreviated to VDQS. This is a kind of junior *appellation contrôlée*, and many wines – after a probationary period as VDQS – are promoted to AC. It is also used for the oddballs which don't quite match AC requirements but are nonetheless interesting.

Third is a relative newcomer – *Vin de Pays* (Country Wine, see page 116). This was created in 1968 (and finalized in 1973) to give a geographical identity and quality yardstick to wines which had previously been sold off for blending. Many good wines are appearing under the *vin de pays* label at very fair prices. It is a particularly useful category for adventurous winemakers because the regulations usually allow the use of good quality grape varieties which are alien to an area and thus debarred from its AC. Some of southern France's most exciting new wines come into this class.

There are seven major areas of control in the AC regulations, which are mirrored to a greater or lesser extent in both VDQS and *vin de pays*:

LAND The actual vineyard site is obviously at the top of the list. Its aspect to the sun, elevation, drainage – all these crucially influence the grape's ability to ripen. The composition of the soil also affects flavour and ripening.
GRAPE Different grape varieties ripen given more or less heat and on different sorts of soil. Some wines are traditionally made from one grape variety – like Chablis from the Chardonnay, some are made from several – like Sauternes' Sémillon and Sauvignon Blanc grapes. Over the centuries the best varieties for each area have evolved and only these are permitted so as to preserve each AC's individuality.
ALCOHOLIC DEGREE A minimum alcoholic degree is always specified as this reflects ripeness. Ripe grapes give better flavour – and their higher sugar content creates more alcoholic fermentation.
VINEYARD YIELD Overproduction dilutes flavour and character – this is as true for vines as it is for pears and plums. So a sensible maximum yield is fixed which is expressed in hectolitres of juice per hectare.
VINEYARD PRACTICE The number of vines per hectare and the way they are pruned can dramatically affect yield and therefore quality. So maximum density and pruning methods are decreed.
WINE-MAKING PRACTICE The things you can or can't do to the wine – like adding sugar to help fermentation, or removing acidity when the crop is unripe. Each area has its own particular rules.
TESTING AND TASTING The wines must pass a technical test for soundness – and a tasting panel for quality and 'typicality'. Every year a significant number of wines are refused the AC.

You may also see words like *grand cru, grand cru classé* or *premier cru* on the label. Sometimes, as in Alsace and Burgundy, this is part of the AC.

But in the Haut-Médoc in Bordeaux, it represents a historic judgement of excellence. In the 1855 Classification 60 red wines from the Haut-Médoc – and one from the Graves (now Pessac-Léognan) – were ranked in five tiers according to the prices they traditionally fetched on the Bordeaux market. Although there are some underachievers, there are at least as many overachievers, and, in general, the 1855 Classification is still a remarkably accurate guide to the best wines of the Haut-Médoc.

Sauternes was also classified in 1855, but Graves had to wait till 1953 for its reds and 1959 for its whites. Pomerol has no classification, though St-Émilion does – and it is revised every ten years to take account both of improving properties and of declining ones.

However, these Bordeaux classifications, though obviously influenced by the best vineyard sites, are actually judgements on the performance of a *wine* over the years – something which is often as much in the hands of the winemaker as inherent in the soil.

Alsace and Burgundy have a classification, enshrined in the AC, which delineates the actual site of the vineyards. So the potential for excellence is rewarded with either *grand cru* (the top in both areas) or *premier cru* (the second rank, so far only in Burgundy). Ideally this is preferable – although a bad grower can still make bad wine from a *grand cru*.

THE 1855 CLASSIFICATION OF SAUTERNES

▲ Château Olivier, like the other Classed Growths of the Graves region, is now in the Pessac-Léognan AC, but it will continue to be described as *cru classé de Graves*.

GREAT FIRST GROWTH (*GRAND PREMIER CRU*)	SECOND GROWTHS (*2ÈME CRUS*)
d'Yquem, *Sauternes*	d'Arche, *Sauternes*
	Broustet, *Barsac*
FIRST GROWTHS (*PREMIERS CRUS*)	Caillou, *Barsac*
Climens, *Barsac*	Doisy-Daëne, *Barsac*
Coutet, *Barsac*	Doisy-Dubroca, *Barsac*
Guiraud, *Sauternes*	Doisy-Vedrines, *Barsac*
Haut-Peyraguey, *Bommes*	Filhot, *Sauternes*
Lafaurie-Peyraguey, *Bommes*	Lamothe, *Sauternes*
Rabaud-Promis, *Bommes*	Lamothe-Guignard, *Sauternes*
Rayne-Vigneau, *Bommes*	de Myrat, *Barsac* (now extinct)
Rieussec, *Fargues*	Nairac, *Barsac*
Sigalas-Rabaud, *Bommes*	Romer-du-Hayot, *Fargues*
Suduiraut, *Preignac*	Suau, *Barsac*
la Tour-Blanche, *Bommes*	de Malle, *Preignac*

THE 1959 CLASSIFICATION OF WHITE GRAVES

CLASSED GROWTHS (*CRUS CLASSÉS*)	Haut-Brion, *Pessac*
Bouscaut, *Cadaujac*	la Tour-Martillac, *Martillac*
Carbonnieux, *Léognan*	Laville-Haut-Brion, *Talence*
Domaine de Chevalier, *Léognan*	Malartic-Lagravière, *Léognan*
Couhins, *Villenave d'Ornan*	Olivier, *Léognan*

A-Z OF WINES, GRAPES AND WINE REGIONS

The lists on the following pages cover all the *appellations contrôlées* for French white wines (including sparkling and sweet wines), plus a selection of the most important VDQS and *vins de pays*, so unless you are travelling in some *very* obscure corner of France you should find here a description of any wine you are likely to come across. There are also profiles of those Bordeaux châteaux and Champagne houses which I consider to be the best. Often these are the most famous names, but not always!. There are also entries on France's main white wine grapes and wine regions.

The wine entries all follow the same format, the left-hand column containing the name of the wine, the classification, the region and the main grape varieties (up to a maximum of four) in order of importance (see below for a sample explained in more detail). The right-hand column gives the wine description with, where appropriate, recommended producers and vintages.

If you cannot find the wine you want in the A-Z, it may mean that it is listed under a different name. In such cases consult the Index.

The most important white wine regions of France (Alsace, Chablis, Champagne, Bordeaux, Burgundy, Côte d'Or, Graves, Loire, Sauternes) are each accorded a whole spread with maps and a list of the main wines and grapes. All the items in these lists can be found in the A-Z. And there is a similar section on *vins de pays*.

The name of the wine; in this case it's a sweet white Barsac and these wines are generally known by the château name (ch. = château). Most wines are listed under the AC name.

BROUSTET, CH.

The classification; some wine regions (for example, Sauternes, Côte d'Or) have particular local systems of classification by which wines are able to style themselves *grand cru*, *premier cru* and so forth. Barsac forms part of the Sauternes classification of 1855. This property is a Second Growth.

Barsac, the *appellation contrôlée* (AC) name.

Barsac AC,   *2ème cru classé*

The region.

BORDEAUX

Sémillon, Sauvignon Blanc, Muscadelle

The grapes in order of importance up to a maximum of four named varieties.

The *appellation*. This wine is a Vin Délimité de Qualité Supérieure (VDQS).

BUGEY VDQS

SAVOIE

The region.

The grape varieties.

Jacquère, Chardonnay, Altesse

◄ An aerial view of Château Suduiraut in the Sauternes area of Bordeaux.

AJACCIO AC
CORSICA
Vermentino, Ugni Blanc

To be frank, the best white wines coming out of Corsica are not *appellation contrôlée* at all, but are the *vins de pays* being made by the more innovative co-operatives, and using such mainland classic grape varieties as Chardonnay. However, there is *one* exception – the Domaine Peraldi in Ajaccio. The wine is fermented cold in thoroughly modern surroundings and the best cuvées are aged briefly in oak to tremendous effect. However, the Ajaccio whites, based on a minimum of 80 per cent Vermentino, are normally only enjoyable when made from early-picked grapes and drunk as young as possible. Ajaccio has several estates which try to be more ambitious, but, with the exception of Peraldi, the effect is thick, oily and unrefreshing.

ALIGOTÉ

Aligoté plays the same role in the white Burgundy world as Gamay does in the red – everyone says how inferior it is, picks out its worst features at the expense of its good ones, and manages to forget, first, that it never claimed to be a world-beater, and second, that in one or two places it can make extremely nice wine. Its basic characteristic is a positively lemony tartness, even though the wine may be quite full, but it can also have a misleading ripe smell rather like buttermilk soap, with sometimes a whiff of pine, and of eucalyptus. It is a grape which gives immeasurably better wine from old vines, and many of the best wines in Burgundy come from vines 50 years old. In ripe years it can make a good stab at resembling a Chardonnay, especially if a little new oak is used for maturing it.

The best area for Aligoté is Bouzeron, the northernmost village in the Côte Chalonnaise where the wine has its own AC, but several Côte d'Or villages also produce fine Aligoté from old vines, though these are only allowed the Bourgogne Aligoté AC. Pernand-Vergelesses makes particularly good examples. Apart from in the Côte d'Or and the Côte Chalonnaise there is some Aligoté planted in the Hautes-Côtes, in the Mâconnais and around Chablis – not in the Chablis AC but in the nearby villages of St-Bris-le-Vineux and Chitry-le-Fort.

Virtually every single one of the 2500 acres (1000 hectares) of French Aligoté is in Burgundy, except for a few vines in the Rhône's Châtillon-en-Diois – where the wine is rather nutty and not half bad.

ALOXE-CORTON AC
CÔTE DE BEAUNE, BURGUNDY
Chardonnay

A hundred years ago you'd be more likely to find Aligoté than Chardonnay growing in the commune of Aloxe-Corton. In fact, the white grape which Charlemagne is supposed to have planted at the top of the great Corton slope, above the tiny village of Aloxe-Corton – to stop his wife nagging him about red wine staining his beard – was almost certainly Aligoté (which I'm sure kept his wife happy with its pale, neutral style). Chardonnay was introduced in the nineteenth century and now dominates the white parts of the vineyards, although Aligoté and Pinot Beurot – Alsace's Pinot Gris – can still be found making very rich wines. Almost all of the white wine of Aloxe-Corton is now sold as *grand cru* (both Corton and Corton-Charlemagne), and straight Aloxe-Corton Blanc is very rare. Senard makes one of the few examples. Annual production of white wine from the *grands crus* may total 150,000 bottles, but Aloxe-Corton Blanc seldom exceeds 3000 bottles a year. Best producers: Chanson, Drouhin, Leflaive, Jadot, Latour, Tollot-Beaut.

ALSACE EDELZWICKER
Alsace AC
ALSACE
Chasselas, Sylvaner, Pinot Blanc and others

This is the usual name for wine from a blend of several grapes in Alsace. In the mid-nineteenth century Edelzwicker was very highly regarded ('edel' means 'noble'), being a blend of the best grape varieties – Riesling, Gewürztraminer and Pinot Gris. It must have been a fascinating wine, but since Alsace gained its AC in 1962 the move has been towards *all* the best grape varieties being vinified separately. So now Edelzwicker is generally a blend of Chasselas,

Sylvaner and Pinot Blanc, beefed up with a splash or two of Gewürztraminer or Riesling. Abroad, the name Edelzwicker is giving way to wines labelled simply Alsace or Vin d'Alsace. Often non-vintage, and never expensive, they can be extremely good value. Best producers: Dopff & Irion, Éguisheim co-operative, Ehrhart, Schoech.

ALSACE GEWÜRZTRAMINER
Alsace AC
ALSACE
Gewürztraminer

One of our more respected wine authorities described Gewürztraminer to me as smelling 'like a French boudoir'. I forbore from asking how he came to be cognizant of such forbidden delights, but as he stumped off muttering 'cheap scent. . . Fifi. . . *hélas, hélas*', I found myself thinking that Fifi must have been quite a girl, and that Gewürztraminer's problem is that it is too absurdly easy to enjoy. Our rather Puritan attitude towards wine can't stand Gewürztraminer's willingness to be enjoyed with no pain and no recrimination. Well, I hope you don't suffer from this torture, because Gewürztraminer must be wallowed in to get the best out of it! Given that Alsace wines are renowned for their flowery spice, the 'Gewürz' (as it is often called) is the most *alsacien* of flavours because the smell is an explosion of roses, grapes, lychees, mangoes and peaches. The flavour is often thick with the richness of oriental fruit, and can also add honey, a tingling sensation like freshly ground pepper and the cool scent of Nivea Creme. Sometimes there's just not enough acidity to cope, but the effect is so luscious, I often don't mind. It's worth emphasizing that these wines are *dry* – even if they don't seem it! The flavours are most evident in late-picked wines from hot years, but even cheap Gewürztraminer from one of Alsace's many co-operatives will be flowery, rather exotic and unmistakable, even if in miniature. The wines can age for several years, but are delicious within a year. Best years: 1985, '83, '81, '79. Best producers: Becker, Beyer, Cattin, Faller, Ginglinger, Hugel, Kientzler, Kuentz-Bas, Rolly Gassmann, Schleret, Schlumberger, Schoech, Trimbach, Zind-Humbrecht.

ALSACE GRAND CRU AC
ALSACE
Riesling, Gewürztraminer or Muscat

This *appellation* is an attempt, beginning with the 1985 vintage, to classify the best vineyards in Alsace. It is fiercely resisted by the merchant *négociants*, who argue that a blend of several vineyards always makes the best wines, but this just isn't so. It is the same now-discredited argument used for generations by the merchants of Burgundy who, anxious to keep tight control over their profitable share of the market, would deny a grower the right to say, 'This slope has always been special and I can show you why by offering you my version of its wine – unblended and undiluted'. Certainly, *négociant* blends may suffer, but in their place we will experience the fascinating variety of Alsace wine.

At the moment 48 vineyards are classified, mostly in the southern Haut-Rhin section, though there are other sites under consideration. Only Gewürztraminer, Riesling, Pinot Gris and Muscat grapes qualify for *grand cru* status and the grape varieties must be unblended. Since several great Alsace wines are blends and since, for instance, the non-designated Sylvaner is capable of very fine wine but cannot use the term *grand cru* even if it comes from a *grand cru* quality vineyard, the arguments are not over yet – and we may see a *premier cru* second tier of vineyards just as in Burgundy. Things do look hopeful, however, especially since the minimum natural alcohol level for *grand cru* is much higher (10 degrees for Muscat and Riesling, 11 degrees for Gewürztraminer and Pinot Gris) and the yield allowed is 70 hectolitres per hectare – as against 100 hectolitres for AC wine – which can dramatically improve quality. But the merchant and co-operative blends will still dominate the market for years to come. Thankfully, Alsace is full of drinkable and affordable wine and eventually there should be a happy co-existence between blends and single-vineyard wines. Best sites: Brand, Eichberg, Frankstein, Geisberg, Goldert, Hengst, Kitterlé, Mandelberg, Rangen, Rosacker, Schlossberg, Schoenenbourg, Sporen, Zinnkoepflé, Zotzenberg.

ALSACE

Some of the most deliciously individual wines in France come from Alsace yet, at first sight (rather than taste), you might well mistake them for German. Alsace bottles are tall, slender and green - just like the bottles from the Mosel region of Germany. The name of the producer is almost certain to be Germanic, and in many cases the name of the wine – Riesling, Sylvaner, Gewürztraminer – will continue the German charade.

Despite the German influence – and years of German rule – Alsace is proudly, independently French. Many of the grapes used may be the same but Alsace winemakers create completely different flavours from them – drier, yet riper, fuller of alcohol, yet quite disturbingly scented.

The key to producing wine of this aromatic, heady character so far north lies in the Vosges mountains –

rising high to the west, they draw off the moisture from the damp westerly winds and leave an east-facing slope of vines to enjoy the second driest climate in all of France. As the rest of the north braces itself against autumn storms, warm, sun-soaked days still linger over Alsace vineyards bringing the grapes to full ripeness year after year.

Although it is now commonplace for us to see bottles labelled according to grape type from all over the world, Alsace was the first area of France to enshrine this practice in its own wine laws. A single AC was created – Alsace AC – and apart from the blends, called Edelzwicker, all table wines are called by the grape name. Usually this is the only description of wine type on the label but the best vineyards have now been designated *grand cru*. Occasionally the grapes are left to overripen in the hottest years and make intense, late-picked wines of positively monumental flavour. And for the grapes which don't ripen, there is a thriving sparkling wine industry making Crémant d'Alsace.

MAIN WINES
Alsace Edelzwicker
Alsace Gewürztraminer
Alsace Grand Cru
Alsace Muscat
Alsace Pinot Blanc
Alsace Pinot Gris (Tokay)
Alsace Riesling
Alsace Sylvaner
Alsace Vendange Tardive
Alsace Sélection de Grains Nobles
Crémant d'Alsace

MAIN GRAPES
Chasselas
Gewürztraminer
Muscat
Pinot Blanc
Pinot Gris
Riesling
Sylvaner

▼Typically, vines cluster close round the village of Itterswiller in northern Alsace.

VOSGES

Strasbourg

Bergbieten•

Bruche

•Obernai

Barr•
•Andlau

Giessen   Sélestat•

Bergheim•
Ribeauvillé•
Hunawihr•
Riquewihr•   •Beblenheim
            •Bennwihr
Kaysersberg• •Kientzheim
Katzenthal •Ingersheim
Turckheim•   •Colmar•
Wintzenheim•

•Eguisheim
•Voegtlinshofen

Fecht   Munster •Gueberschwihr

•Bergholtz
Guebwiller•

Ill

Thann•   Mulhouse•

N

Vineyard areas

0   10 km
0   5 miles

15

ALSACE MUSCAT
Alsace AC
ALSACE
Muscat Ottonel, Muscat Blanc à
Petits Grains

This can be sheer heaven. If it continually amazes me how few wines have any taste of grape at all, it also amazes me how Alsace Muscat can seem like the purest essence of fresh grape – and yet be totally dry. It is a magical combination – the heady, rather spicy, hothouse smell of a vine in late summer, the feel in your mouth delicate and light, yet the gentle fruit as perfumed and refreshing as the juice crunched from a fistful of ripe muscatels. There is a little green acidity and a slight muskiness like fresh coffee, which adds to the pleasure. The Muscat à Petits Grains variety (the same Muscat found widely in southern France) used to predominate in Alsace, but its susceptibility to rot meant that producers turned increasingly to Muscat Ottonel. Between the two varieties they cover less than four per cent of the vineyard area in Alsace, because they are prone to disease and often only ripen well one year in two. If you see one – snap it up, chill it for an hour, and serve it either as the perfect aperitif or after dinner – the Muscat flavour in a light, dry wine is far more reviving than a bumper of port or brandy! And drink it young to catch that perfume. Best years: 1987, '86, '85. Best producers: Albrecht, Becker, Cattin, Dirler, Dopff & Irion, Ginglinger, Klipfel, Kreydenweiss, Kuehn, Kuentz-Bas, Zind-Humbrecht.

ALSACE PINOT BLANC
Alsace AC
ALSACE
Pinot Blanc, Auxerrois Blanc

For such a simple wine Pinot Blanc can have an awfully complicated make-up. Usually it consists of a blend of Pinot Blanc and the similar, but unrelated Auxerrois and is a soft dry white, slightly appley, slightly creamy – perfect wine-bar white with or without food. However, Pinot Blanc wine can also be made from *three* other grape varieties: white wine from the red Pinot Noir is called Pinot Blanc and can be delicious, full and creamy; Pinot Gris wine, too, can be called Pinot Blanc; and there is a little Chardonnay *also* called Pinot Blanc! The wines all share the same fresh, soft easy-drinking style, excellent young, but capable of ageing well. The term Klevner or Clevner, the Alsace name for Pinot Blanc, seldom appears on a label – if it does, it generally applies to a Pinot Blanc-Auxerrois blend. Best producers: Bechtold, Cattin, Gisselbrecht, Hugel, Jossmeyer, Kreydenweiss, Schleret, Sipp, Weinbach, Willm.

ALSACE PINOT GRIS
Alsace AC
ALSACE
Pinot Gris (Tokay d'Alsace)

Well, *I* love Pinot Gris. If that sounds a bit defensive, it's because so many people criticize this delicious wine as being flat and mawkish. I mean, what is mawkish supposed to imply? As far as I'm concerned, top-line Pinot Gris wines are frequently the greatest wines in Alsace and even the basic ones have a lovely lick of honey to soften and deepen their attractive peachy fruit. But first things first – that name, Tokay.

The legend is that an Alsatian soldier, de Schwendi, attacked the Hungarian fortress of Tokaj in 1565, captured 4000 vats of their Tokay wine, and liked it so much that he sent his servant to fetch some Tokay vine cuttings to plant in Alsace. Which· he did. Or he thought he did. Tokay is made from Furmint grapes. He brought back Pinot Gris. Which was already well-known in much more hospitable Burgundy. So perhaps he skived off there and only pretended to go to Hungary. Or. . . Or does it really matter? Wine legends are all the same, all suffering from that carefree unconcern with facts which is quite natural among story-tellers after a few glasses. Anyway, the name Tokay stuck – though the EEC tried to ban it in 1980, at the Hungarians' insistence – what cheek! And Tokay is always made from Pinot Gris, although nowadays the label usually says Tokay Pinot Gris.

It is golden wine, often seeming too dark in colour for its own good. Acidity *is* low, but that doesn't stop the wine ageing brilliantly, blending a treacly, honey and raisin richness with flavours like the sweet essence from the skins of peaches and apricots, and a smokiness like lightly burnt toast. And, as I keep saying in Alsace, this is a *dry* wine! The Vendange Tardive styles of Pinot Gris are particularly exciting but even at the basic level you should catch a glimpse of these flavours. The wine can be drunk straight away or matured for some years. It is the most suitable Alsace wine for the rich cream, game and *foie gras* dishes which indulgently clutter the local cuisine. About five per cent of the vineyards are planted with Pinot Gris. Best years: 1985, '83, '81, '78, '76. Best producers: Albrecht, Boxler, Cattin, Gisselbrecht, Hugel, Adam Josmeyer, Kreydenweiss, Kuentz-Bas, Muré, Ostertag, Schaller, Schleret, Schlumberger, Zind-Humbrecht; co-operatives at Éguisheim, Guebershwihr and Pfaffenheim.

ALSACE RIESLING
Alsace AC
ALSACE
Riesling

Wherever Riesling is planted people immediately call it the 'king of wines'. Alsace included. And if here king means the least approachable, the haughtiest, the slowest to unwind and the most reserved in manner, then I suppose I'll buy that – just! Certainly Riesling does have a rather proud, austere style in contrast with the perfumed headiness of Gewürztraminer and Pinot Gris, and the easy-come drinkability of Pinot Blanc and Muscat. Even among the Alsace winemakers themselves it is the most revered grape variety. I suspect the reason Riesling is so popular with the producers is that although it is the great grape of Germany – which between 1870 and 1918, and 1940 and 1945 controlled the region – they take positively provocative pleasure in asserting that their totally dry, yet full-bodied style is superior to Germany's lighter, sweeter product. And although Germany is now making dry 'Trocken' styles, they're not, so far, a patch on Alsace Rieslings.

About 18 per cent of the region is planted with Riesling and this is increasing. When the wines are young they should have a steely streak of acidity, cold like shining metal splashed with lemon and rubbed with an unripe apple. As the wine ages, sometimes after two years but sometimes not until ten years or more, a pure, strangely unindulgent honey builds up, a nutty weight balancing the acid which itself slowly turns to the zest of limes and the quite unmistakable wafting pungency of petrol fumes. You can see why Alsace Riesling is not so easy to appreciate as Muscat or Gewürztraminer, but it certainly is 'something else'! The Vendange Tardive and special Sélection wines are most likely to show this style. Ordinary blends of Riesling can be a bit bland and floral. Don't age these, but do age the 'specials' – and don't neglect lesser years. 1984, '86 and '87 all produced good, lean, steely Rieslings. But the best years are: 1985, '83, '81, '79, '76. Best producers: Adam, Albrecht, Bennwihr co-operative, Beyer, Blanck, Cattin, Deiss, Faller, Ginglinger, Josmeyer, Kientzler, Kreydenweiss, Lorentz, Rolly Gassmann, Schaetzel, Schoech, Sick-Dreyer, Sparr, Trimbach, Weinbach, Willm, Zind-Humbrecht.

ALSACE SYLVANER
Alsace AC
ALSACE
Sylvaner

This used to be the most widely planted of Alsace's grapes and even as recently as 1982 accounted for 20 per cent of the vineyard area. This figure is gradually falling as Sylvaner is supplanted by Pinot Blanc and Riesling, both superior varieties of the non-aromatic sort (Gewürztraminer, Pinot Gris and Muscat are the 'aromatics'). It has quite good acidity and ripens well in the less-than-ideal vineyards of the northern Alsace *département* of the Bas-Rhin, and in flat vineyards down on the plain. From a good producer, young Sylvaner can be pleasant and slightly tart in an appley way. Mature Sylvaner *can* get quite a nice earth and honey fullness to it, though it often brings along a whiff of tomato too – which is *not* really what you expect in a white wine! Best producers: Boeckel, Kientzler, Rolly Gassmann, Schlumberger, Seltz, Wantz.

ALSACE VENDANGE TARDIVE
AC
ALSACE
Riesling, Muscat, Pinot Gris or Gewürztraminer

Vendange Tardive means 'late-picked'. The grapes are picked almost overripe, giving much higher sugar levels and therefore much more intense exciting flavours. The minimum natural strength is 12·6 degrees for Riesling and Muscat and 14 degrees for Gewürztraminer and Pinot Gris. Fourteen degrees is quite à mouthful, and given the aromatic personality of Alsace wines, there are

some exceptional late-picked wines to be had from years such as 1983 and '85. The wines are totally dry, but usually rich and mouthfilling, and often they need five years or more to show their personality. They can be disappointingly 'shut-in' at two to three years old, but super five years later. This is very much the trend among top estates now, as they attempt to find a way to challenge the white wines of Burgundy, both in reputation and in price.

There is a further subcategory of special wines – Sélection de Grains Nobles. These wines are from very late-picked grapes affected by noble rot (the fungus which creates the sweetness in Sauternes). The minimum natural alcohol here is 14·6 degrees for Riesling and Muscat and 16 degrees for Gewürztraminer and Pinot Gris. In years such as 1976 and '83 the actual sugar levels are often much higher. Since the yeasts cannot continue to ferment wine much after 15 degrees, these wines are often notably sweet and incredibly concentrated, able to age for decades. Very little is made, and it is always wildly expensive. Best years: 1983, 1976. Best producers: Beyer, Dopff & Irion, Faller, Heim, Hugel, Muré, Schlumberger, Trimbach, Wolfberger from the Éguisheim co-operative, Zind-Humbrecht.

ANJOU AC
CENTRAL LOIRE
Chenin Blanc, Chardonnay, Sauvignon Blanc

Basic Anjou Blanc – usually dry or off-dry, normally harsh and positively alive with the reek of sulphur fumes – has quite rightly for many years been the Cinderella of French white AC wine. The Chenin grape dominated the area, hardly ever ripened properly and a succession of seedy merchants and mediocre co-operatives contrived to make the worst of what little there was. But things have changed! The region now has a resident wine chemist committed to raising standards, modern cool-fermentation methods are revealing unexpected pleasures in the Chenin grape, and both Sauvignon Blanc and Chardonnay, although legally only allowed to a maximum of 20 per cent, are contributing massively to produce dry, surprisingly fruity whites. We see some medium wines and they, too, are increasingly attractive – fresh, slightly honeyed and cheap.

The AC covers the whole Maine-et-Loire *département*, as well as bits of Deux-Sèvres and Vienne. The best whites have their own local ACs, such as Bonnezeaux, Coteaux du Layon or Saumur, but at least Anjou Blanc is now increasingly a source of good straight French whites, dry or semi-sweet, with some of the better ones using the Anjou Coteaux de la Loire label. There is also an increasing amount of sparkling Anjou Mousseux – which can be good, but *very* dry. Anjou whites can age well although the wines sold are usually of the previous vintage. Best years: 1986, '85, '83, '82. Best producer: Ackerman-Laurance.

ARBOIS AC
JURA
Chardonnay, Savagnin

This is the largest of the specific ACs in the Jura region of eastern France, centred round the busy town of Arbois. Over one million bottles of white are made each year, in several different styles, all unified by the death-defying Savagnin grape. This is the archetypal Jura white grape, though there is an increasing amount of very good light Chardonnay. The Savagnin manages, uniquely and disconcertingly, to infect the amiable qualities of mountain vineyard dry white wine with the palate-numbing, sweet-sour properties of a really dry *fino* sherry. In an ordinary Arbois white wine this effect is to make you question whether you should send the wine back as being 'off'.

However, there is a type of white Arbois wine called *vin jaune* (yellow wine), made only from Savagnin, which develops a *flor* yeast growth on its surface similar to that of *fino* sherry. *Vin jaune* is also made in other Jura ACs, at its best in Château-Chalon. The wine is left in barrel with the *flor* for six years, during which time it oxidizes, develops a totally arresting damp sourness like the dark reek of old floorboards, and yet also keeps a full fruit, albeit somewhat decayed. To be honest, I prefer *fino* sherry, partly because it has *less* flavour! But just

because *vin jaune* exists, I will support it – even if I don't much want to drink it. It comes in strange 62cl, dumpy *clavelin* bottles – and since they are totally out of step with the dead hand of EEC standardization, I'll support those too! And, probably for the only time in my life, I support a 'smaller than average' size because it means, if I'm cornered one day with a demented *vin jaune* producer, we'll get through the bottle quicker!

There is also a sweet *vin de paille* (straw wine) – from grapes supposedly dried on straw mats – which is hardly made nowadays and is therefore very expensive. A very good Arbois Mousseux is made by the Champagne method and using the Chardonnay grape. The co-operative at Pupillin, just south of Arbois, makes a good example. Best producers: Arlay, Bourdy, Rolet; Arbois and Pupillin co-operatives.

AUDE
LANGUEDOC-ROUSSILLON

▼In the Aude, vines grow everywhere among the hot, harsh hills. Over half the region's wine is made by co-operatives.

The Aude *département* produces an amount of wine second only to its neighbour, the Hérault, and between them they have much to answer for concerning France's contribution to the dreaded EEC wine lake – since the overproduction of unsalable, undrinkable wine was, until recently, a way of life in this part of the Midi. Yet the Aude is a region of massive potential, running down the Mediterranean shore from the Hérault in the north to the Pyrénées-Orientales in the south – but, crucially, with far less of the flat, lifeless sea-front which dominates the Hérault.

The predominance of mountainous land, particularly in the vast ACs of Corbières and Minervois, and the smaller ones of Fitou and Blanquette de Limoux, means that the potential for quality is enormous, and as estate owners recover their confidence each vintage brings a new crop of exciting, gutsy wines. Yet they are almost without exception *red*. There is no white Fitou and only a small amount of white Minervois and Corbières. Blanquette de Limoux in the hills south-west of Carcassonne is a totally white AC for its high-quality Champagne-method sparkling wine and there is a tiny production of sweet Muscat de St-Jean-de-Minervois.

About two-thirds of the *vin de pays* wines go under the departmental name Vin de Pays de l'Aude and the rest are divided between 21 *vins de pays de zone*. The Vin de Pays de l'Aude, however, is almost 100 per cent red and rosé, yet in that tiny fraction which is white lurks the kernel of great things. Local co-operatives and big companies such as Chantovent and Nicolas alike have pioneered Chardonnay, Sauvignon Blanc, Sémillon and Chenin Blanc alongside the local varieties – Ugni Blanc, Bourboulenc, Macabeo, Grenache Blanc and their neutral-flavoured cronies. The first results show clean, fresh whites of pure varietal character at a low, low price. I think I'm going to keep my eye on Aude whites in the next year or two. Drink as young as possible.

AUXEY-DURESSES AC
CÔTE DE BEAUNE, BURGUNDY
Chardonnay, Pinot Blanc

Auxey-Duresses is one of the out-of-the-way Côte de Beaune villages, which – in times of inflated prices for wines from top villages like Meursault and Puligny-Montrachet – can be a crucial source of supply for those who still want to drink top white Burgundy yet are damned if they'll pay a loony sum. It makes it all the more incomprehensible that the standard of Auxey-Duresses wine varies so dramatically. At its best – from a producer such as the Duc de Magenta or Roulot – the white is dry, soft, nutty and hinting at the kind of creaminess which should make a good Meursault. Too often, though, the wines have ended up rather flabby and flat. It's the kind of village I really like to write about precisely because it is a rare oasis of good-value Burgundy, but despite my desire to write about it, I'm too often thwarted by the shrug-shouldered Burgundian laxness which seems to say – we can sell the wine, so. . . Sure, you can sell it now, but it's not so many years ago you couldn't sell it for a plate of potatoes, and fashions do change. . .

So where is this den of iniquity? Auxey-Duresses is a little village west of Meursault, leading up to St-Romain. The white vines are mostly on the left as you drive from Meursault and that makes them basically north-facing – which explains some of the inconsistency in the wines. The whites make up about 25 per cent of the production of 600,000 plus bottles annually. The wines can age but, given their slight unpredictability, it's best to drink them fairly young, between three and five years old. Best years: 1987, '86, '85, '83, '82. Best producers: Diconne, Duc de Magenta, Leroy, Prunier, Roulot.

BANDOL AC
PROVENCE
Clairette, Ugni Blanc, Sauvignon Blanc, Bourboulenc

This AC does make white wine, but Bandol's reputation rests heavily on its ability to make one of Provence's best reds. The reason is simple: this small coastal region – just west of Toulon – has an excellent red grape, the Mourvèdre, which is ideally suited to Bandol's hilly vineyard sites, but most white plantings are made up of the fairly dull Clairette, Ugni Blanc and Bourboulenc. These produce neutral, vaguely nutty but unmemorable wines at horrendous prices. Now, however, growers are allowed to add Sauvignon Blanc, and there has been a considerable improvement in the freshness of the wines which use it, a green appley fruit balancing a vaguely aniseed perfume. The wines are still for drinking young, but the excessive price tag doesn't hurt quite so much. Out of Bandol's three million plus bottles a year, whites account for only about five per cent. Drink these wines as young as possible. Best years: 1986, '85. Best producers: Bastide Blanche, Laidière, Vannières.

BARSAC AC
BORDEAUX
Sémillon, Sauvignon Blanc,
Muscadelle

▲Château Coutet is the largest estate in Barsac. Its vineyards, 75% Sémillon, produce about 85,000 bottles a year. The château itself is over 700 years old.

Barsac has the dubious distinction of being the only AC in Bordeaux to have suffered the ignominy of having one of its Classed Growths rip up the vines and go back to sheep grazing – within its very boundaries! That's what Château Myrat did in 1976 after the owner gave up the struggle of trying to make ends meet in the face of consumer indifference to his wine. (Stop Press. I've just been down there and unless someone put magic mushrooms in my drink at lunchtime, they've replanted. Ah well, another great story bites the dust!) Barsac is the largest of the five communes entitled to the Sauternes AC – it comprises about 1750 acres (700 hectares) out of a total for Sauternes of 4905 acres (1985 hectares). The sweet wines of Barsac can also call themselves Barsac AC if they want – and most of the good properties do this. Some, leaving nothing to chance, label themselves Sauternes-Barsac – just to make sure you get the message!

Barsac is a little village close to the Garonne in the north of the Sauternes AC. Along its eastern boundary runs the diminutive river Ciron – source of the humid autumn mists crucial to the development of noble rot which intensifies the sweetness in the grapes and without which you can't make truly sweet wine. The important grapes are Sémillon, which can produce syrupy, viscous wines in the best years, and Sauvignon Blanc, which adds fruit and acid balance. There is a little Muscadelle, which is particularly useful for its honeyed spice in less good years. In general, Barsac wines are a little less luscious, less gooily indulgent than other Sauternes but from good properties they should still be marvellously heady, richly satisfying, full of the taste of peaches and apricots and creamy nuts. But they're expensive, especially the Classed Growths, of which there are nine in Barsac. Best years: 1986, '83, '81, '80, '76, '75. Best properties: (Classed Growths) Broustet, Climens, Coutet, Doisy-Daëne, Doisy-Dubroca, Doisy-Védrines, Nairac; also Cantegril, Gravas, Guiteronde, Liot, de Menota, Piada.

BASTOR-LAMONTAGNE, CH.
Sauternes AC, *cru bourgeois*
BORDEAUX
Sémillon, Sauvignon Blanc,
Muscadelle

There's no such thing as a good, cheap Sauternes. The process of making good Sauternes is fiendishly expensive, the vineyard yield is low and the incidence of sweetness-inducing noble rot erratic and unpredictable. But there is one shining exception – Château Bastor-Lamontagne. Year after year, regardless of the vintage, this Sauternes property on a good site in the commune of Preignac, just north of the great Château Suduiraut, produces luscious, honeyed wine at a price which still allows us to wallow in the delights of high-class Sauternes without taking out a second mortgage. This 208-acre (84-hectare) property is actually owned by a bank. I wish I had an account with them. Best years: 1986, '85, '83, '82, '81, '80.

BÂTARD-MONTRACHET AC, BIENVENUES-BÂTARD-MONTRACHET AC
grands crus
CÔTE DE BEAUNE, BURGUNDY
Chardonnay

Yes, I'm afraid this means exactly what you think it means. But maybe it's just a drawn-out French joke in questionable taste, because Bâtard has a near-neighbour vineyard called Chevalier, and lo and behold the Chevalier (French for 'knight') has Les Desmoiselles (French for 'damsels') next-door as well as Les Pucelles (French for. . .oh, I think you get the message!). Right, where were we? Bâtard-Montrachet is a *grand cru* white Burgundy. And it's superb. This 29-acre (11·8-hectare) vineyard, straddling the border between the villages of Puligny-Montrachet and Chassagne-Montrachet, gives wines of enormous richness and grandeur, with flavours of freshly roasted coffee, hot toasted bread, brazil nuts and spice – and honey which after six to eight years of maturity becomes so strong it seems to coat your mouth. Yet despite all this, Bâtard-Montrachet is a dry wine. There is not a hint of sugar, just the alchemy of a great vineyard, a great grape variety – Chardonnay – and the careful, loving vinification and ageing in good oak, which has given *grand cru* white Burgundy its reputation as the world's greatest dry white wine.

There are two other parts of Bâtard – Bienvenues-Bâtard-Montrachet of 5·7 acres (2·3 hectares) just to the north (*bienvenues* means 'welcome') and Criots-Bâtard-Montrachet, 4 acres (1·6 hectares) directly to the south. These are also great wines, although generally a little less overwhelming than straight Bâtard-Montrachet. Best years: 1986, '85, '84, '83, '82, '79, '78. Best producers: Bachelet-Ramonet, Blain-Gagnard, Delagrange-Bachelet, Leflaive, Ramonet-Prudhon, Sauzet.

BEAUJOLAIS AC
BEAUJOLAIS, BURGUNDY
Chardonnay

Statistics differ as to how much white Beaujolais there is, some claiming that five per cent of all Beaujolais is white, others claiming less than one per cent. Well, 98 per cent of the vineyards are planted with the red Gamay grape, which leaves two per cent to divide between Chardonnay and Pinot Noir. Let's say one per cent of the vineyards are Chardonnay – that's *not* going to produce five per cent of the total, is it?

Until recently I wasn't much of a fan of white Beaujolais, finding it rather hard and fruitless. But as the white wines from the neighbouring Mâconnais just to the north have become increasingly shapeless and musky-fruited I've begun to appreciate the dry, stony charms of Beaujolais a bit more. There used to be quite a bit of Beaujolais Blanc made in the far north of the Beaujolais AC, near St-Amour and Leynes, but this is now usually sold as St-Véran AC. The best white Beaujolais now comes from old Chardonnay plantations in the southern part of the region, down towards Lyon. Village names to look for are Theizé, Le Breuil, Châtillon-d'Azergues. Best years: 1987, '86, '85. Best producers: Charmet (the best; lovely, peachy wine), Dalissieux, Jadot, Mathelin.

BEAUNE AC
CÔTE DE BEAUNE, BURGUNDY
Chardonnay, Aligoté

Most people think of Beaune as a 100 per cent red wine commune, but in fact, five per cent of the 1330 acres (538 hectares) of vines are planted with white grapes, usually on the higher sections of vineyards where outcrops of limestone create good conditions for Chardonnay. The two most important producers are

Bouchard Père & Fils with their rather erratic Beaune du Château – a blend of white wine from several *premiers crus* – and Drouhin, whose Clos des Mouches is outstandingly good creamy, nutty wine, similar to a Puligny-Montrachet in style and only just lacking the extra complexity of the very best white Burgundies. The wines age well, particularly the attractive oaky Clos des Mouches, but are also delicious at only two years old. Best years: 1987, '86, '85, '84, '83, '82.

BELLET AC
PROVENCE
Rolle, Chardonnay

This rare white wine from a tiny AC a few miles up in the hills above the fashionable Promenade des Anglais is mostly consumed in the chic eateries of Nice by flashy folk with more money than sense. And I'm perfectly happy for it to stay that way, because I have yet actively to 'enjoy' a bottle of white Bellet. There is a stale, nutty meatiness about the wines, which I find unattractive in these cold northern climes, and which would be positively off-putting if I were expecting it to provide refreshment after an hour or two of bronzing in the noon-day Riviera sun. Anyway, there's not a lot of it – only about 40,000 bottles a year of white, based chiefly on the Rolle grape, out of a total production of less than 150,000 bottles. And the prices are a bit batty too, so I'm happy to give the wines a miss. If I *did* want a bottle, the only producer I'd go to would be Château de Crémat, who blend in a little Chardonnay and make quite an interesting wine.

BERGERAC SEC AC
SOUTH-WEST
Sémillon, Sauvignon Blanc,
Muscadelle and others

Bergerac is the main wine region of the Dordogne, and might consider itself unlucky to be denied the more prestigious Bordeaux AC, since its vineyards abut those of St-Émilion and Bordeaux Supérieur Côtes de Castillon, and for centuries Bergerac wines *were* sold as Bordeaux. However, the *appellation controlée* laws took little notice of historical practice in the south-west of France, and the Bordeaux AC stops dead at the departmental boundary of Gironde. There is also no reason why Bergerac cannot build its own reputation. The vineyards are good, the grape varieties are the same as those of Bordeaux, but there is a certain lack of ambition to create anything more than a simple white wine. Production is dominated by the functional and fairly efficient co-op, whose wines are mostly clean and slightly grassy. However, good Bergerac Sec can have a very tasty strong nettles and green grass tang to it, with a little more weight than an equivalent Bordeaux Blanc. In general drink them as young as possible. Best years: 1988, '87, '86. Best producers: Bellingard, Court-les-Mûts, Gouyat, la Jaubertie, Panisseau.

BLANQUETTE DE LIMOUX AC
LANGUEDOC-ROUSSILLON
Mauzac, Clairette, Chenin Blanc,
Chardonnay

The publicity people for Blanquette de Limoux have made great play of the claim that their product is the oldest sparkling wine in the world and that Dom Pérignon and his chums, who are supposed to have 'invented' Champagne in the Champagne region of northern France, nicked the idea on their way back from a pilgrimage to Spain. These wine legends are good fun, impossible to prove or disprove, and totally irrelevant to the quality of the drink, which in this case is pretty high.

Blanquette de Limoux comes from a hilly region just south-west of Carcassonne in the Aude *département*. It's a surprising place to find a sharp, refreshing white wine, since most southern whites are singularly flat and dull, but the secret lies in the Mauzac grape which makes up over 80 per cent of the wine and gives it its striking 'green apple skin' flavour. The Champagne method of re-fermentation inside the bottle is generally used to create the sparkle, although the more rustic *méthode rurale*, which entails finishing off the original fermentation inside the bottle, is also occasionally employed.

For some time this very dry, lemon and appley-flavoured sparkling wine was accorded second place after Champagne among France's sparkling wines, but the improvement in quality in the Loire, Burgundy and Alsace means that this position is now hotly disputed. A certain amount of Chardonnay, as well as Clairette and Chenin Blanc, has now been planted to give a rounder, deeper-flavoured wine – less unique a taste, but certainly more like Champagne. Best producers: the co-operative at Limoux (making the bulk of the six million bottles produced annually); also Froin, Martinolles.

BOLLINGER
Champagne AC
CHAMPAGNE
Pinot Noir, Chardonnay, Pinot Meunier

Far too much Bollinger gets drunk in the wrong way. I don't mean to be stuffy, but Bollinger has long been the preferred tipple of the English upper classes baying for the sound of broken glass, and their more recent imitations, the new wave of financial whizz-kids with more money than manners. 'More Bolly, more Boll', has long been the cry to send shivers down the spines of right-thinking citizens and make them shut up their houses, rein in their daughters and hope they are spared the fizz-fuelled rampage. Which is *very* unfair on poor old Bollinger (though obviously it doesn't do their sales figures any harm!) because Bollinger is just about the most *serious* Champagne company imaginable. Its wines are full-flavoured, though frequently rather hard when released for sale, and always certain to benefit from a year or two's extra ageing.

The non-vintage is the best-known wine, but the company does a unique range of vintage wines too. As well as a normal vintage release, they do a Vintage RD. RD stands for *récemment dégorgé* – recently disgorged – showing that the wine has been lying in bottle on its yeast for longer than usual, picking up loads of flavour on the way. They also produce Vintage Année Rare – an RD which has spent even longer on its lees, and Vieilles Vignes Françaises Blanc de Noirs – from a single vineyard of incredibly ancient, ungrafted vines in Ay. Impressive stuff – but, as I said, *serious*. If I were celebrating with Bollinger, I'd only use it for something really momentous, like becoming a bishop.

▶ In Champagne, the stark-white chalk soil is crucially important: it provides ideal drainage, aids ripening by reflecting back the sun's heat, and produces grapes with high acidity – vital for good Champagne.

BONNEZEAUX AC
grand cru
CENTRAL LOIRE
Chenin Blanc

You pronounce it 'Bonzo' and for years I wanted to try the wine simply to check its canine credentials. Luckily, nowadays most people have stopped calling their dogs Bonzo, and a wise and prudent few are at last taking an interest in the great sweet wines of the Loire. Because Bonnezeaux *is* one of the two greatest Loire 'stickies', a *grand cru* covering about 125 acres (50 hectares) inside the larger Coteaux du Layon AC, on gentle slopes between the villages of Bonnezeaux and Thouarcé. The whole Layon valley, which extends south-east from the Loire near Angers, makes sweet wines, but Bonnezeaux (and Quarts

de Chaume, the other *grand cru*) are by far the best. They have the lowest yields – Bonnezeaux is allowed just 25 hectolitres per hectare and often achieves only 15 hectolitres per hectare – and because they can request a higher price than their neighbours, Bonnezeaux and Quarts de Chaume growers generally wait for noble rot to affect their grapes in late October, or even November. The best growers then make several trips through the vines, picking only the most shrivelled, raisiny grapes. These tiny amounts of ultra-sweet juice will then ferment slowly, sometimes on into the New Year. The fermentation stops between about 13·5 and 14·5 degrees of alcohol and the remaining grape sugar gives the wine its sweetness.

This is the same wine-making method as that used in Sauternes, but the flavours are different. In the Layon valley only the Chenin Blanc grape is used, with its very high natural acidity and a sugar content rather lower than Sauternes' Sémillon. Consequently Bonnezeaux can seem surprisingly dry at first, because the acidity is masking the sweetness. But give it 10, 20 or even 40 years, and the colour deepens to an orange gold, and the sweetness builds to an intense, yet always acid-freshened, peach and apricot richness, scraped by a slight bitterness of peach kernels. Never quite as luscious as Sauternes, it is nonetheless unique sweet wine, best drunk by itself, or perhaps with some of those peaches and apricots. Best years: 1985, '83, '82, '78, '76, '70, '64, '59, '47. Best producers: Fesles, Petit Val, Renou.

BORDEAUX BLANC AC
BORDEAUX
Sémillon, Sauvignon Blanc,
Muscadelle

The simple Bordeaux AC is one of the most important French ACs and, at the same time, one of the most abused. Its importance lies in the fact that it can apply to the dry, medium and sweet white wines of the entire wine-producing area of the Gironde, the largest fine wine vineyard area in the world. Most of the best wines are allowed more specific geographical ACs, such as Sauternes or Graves, but there is a vast amount of unambitious but potentially enjoyable wine sold as Bordeaux AC.

The problem was that since prices remained obstinately low, incentive disappeared and quality slipped, so that Bordeaux Blanc came to be a byword for flabby, fruitless, off-dry, over-sulphured brews of the sort which could put you off wine-drinking for good. But as prices of white Burgundies and the Sauvignons of the Loire valley have risen year by year, demand for decent white Bordeaux has picked up, and there is now an increasing number of pleasant, clean wines, frequently under a merchant's rather than a château label, which make refreshing drinking. Cool fermentation in stainless steel tanks, to preserve the fruit aromas of the grapes, and occasional steeping of the juice and grape skins together after crushing but before fermentation (a process which dramatically increases fruit flavours), are the keys to improved quality.

The simple Bordeaux AC applies to wines which have more than four grams of residual sugar per litre. In a wine of high acidity, this is hardly noticeable, but there is a subdivision of the AC for wines with less than four grams of sugar per litre. These are labelled Bordeaux Sec or Vin Sec de Bordeaux. Since many of these are 100 per cent Sauvignon wines, the grape name may also be used on the label.

The Bordeaux AC also applies to wines made in superior *appellations*, but in the wrong style. Consequently, white wine made in the red wine ACs of the Médoc can only be Bordeaux AC, and dry wines made in the sweet wine ACs of Sauternes and Barsac are also only allowed the Bordeaux AC. With rare exceptions (like Ygrec from Château d'Yquem, and Pavillon Blanc du Château Margaux), all Bordeaux Blanc AC wines should be drunk as young as possible. Best years: 1988, '87, '86. Best wines: Caillou Blanc de Château Talbot, Loudenne, Moulin-de-Launay, Pavillon Blanc de Château Margaux, Peyrouley, Pierrail, Renon, Sirius (a Sichel merchant's brand), Tanesse, Thieuley, Tour Mirambeau, Trois Moulines, Vin Sec de Doisy Daëne, "Y" (Ygrec). Best merchants: Coste, Dourthe, Dubroca, Ginestet, Joanne, Mau, Sichel.

BORDEAUX

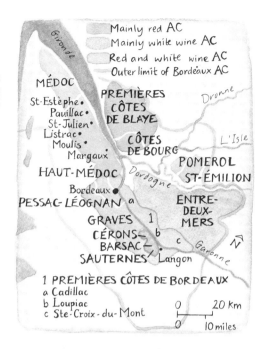

On any wine list the biggest section is likely to be Bordeaux. Different vintages abound. Long lists of properties under the title 'Château this' or 'Domaine that' fill the pages. Yet these will almost all be red wines, and it is easy to forget that Bordeaux is a major producer of white wines as well. In fact, some of the greatest whites in the world – the unctuously sweet wines of Sauternes and Barsac, and the spicy dry whites of Graves and Pessac-Léognan – are grown in the Bordeaux area.

Bordeaux is situated way down in the south-west of France. As the river Dordogne flows in from the east and the Garonne from the south-east, the climate becomes mild and the fierce heat of the south is tempered by the influence of the sea. To make great white wine you must avoid the extremes of heat which affect most of southern France throughout the summer because an element of fruit acid is crucial in the grapes if the wine is to be refreshing – one of the chief objectives in a white wine. But here there is an ever-present hint of moisture in the air, even as the August sun beats down. And the landscape – even when thick with vines – always imparts a sense of cool greenness.

North of the city of Bordeaux lie the great vineyards of the Médoc where only a tiny proportion of wines are white, and on the right bank of the Garonne and the Gironde estuary, there are just a few whites in the Bourg and Blaye areas.

To the south of the Garonne, however, are the white wine ACs of Sauternes, Barsac and Cérons, and the Graves where both red and white wines are made. Between the Garonne and the Dordogne is the large Entre-Deux-Mers *appellation* (the name means 'between two seas'). This is where much of the best light dry Bordeaux white is coming from today. And in the south of the Entre-Deux-Mers, facing Sauternes across the river, are the vineyards of Cadillac, Loupiac and Ste-Croix-du-Mont, which make sweet wine in the Sauternes style, but without quite the richness.

The Sémillon grape is the most important variety for white Bordeaux and it gives a round, rather fullbodied wine, which can be a little too fat to be refreshing by itself, and so the Sauvignon Blanc is usually blended in to provide a sharper, green acid tang. Sauvignon Blanc is also frequently made into a dry wine on its own.

MAIN WHITE ACs
Barsac
Bordeaux
Cadillac
Cérons
Côtes de Blaye
Côtes de Bourg
Côtes de Francs
Graves
Entre-Deux-Mers
Loupiac
Pessac-Léognan
Premières Côtes de Blaye
Premières Côtes de Bordeaux
Sauternes
Ste-Croix-du-Mont

MAIN GRAPES
Sauvignon Blanc
Sémillon

◄Some of the freshest dry white in Bordeaux now comes from Entre-Deux-Mers where vines share the lush landscape with trees and meadows.

See also *Graves and Pessac-Léognan*, pages 68–69, and *Sauternes*, pages 104–105.

BOUCHES-DU-RHÔNE
PROVENCE

This *département* stretching across the wide Rhône delta is very much a red and rosé region, although the good white Cassis AC lies on the Mediterranean coast between Marseille and Toulon. The *département* encompasses the Coteaux d'Aix-en-Provence AC with its sub-area, Coteaux des Baux-en-Provence, both of which do make white wine, but whose fame rests on excellent reds. The most important white production in the *département* takes place in the Camargue, out on the marshes of the Rhône delta. Often utilizing the title Vin de Pays des Sables du Golfe du Lion (what a mouthful), experimental plantings of Sauvignon Blanc and Chardonnay to supplement the more usual Ugni Blanc, Clairette and Muscat are producing some pleasant light whites for immediate drinking and one or two, like the Sauvignon Blanc, which really do show a lot of personality. The departmental Vin de Pays des Bouches-du-Rhône produces very little white and none of it is exciting.

BOURGOGNE ALIGOTÉ AC, BOURGOGNE ALIGOTÉ DE BOUZERON AC
BURGUNDY
Aligoté

This used to be a byword for sharp, sour wine, and the Burgundians themselves could be seen in the region's cafés, lacing it liberally with blackcurrant liqueur to hide the flavour. But the wine is not as bad as that. The marked lemon acidity and the almost neutral fruit do make it an excellent base for *kir* – just add a dash of blackcurrant liqueur. Yet Aligoté is a vine which benefits enormously from maturity and those growers who possess old vines can make delicious, full, almost Chardonnay-type wines, with a smell of buttermilk and a nuttiness coating the striking lemon acidity. The wine is never complex but can be pretty good. The best examples come from Côte d'Or growers with old vines like Rion, Coche-Dury, Jobard and Confuron. The merchants Dupard also make a good example.

Bourgogne Aligoté de Bouzeron is a separate AC for one village at the northern end of the Côte Chalonnaise – the only village producing Aligoté that is allowed to use its own name. This is generally reckoned to be the finest Aligoté, and certainly that buttermilk soap nose can be quite marked, and the lemony flavour can have a peppery bite as well. Aligoté is supposed to be the perfect accompaniment for snails (the growers of Aligoté in the Hautes-Côtes have even started a snail brotherhood – the Confrérie de l'Escargot). Bouzeron's best producers are Bouchard Père & Fils, Chanzy, de Villaine. Other Aligoté producers: Coche-Dury, Cogny, Confuron, Dupard, Jobard, Rion.

BOURGOGNE BLANC AC
BURGUNDY
Chardonnay, Pinot Blanc, Pinot Beurot

Bourgogne Blanc or white Burgundy is either an elegant, classy, dry white of marvellous, nutty character or an overpriced washout, depending entirely on how the *appellation* has been interpreted. At its most fundamental, white Bourgogne can come from anywhere in the Burgundy region – that means it could be from near Chablis in the north, or from the Mâconnais and Beaujolais, some 180 miles (290km) further to the south near Lyon. In general, the Chardonnay grape is used, although there is some Pinot Blanc and Pinot Beurot which is often thrown in for good measure.

Usually Bourgogne Blanc will be a bone dry wine from vineyards not considered quite good enough for a classier *appellation*, but vaguely in the same style. So a Bourgogne Blanc from the Yonne region round Chablis will usually be light, slightly tart and refreshing, one from the Côte d'Or might have some of the nutty fullness of nearby Meursault while a Bourgogne Blanc from the Mâconnais will probably be fatter and rather appley. Often you can guess at the style from the label: if the wine is from a grower the flavours will follow regional style. However, if the address on the label is of a Côte d'Or merchant, the wine could be from anywhere in Burgundy.

Some good growers in the Côte d'Or and Côte Chalonnaise declassify some of their Chardonnay which isn't quite good enough for their top labels, but still age it in newish oak barrels. Such wines can be absolutely superb and far superior to many Meursaults and Puligny-Montrachets from the less reputable merchants. Wines matured in oak (sometimes marked *vieilli en fûts de chêne*) can age well, but most Bourgogne Blanc should be drunk within two years. Best years: 1987, '86, '85. Best producers: Boisson-Morey, Boisson-Vadot, Bouchard, Boyer-Martenot, Buxy co-operative, Henri Clerc, Coche-Dury, Drouhin, Faiveley, Jadot, Jaffelin, Javillier, Jobard, Labouré-Roi, René Manuel, Millau-Battault.

BOURGOGNE GRAND ORDINAIRE AC
BURGUNDY
Chardonnay, Aligoté, Pinot Blanc and others

You hardly ever see this – 'BGO' as they call it. I haven't tried a bottle, except in Burgundy itself, for years. It is almost impossible to know what you're getting because this is the Burgundian catch-all to end all catch-alls. Just about any grape which will grow can be included in the blending cauldron – Chardonnay (though anyone who uses this for 'BGO', the cheapest AC, must be nuts), Aligoté, Pinot Blanc, Pinot Beurot, Sacy, and Melon de Bourgogne (the Muscadet grape which was supposedly banished from Burgundy generations ago for being too boring). You won't find the wine abroad and even in Burgundy it's mostly sold as quaffing wine for the bars – for which it can be perfectly suitable, so long as you have a bottle of *crème de cassis* (blackcurrant liqueur) very close to hand in case the first mouthful explains with awful clarity that epithet 'Ordinaire' – the only French AC to admit in writing that the wine may actually be pretty duff stuff.

BROUSTET, CH.
Barsac AC, *2ème cru classé*
BORDEAUX
Sémillon, Sauvignon Blanc, Muscadelle

This is good wine, and so it should be, because this Second Growth Barsac is owned by Eric Fournier, who creates wonderful reds at his First Growth St-Émilion property, Château Canon. Monsieur Fournier is extremely strict about only selecting the best barrels for bottling under the Broustet label (the rest goes under the label Château de Ségur) and this results in a very small production – the 40 acres (16 hectares) only produce around 2000 cases of Broustet, less than half the yield of many other Classed Growths in the region. The wine doesn't have great fruit but does have thick, lanolin-like richness, syrup and honey coating your mouth, which is pretty satisfying. Best years: 1986, '83, '81, '80, '75, '71.

BUGEY VDQS
SAVOIE
Jacquère, Chardonnay, Altesse

A few years ago you could have said 'Bugey? Don't waste space on a sour little country wine most people will never have heard of, and if they've got any sense, won't waste time searching for'. And I'd have agreed. These straggly little vineyards covering 625 acres (250 hectares) halfway between Savoie and Lyon in the *département* of Ain, made thin, lifeless stuff from the Savoie grapes Altesse and Jacquère, hindered even further now and then by Aligoté. But a couple of summers back I stopped in the little town of Belley and stayed at the local hotel. Bugey was the house wine and, having sniffed the red and found it distinctly reminiscent of a turnip field, I had a jug (small) of the white. It was fantastic. Another jug (larger) later, I discovered I was drinking one of the trendiest white wines in France – Chardonnay du Bugey. It's light, wonderfully creamy and fresh as mountain pasture and one of the crispest, cleanest, snappiest Chardonnays in France. But you'll have to go to Belley to get it. Rumour has it they even make a pretty decent fizz too. Best producers: Cellier de Bel-Air, Crussy, Monin.

BUZET AC
SOUTH-WEST
Sémillon, Sauvignon Blanc, Muscadelle

Buzet shot to prominence in the 1980s with its red wines – and red is still the bread and butter of this region which lies south-east of Bordeaux, between Agen and Casteljaloux. Since this area nudges Armagnac, which relies on white wine for distilling, you'd expect Buzet to turn over some decent whites as well, but they aren't terribly exciting – dry, rather full-feeling, but short on freshness and perfume. Best producer: Buzet-sur-Baïse co-operative.

BURGUNDY

Côte de Nuits } Côte d'Or
Côte de Beaune
Côte Chalonnaise
Mâconnais

Dijon ●

0   20km
0   10miles

N̂

Vougeot
Nuits-St-Georges
Aloxe-
Corton
● Corton
● Beaune
● Meursault
HAUTES-CÔTES
Bouzeron ● Chagny
● Rully
● Mercurey
Givry ●
● Chalon-sur
-Saône
● Montagny
Dheune
Saône
Grosne
● Mancey
Tournus ●
Lugny ●
Cluny ● Viré ●
Clessé ●
Saône
Mâcon ●
Pouilly. ● Loché
Fuissé. ● Vinzelles
St-Véran

► The tiny village of Aloxe-Corton is famous for the magnificent gilded roof of its château and for its two great *grand cru* wines: the red Corton and the white Corton-Charlemagne.

The name Burgundy always seems to be more suitable for red wine than white. BUR-GUN-DY. It sort of booms: it's a rich, weighty sound, purple rather than pale, haunches of venison and flagons of plum-ripe red rather than a half-dozen oysters and a glass of Chablis.

Yet white Burgundy is nowadays at least as important as red Burgundy, possibly more so, since the term Burgundy applies to a large swathe of eastern France starting, only a few miles from the chilly vineyards of Champagne, at Chablis in the north (which has its own map on page 34) and stretching down through the Côte d'Or south of Dijon, the Côte Chalonnaise and on to the Mâconnais, where France seems to change from being a cold northern nation to a warm, Mediterranean one. In all of these areas, white wine is of crucial importance, and in two – Chablis and the Mâconnais – red wine is almost an irrelevance!

The most important grape right through Burgundy is the Chardonnay, and it is because of the tremendous renown of the white wines of Chablis and the Côte d'Or that Chardonnay became planted worldwide as winegrowers everywhere sought to emulate the flavour of Meursault, Puligny-Montrachet and Chablis. It is now thought of as the world's greatest white wine grape and its birthplace is Burgundy. Aligoté is the second-line grape and rarely sets the world on fire, but can produce some decent tangy whites and can also add a useful acid nip to the sparkling Crémant de Bourgogne.

Between Dijon and Chagny lies the long thin sliver of land called the Côte d'Or – the Golden Slope. The northern section, the Côte de Nuits, is almost entirely given over to red wines, but the Côte de Beaune to the south produces fabulously rich, compellingly powerful white wines – from the villages of Aloxe-Corton, Meursault, Puligny-Montrachet and Chassagne-Montrachet.

The Côte Chalonnaise is a small area whose whites were mostly made into sparkling wine, but both Rully and Montagny are now showing they can produce lovely white wines without the help of bubbles. And the Mâconnais is the broadest expanse of white Chardonnay vines in Burgundy. Most of the wine is simple and refreshing, but in the ACs of Pouilly-Fuissé and St-Véran, a few producers are creating some of Burgundy's finest wines.

MAIN WINES
Bourgogne
Bourgogne Aligoté
Bourgogne Grand Ordinaire
Côte d'Or ACs
Crémant de Bourgogne
Givry
Mâcon
Mâcon-Villages
Mercurey
Montagny
Pouilly-Fuissé
Pouilly-Loché
Pouilly-Vinzelles
Rully
St-Véran

MAIN GRAPES
Aligoté
Chardonnay
Pinot Blanc

See also *Chablis*, page 34–35, and *Côte d'Or*, page 52-53.

31

CADILLAC AC
BORDEAUX
Sémillon, Sauvignon Blanc,
Muscadelle

This is a rather forlorn little AC, bordering the Garonne, in the southern part of the Premières Côtes de Bordeaux AC. It covers a mere 200 acres (80 hectares), and even this paltry acreage seems to be dwindling. The AC was only created in 1981, with the aim of giving the best wines in the southern Premières Côtes their own AC to help boost sales. This was fair enough, except that the AC specifies the wines must be semi-sweet or sweet and the market is moving fast and furiously towards dry whites – which, of course, the area around Cadillac is capable of producing very well. Cadillac does get affected by noble rot – the fungus which, on the opposite bank of the Garonne, intensifies the sweetness of Sauternes, but since it is extremely expensive to separate the noble-rotted grapes from the rest, and since Cadillac has no reputation which might allow it to charge higher prices, most Cadillac wines are merely sweetish with no real lusciousness to write home about. Château Fayau is the one exception. Sémillon, Sauvignon Blanc and Muscadelle grapes are used to make the wines, and the allowed yield is 40 hectolitres per hectare as against 25 hl/ha for Sauternes – another reason why Cadillac is rarely special.

CARBONNIEUX, CH.
Pessac-Léognan AC, *cru classé de Graves*
BORDEAUX
Sauvignon Blanc, Sémillon,
Muscadelle

▼ Carbonnieux has been making wine since the 12th century. The present château dates from the 1300s.

This is the largest of the Graves Classed Growth properties which now lie within the new Pessac-Léognan AC. The property's 175 acres (70 hectares) are divided equally between red and white grape varieties. Sauvignon Blanc dominates the vineyard at 65 per cent, with 30 per cent Sémillon and 5 per cent Muscadelle, which might explain why the wine is bright and breezy when it's very young – I've drunk it happily at less than a year old. However, the wine isn't cheap and a Classed Growth wine should mature and develop extra nuances of personality if it is going to be worth the money. But I haven't had any mature Carbonnieux which roused the old tastebuds from their slumbers. There is now evidence of a little new wood being used – I'd like more, but I suspect the vintages since 1983 will have a more exciting maturity than the preceding ones.

CASSIS AC
PROVENCE
Ugni Blanc, Clairette, Marsanne and others

This is the most famous and most overpriced white wine of the French Riviera, but I can't help wondering whether the stunning views of the vineyards rising up towards the steep cliffs, the port's daily catch of the Mediterranean's freshest fish, and the cavalcade of quayside restaurants crushed tight with trendies from nearby Marseille and Toulouse don't have something to do with it. The wine isn't *that* special. The actual flavour is mild to put it politely but, I don't know. . .sit me down on the harbour walls, chill the wine and wait until tomorrow to send me the bill. . .mmm. Just over half the 420 acres (170 hectares) of vines are white. The wine ages well, but drink it young to enjoy its freshness. Best producers: Clos Ste-Magdeleine, Ferme Blanche, Paternel.

CÉRONS AC
BORDEAUX
Sémillon, Sauvignon Blanc, Muscadelle

Cérons is a little enclave within the Graves region of Bordeaux, on the northern boundary of Sauternes-Barsac. The AC is for sweet white wine which is not quite so sweet as Sauternes, and for that reason not so well known, not so highly priced. This should mean that Cérons is a bargain. Well, a generation ago perhaps it was, but throughout the 1960s and '70s the interest in sweet white wine waned and hard times hit Cérons and Sauternes alike. The only solution was to use the grapes to make dry wine – and here Cérons saved its neck by being really crafty! Dry white wine from Sauternes only qualifies for the basic Bordeaux AC and so can never command much of a price, but the Cérons growers persuaded the AC authorities to allow them to use Graves AC for their dry reds and whites. With the stroke of a bureaucrat's biro, Cérons' dry wines doubled in value. (The Sauternes growers still battle in vain for a similar arrangement.)

In fact, dry wines are now more important in Cérons than 'sweeties'. There are still a few producers making rather soft, mildly honeyed wines, with the restrained sweetness of a ripe apple rather than the syrupy richness of pineapple and peach. Best years: 1986, '83. Best producers: Château de Cérons, Grand Enclos du Château de Cérons, Haura, Mayne-Binet.

CHABLIS AC
BURGUNDY
Chardonnay

Fact: Chablis wine can only come from 5500 acres (2200 hectares) of vineyards clustered round the town of Chablis in the Serein valley between Dijon and Paris, in France. But you try telling that to an American wine producer who happily produces his Chablis in the Central Valley of California. Fact: Chablis wine can only come from the Chardonnay grape. Nonsense, the New Zealanders call their Chardonnay Chardonnay and sell it at a fair price. They use Müller-Thurgau and Chasselas for their Chablis – it helps to keep the price down. Fact: Chablis is a still dry white wine. Not on your nelly, *mon vieux* gringo. An Argentinian producer may find that the sweeter style of Chablis sells best, and he has a surplus of red grapes. So he thinks he'll make his Chablis pink this year – and why not sparkling?

Chablis' trouble is that its name has become synonymous in many parts of the world with some sort of dry-to-medium, white-to-off-white wine from any available grape and all with one thing in common – a low, low price. Real Chablis couldn't be more different. It is always white and dry, often bone dry, so green-edged, so flinty – like the click of dry stones knocked together.

The Serein river valley is Burgundy's northernmost outpost where Chardonnay only ripens with difficulty, and where there is a dreadful record of devastation by frost – in 1985 many vineyards hardly survived. Consequently the price is high. Too high as it happens because much Chablis can be rather mean and not a lot better than a decent Muscadet. In general, straight Chablis AC is drunk at one to two years old, but the better producers often produce wine which can improve for three to five years. Best years: 1987, '86, '85, '84, '83. Best producers: Brocard, Defaix, Droin, Durup, Fèvre, Laroche, Long-Depaquit, Louis Michel, Pico-Race, Pinson, Raveneau, Régnard, Rottiers-Clotilde, Simmonet-Febvre, Vocoret.

CHABLIS

Map legend:
- Chablis grand cru
- Chablis premier cru
- Chablis
- Limit of Chablis AC

Map locations: Maligny, La Chapelle-Vaupelteigne, Poinchy, Milly, Fleys, Chablis, Chichée, Serein (river)

C hablis has managed to make a virtue out of the fact that in most years it barely manages to ripen its grapes and the resulting wines have long been a byword for green, ultra-dry whites of no discernible richness and little discernible fruit. Yet that just shows how easy it is for a reputation to linger on long after it bears little resemblance to the truth. Chablis is certainly dry, but it is very rarely green or raw nowadays, and although it doesn't have the almost tropical fruit ripeness of some white wines from further south in Burgundy, it does have a gentleness and a light unassertive fruit which can make for delicious drinking.

Also, Chablis does come from one small, decidedly marginal area in the frost-prone, autumn-cool valley of the river Serein between Dijon and Paris – and from there alone. Sadly for Chablis, non-French winemakers and marketing men found the name beguiling to the eye, and extremely easy to pronounce and remember. Consequently all over the world the name Chablis has been adapted to local wines. Spanish 'Chablis' was, for a long time, a common sight on British wine-shop shelves; and today, California, Australia, New Zealand, South Africa and many others all produce their Chablis versions – which are limited by one thing only – not the grape type, not the wine style, but by the fact that they are *cheap*.

True Chablis comes only from the Chardonnay grape, comes only from the French AC region, and is always white and dry. And it is *never* cheap. It *cannot* be cheap because the vineyards are at the northern limit for fully ripening Chardonnay grapes. The Champagne region is a mere 19 miles (30km) to the north, and you only have to taste a still 'Coteaux

◀Three of Chablis' top-quality – or *grand cru* – vineyards, in the foreground, Vaudésir, with Grenouille and Valmur behind.

MAIN WINES
Chablis
Chablis Grand Cru
Chablis Premier Cru
Petit Chablis

MAIN GRAPES
Chardonnay

Champenois' Chardonnay to realize how tart and thin unripe Chardonnay can be. The better Chablis vineyards – especially the seven *grand cru* sites – are all on slopes to catch the maximum heat from the sun, which automatically increases labour costs, and the harvest is notoriously unreliable due to the ever-present risk of spring frosts, the likelihood of bad weather when the vines flower, and the probability of winter setting in before the crop ripens.

All of which might make one wonder if it is worth continuing the effort. Well, it is. New methods of frost prevention are cancelling out the worst effects of a spring-time relapse into winter. A better understanding of the malolactic fermentation (which converts tart malic acid into softer, creamier lactic acid) means that very few wines are now harsh and green, though some may be too creamy and dull. And, despite Chablis' 'bone-dry' reputation, an increasing number of producers are experimenting with oak barrel ageing – resulting in some full, toasty, positively rich dry whites which makes me almost prepared to pay the high prices asked.

CHABLIS GRAND CRU AC
BURGUNDY
Chardonnay

This is the heart of Chablis: the vineyards of Bougros, Preuses, Vaudésir, Grenouilles, Valmur, Les Clos and Blanchots, which comprise a single swathe of vines rising steeply above the little river Serein, facing serenely towards the south-west and able to lap up every last ray of the warm afternoon sun. It is only because of the perfect exposure, the steep elevation and the unique Kimmeridgian limestone that the Chardonnay grapes can fully ripen and gain the fatness and strength which should mark out a *grand cru*. And while the quality of much Chablis has become rather haphazard in recent years, *grand cru* growers, in general, have been making exceptional wines during the 1980s, especially those who have used oak to mature their wines, adding a rich warmth to the taut flavours of the wine.

Prices are high, naturally, because supplies are very limited – especially since the *grands crus* suffer more than the other vineyards from the late frosts which can decimate Chablis' crop in the spring. There is much argument between those who use new wood to age their wines and those who don't. The anti-new wood brigade *do* make the *vrai* Chablis – if you're after a wine which always keeps a firm grip on that lean, streak of self-denial which, even after ten years, stops a *grand cru* ever wallowing in its own deliciousness. If you use new oak barrels, the wine gains a rich, almost tropical, apricoty fruit, nuts and cream flavour and the spicy butter of the oak completes a picture of high-quality indulgent white. And then, just when you're about to say 'this is as sumptuous as Montrachet' you find that reserved, minerally restraint clambering back to centre stage. Never drink *grand cru* too young – it's a total waste of money. Or too old. Five to ten years is the normal timescale. Best years: 1987, '86, '85, '84, '83, '82, '81, '78. Best producers: Dauvissat, Defaix, Droin, Fèvre, Long-Depaquit, Louis Michel, Pinson, Raveneau, Régnard, Robin, Servin, Simmonet-Febvre, Vocoret.

CHABLIS PREMIER CRU AC
BURGUNDY
Chardonnay

Of Chablis' 4620 acres (1870 hectares), 580 are designated *premier cru* or First Growth. In true Burgundian style *premier cru* is the second tier of quality, *grand cru* (Great Growth) being the top. There's no doubt that *some* of these *premiers crus* are on splendid slopes, ideally suited to producing fine wine, but Chablis has been the scene of much contentious politicking recently as 'interested' parties (those owning the relevant vineyards) have sought to upgrade Petit Chablis land to Chablis AC, and much straight Chablis land to the superior AC, Chablis Premier Cru. There is a good argument for upgrading the majority of Petit Chablis land since it can produce perfectly good wine from the Chardonnay grape. However, there is little evidence yet that the 'new' *premiers crus* are doing anything except lessening the expectations of the consumer when confronted by a *premier cru* label – because I can't detect any difference with many of them and I don't expect the consumer can either. But what am I saying? Of *course* I can tell the difference. *Premier cru* prices kick off at up to twice as much as straight Chablis. Once again, is the consumer being taken for a ride? Of those 1435 acres (580 hectares) of *premier cru*, 500 acres (200 hectares) are brand new – and of these some historically have names like *Verjus* (sour grapes) and *Champs des Raves* (turnip fields).

So what of the good *premiers crus*? The best are Montée de Tonnerre, Vaillons and Mont de Milieu, just south of the *grand cru* slopes, and some examples of Côte de Léchet and Montmain, south-east-facing slopes to the west of the town of Chablis. The flavours are still dry, and are often nutty, fairly full, with a streak of something almost mineral there. They should feel bigger and more intense than straight Chablis AC, and if the winemaker has used wood rather than stainless steel to make his wine, they probably will. But at these prices, satisfaction, I'm afraid, is *not* guaranteed, and the sincerity and dedication of the producer are actually more important than the particular vineyard site in the long run.

A good *premier cru* may take as much as five years to show its full potential.

Best years: 1987, '86, '85, '83, '82, '81. Best producers: La Chablisienne co-operative, Dauvissat, Defaix, Droin, Drouhin, Fèvre, Laroche, Louis Michel, Pinson, Raveneau, Régnard, Rottiers-Clotilde, Simmonet-Febvre, Testut, Tour Vaubourg, Vocoret.

CHAMPAGNE AC
CHAMPAGNE
Pinot Noir, Chardonnay, Pinot Meunier

The renown of Champagne is such that it is the only *appellation contrôlée* wine which does not have to bear the words *appellation contrôlée* on its label. Yet Champagne *is* an AC – very definitely so – and one more tightly controlled than most because of the insatiable thirst of the world for this most exciting of sparkling wines, and the consequent intense pressure which is brought to bear on supply.

Champagne is thought of as a general term for sparkling wine, and there are countries – mostly in the New World – which still use the term Champagne to describe their sparkling wines, but in fact the AC applies only to sparkling wines (mostly white but occasionally rosé), which have gained their effervescence by undergoing a second fermentation in the actual bottle from which they will eventually be served (called the 'Champagne method') and which come from one precise geographical location, centred on Épernay and Reims, to the east of Paris. Nothing else, coming from anywhere else in France or the world, can be true Champagne.

This northerly origin for Champagne wines means that the grape varieties rarely ripen fully, and the result is a light wine of very high acid. This isn't much fun to drink by itself, but is perfect for making sparkling wine, so long as the wine comes from good grape varieties. In Champagne it does. The Chardonnay is the world's greatest white grape and here produces lovely, fragrant wines which become surprisingly creamy with a little maturity. Pinot Noir and Pinot Meunier are both high quality *black* grapes (Pinot Noir is the grape of red Burgundy). Because it is so far north, the skins of these grapes never develop much colour and so the juice can be removed by careful pressing with virtually no coloration at all. The Pinot Noir provides a full, strong wine, needing time to soften and the Pinot Meunier a gentle quick-maturing wine.

Although there are some wines made only from a single grape variety – usually Blanc de Blancs from Chardonnay, or Blanc de Noirs from Pinot Noir – most Champagnes are the result of blending the three grape varieties together. Blending of the produce of different villages is also crucial, and most Champagnes will blend wines from perhaps a dozen different villages throughout the region. The villages are classified according to quality. There are 17 *grand cru* villages at the top followed by 38 *premier cru* villages.

Most wine is made by large merchant houses, and becomes known by the title of the house – Moët & Chandon, Bollinger, etc. However, an increasing amount of wine is released under the name of the retailer and on the export markets, large supermarket groups, selling Champagne under their own name, are some of the most important suppliers. A smaller amount of Champagne is made by the vine-grower himself – this is usually unblended, and is only exciting when it comes from a *premier cru* or *grand cru* village. This will be clearly marked on the label. Champagne comes in sweet, medium, medium dry, very dry (brut) and very, very dry (ultra-brut) styles. It is usually a blend of two or more years, labelled 'non-vintage', but when the vintage is good, a 'vintage' cuvée is released of wine from a single year's harvest. There are also 'de luxe' cuvées, which are normally (but not always) vintage and are supposed to be the *crème de la crème* of Champagne. Frequently, they are more remarkable for the weirdness of their bottles and absurdity of their price, than the perfection of their flavours. Best years: 1985, '83, '82, '81, '79, '78, '76, '75. Best producers: Billecart-Salmon, Bollinger, Deutz, Duval-Leroy, Gosset, Alfred Gratien, Henriot, Jacquesson, Krug, Lanson, Laurent-Perrier, Moët & Chandon, Paillard, Perrier-Jouët, Piper-Heidsieck, Pol Roger, Pommery & Greno, Roederer, Taittinger, Veuve Clicquot.

CHAMPAGNE

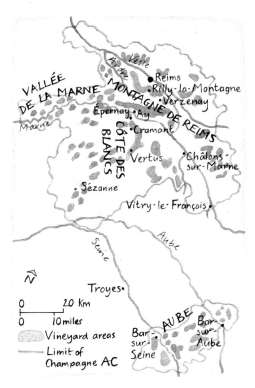

Argentina – where sunshine to ripen the grapes is taken for granted – would ever risk planting vines in such an unfriendly, hostile environment as the stark chalklands of France's far north, where it never gets warm enough for a grape to ripen totally, where the acidity stays toothachingly high and where the thin, meagre flavour of the young still wine makes it virtually undrinkable on its own.

But I've just described the perfect base wine for great bubbly. If you make sure this workhouse gruel of a wine is made from top quality grape varieties like the white Chardonnay and the black Pinot Noir and Pinot Meunier (they ripen so feebly that the skins have little pigment and the juice pressed off is almost colourless) then you literally can't go wrong. It's a good thing, though that the Romans decided to plant grapes in the region. It must have been warmer then, and I doubt if anyone would do it now.

'La Champagne' – the only place in the world real Champagne can come from – is mostly a charmless, treeless, bitingly cold prairie land to the east of Paris. Yet centred on the towns of Reims and Épernay, and stretching down towards the northern tip of Burgundy at Chablis, there are five areas where the combination of chalk soil and well-drained, protected microclimates allows the grapes to ripen. The Montagne de Reims is a low, wide hill south of Reims where Pinot Noir excels. Côtes des Blancs is a long east-facing slope, south of Épernay, almost exclusively planted with Chardonnay. Vallée de la Marne runs east-west through Épernay and grows good Pinot Meunier and Pinot Noir. And there are two less important areas to the south – the Aube and the Côtes de Sézanne. There are actually a very few still wines made in the Champagne region, but they're not exactly a bundle of laughs, and they have their own AC, Coteaux Champenois.

The Champagne region of France has given its name to the whole concept of sparkling wine. Fizz is thought of and described as 'Champagne' even when it's made thousands of miles away from this chilly, windswept northern area. And although the hordes of imitations throughout the world relentlessly pursue a style as close as possible to that of true Champagne, they never achieve it – for one simple reason. No-one in their right mind in a country like Spain, Italy, Australia, America or

▶ The characteristic chalk of Champagne. True Champagne can only come from this region and must have got its bubbles through a second fermentation in the bottle.

MAIN ACs		Pol Roger
Champagne		Louis Roederer
Coteaux Champenois		Taittinger
		Veuve Clicquot
MAIN CHAMPAGNE HOUSES		
Bollinger		MAIN GRAPES
Alfred Gratien		Chardonnay
Krug		Pinot Noir (black)
Moet et Chandon		

CHARDONNAY

A thin, rasping white, all raw edges and streaked with enough acidity to make an unripe cooking apple blush – that's Chardonnay-Coteaux Champenois from the northernmost climes of France. A rich and buttery wine, so heady with spice, honey and cream that you think it must be sweet, yet it isn't – merely dry wine in its succulent, ripest state; that's Chardonnay too, a single-vineyard Meursault from Burgundy's Côte d'Or. Chardonnay is chalk-dry but nutty in Chablis, lemony and racily tasty as a Vin de Pays from the Muscadet region, as fleeting but thrilling as melting mountain snow in Bugey, but packed with the flavours of peaches, melons, apricots and cream in Pouilly-Fuissé, clean, round and simple like a fat apple in a Vin de Pays de l'Aude, and frothing with cream, honey and excitement as a Blanc de Blancs sparkler from Champagne. All these are Chardonnay, and show why this wonderfully adaptable grape is now the white wine star worldwide.

In a way, it is a less recognizable grape than varieties like Sauvignon Blanc, Riesling or Gewürztraminer, whose basic personality shouts at you from the glass. But the full yet unassertive flavour is what attracts winemakers. Just as chefs' top creations often use veal and chicken rather than stronger-tasting meats – so Chardonnay becomes the canvas on which a winemaker can test all kinds of styles. The most famous of these is the use of oak barrels. Chardonnay extracts a delicious spicy, creamy fullness from new oak barrels, and in Burgundy's Côte d'Or this mixture of Chardonnay, ideal soil and oak barrel-ageing is reckoned to produce the greatest white wine in the world.

Chardonnay plantings are taking place at a hectic pace all over France, and figures become out of date as soon as they are published – yet there are certainly over 37,000 acres (15,000 hectares) already in production. The Côte des Blancs in Champagne is virtually all Chardonnay, and Burgundy – from Chablis in the north, through the heartland of the Côte d'Or, and on to the Côte Chalonnaise, the Mâconnais and even, to a slight degree, the Beaujolais – has Chardonnay as its focal white grape. The Loire is not reckoned to be Chardonnay land, but many producers in Touraine, Anjou and the Muscadet region are planting it – either to release on its own, or else to soften up the Chenin Blanc. The VDQS regions in the centre of France make lean, slightly tart wines from it, while Jura, Savoie and Bugey to the far east have considerable success with it. Although Château Rayas in Châteauneuf-du-Pape makes a remarkable mouthful from Chardonnay, in the south it generally appears in the *vin de pays*, not the AC, wines, because it isn't traditional to the area. Even so, it is having a massively positive effect upon the flavour of southern whites. Chardonnay from the Coteaux de l'Ardèche is already making waves worldwide, and plantations in Provence, the Gard, Hérault and Aude are producing delicious flavours at low, low prices.

CHARENTAIS, VIN DE PAYS
SOUTH-WEST
Ugni Blanc, Folle Blanche, Colombard

The Charentais, lying between La Rochelle on the Atlantic coast and the upper reaches of the Charente river beyond Angoulême, is the Cognac region, and the best wines for distilling have traditionally been both neutral and acid. Since the Ugni Blanc is the chief grape variety, here grown at the northern limits of its ability to ripen at all, neutrality and acidity aren't a problem. However, with the decline in Cognac production there has been an increasing surplus of grapes and thin white wine, and many growers are now allowing some of their harvest to ripen as fully as possible and making Vin de Pays Charentais – still light, lemony and sharp, and actually not a bad drink.

CHASSAGNE-MONTRACHET AC
BURGUNDY
Chardonnay

This is the least fashionable of the great Côte de Beaune white wine villages. One explanation might be that over half the production of this supposedly white wine village is in fact *red*. Another explanation is that Chassagne, a village of some reasonable size, has no restaurant, no café – not even a bar! You have to walk across the dangerously busy Route Nationale 6 (the old main road

between Paris and the south), past Puligny-Montrachet, to Meursault to find somewhere to relax over a drink and a bite – just the kind of hardship to dissuade opinion-forming journalists from reporting favourably.

Well, that can be turned to our advantage, because the general price level in Chassagne is lower than in Puligny or Meursault and the quality right now is increasingly good. There are 880 acres (356 hectares) of vines in this AC between Puligny and Santenay, at the southern end of the Côte de Beaune. Only 40 per cent of these vines are for white grapes, but they include 8½ acres (3·5 hectares) of the great Montrachet *grand cru* as well as 15 acres (6 hectares) of Bâtard-Montrachet and the entire 4 acres (1·6 hectares) of the smallest white *grand cru* – Criots-Bâtard-Montrachet.

The *premiers crus* are not well-known, but can offer big, nutty, toasty wines with more traditional savoury richness, and less of the currently fashionable exotic fruits taste which is increasingly occurring in Meursault and Puligny-Montrachet. En Cailleret, Les Ruchottes, La Romanée, Morgeot and Les Embrazées can be exciting wines – especially if aged for four to eight years. Ordinary Chassagne-Montrachet may lack the complexity of the *premier cru* wine, but since the village is not that 'chic', there is less temptation to 'stretch' and it is usually a thoroughly enjoyable high-quality Burgundy. Best years: 1987, '86, '85, '84, '83, '82. Best producers: Bachelet-Ramonet, Blain-Gagnard, Colin, Delagrange-Bachelet, Duc de Magenta, Fontaine-Gagnard, Gagnard-Delagrange, Lamy, Albert Morey, Marc Morey, Pillot, Ramonet-Prudhon.

CHASSELAS

The Swiss drink copious amounts of Chasselas under the names Fendant, or Dorin or even Perlan. But if you're looking for it in France, you won't find the name Chasselas on a label, since it is very definitely a variety on the way out. I can see why. The wine it produces is about as neutral as wine can get, and although it might be pleasant enough as a thirst-quencher during an alpine hike, it doesn't have enough personality to survive a few months in bottle. There is a little planted in Savoie, and also at Pouilly on the Loire where it confusingly makes the Pouilly-sur-Loire AC in the same area as the far more exciting Sauvignon-based Pouilly Blanc Fumé. However, the main plantations, still about 1000 acres (400 hectares), are in Alsace, where it is turned into simple jug wine, or occasionally, if spiced up with Pinot Blanc or Gewürztraminer, it can be part of the blend for Edelzwicker.

CHÂTEAU-CHALON AC
JURA
Savagnin

This is a tiny AC covering only 86 acres (35 hectares) in the centre of the mountainous Jura vineyard, and applies to one of the most daunting wine types yet invented – *vin jaune* or yellow wine. Château-Chalon *vin jaune* offers the same kind of experience as potholing, hang-gliding and taking your afternoon nap on a bed of nails – the first taste will be so distasteful and distressing that you never countenance a second for one moment. Yet for a brave, indeed demented few, the eventual pleasures far outweigh the initial torments.

The Savagnin grape is the only variety used to make *vin jaune*: I see I recently described it in my tasting notes as producing a fierce, farmyardy white, blending oily thickness with a raw volatile acidity and a strong whiff of damp straw. In kinder mood, I then said that it can develop a raging, sour, woody brilliance that only the very best sherries ever get. So you can see I'm a fan!

Well, in a funny way, I *am* a fan of *vin jaune* because there is nothing like it in the world of wine. Its nearest equivalent in taste would be an old *fino* sherry – and the reason is that they both grow a *flor* yeast on their surface as they age in barrel, which imparts this strange sweet/sour intensity. *Vin jaune* lies in barrel for six years, developing this film of white yeast; during this time the wine evaporates by perhaps one-third, but is protected from oxidation by the *flor* yeast. This painfully concentrated liquid is bottled in dumpy 62cl *clavelin* bottles, and you can age it for, well, no one really knows how long, but certainly up to 100 years. The intensity of the flavour – a surge of stale, nutty richness, slapped about by a cruel searing sourness, makes this monstrous beauty a wine to be approached with trepidation and a good life assurance policy – but I've survived it, and in a helpless sort of way I'm rather looking forward to my next glass – just so long as it's a small one. Best producers: Bourdy, Courbet, Macle, Perron.

CHÂTEAU GRILLET AC
NORTHERN RHÔNE
Viognier

A single estate renowned as the smallest AC in France at 6½ acres (2·6 hectares) – but actually there are several *grands crus* in Burgundy with their own AC which are even smaller! This rare Rhône white from the village of Vérin south of Vienne is pretty remarkable stuff. The Viognier is the only permitted grape variety and it does produce a most exciting dry wine – all apricots and slightly soured cream, spring blossom floating on the wind and honey tinged with tangerine spice. It will cost you an arm and a leg, though. It is *very* expensive – but then there's very little of it – the allocation for the British market last year was only 60 bottles! Would I buy it? At approaching £50 a bottle? No, I wouldn't. I'd save myself at least £30 and buy Condrieu – same grape, same taste and no feeling that perhaps you're being taken for a bit of a ride. Best years: 1986, '85, '83.

▼The Viognier-planted terraces of Château Grillet rise steeply above the river Rhône.

CHÂTEAUNEUF-DU-PAPE AC
SOUTHERN RHÔNE
Grenache Blanc, Clairette,
Bourboulenc and others

There is very little white Châteauneuf-du-Pape, but that hasn't stopped it becoming extremely trendy. In fact, knowing how things become trendy in France, if there were more of it the chic trend-setters wouldn't be interested. There are 7700 acres (3100 hectares) of vines in Châteauneuf-du-Pape, which lies north of Avignon in the blistering hot southern Rhône Valley. Only three per cent of the production is white, although white grapes are quite often used for softening the red wines. The vast vineyards of bleached earth and shining, smooth-faced pebbles sucking in the summer's heat don't look as though they could possibly produce a decent, refreshing white wine – but they can. The main grapes are the Grenache Blanc and Clairette, helped along by Bourboulenc, Picpoul and Roussanne. None of these are exciting, aromatic grapes and yet, with modern cool-fermentation methods, the wines can be brilliant – exciting liquorice and peach fruit, freshened up with mountain herbs and the snappy acidity of a lime. The wines are good when very young, between one and two years old. They *can* age – becoming full, round and nutty, still good, but the specialness is lost. Best years: the most recent. Best producers: Beaucastel, Bérard, Font de Michelle, Fortia, Mont-Redon, Nalys, La Nerte, Vieux Télégraphe (the very best).

CHÂTILLON-EN-DIOIS AC
CENTRAL RHÔNE
Chardonnay, Aligoté

A fairly firm favourite for the title of 'most obscure French white wine AC'. There are smaller ACs – like Château Grillet in the Rhône valley – but the vineyards for Châtillon-en-Diois are miles off the beaten track way up the lovely, lost Drôme valley, on the road to nowhere except the alpine foothills. All the best wines in the Die area are sparkling and go under the Clairette de Die Tradition AC. But there are a few vineyards planted with Aligoté and Chardonnay, and this is one of those rare times when the Aligoté seems to perform as well as Chardonnay. Neither is memorable, but both do just about enough to explain why anyone thought of creating the AC back in 1974.

CHENIN BLANC

My goodness, you have to be a good winemaker to coax anything enjoyable out of the thin-lipped Chenin grape. Much of the nastiest, sourest, dry and medium white wine of the Loire valley is the result of this late-ripening, high-acid variety's raw juice being casually ripened and then foisted on to an unwilling public (at admittedly give-away prices). But, like all the best things in life, you must take up the challenge, and then there is great wine to be had from the Chenin grape. In fact, the Chenin could lay claim to being the most underrated great white wine grape in the world. Although there is a little Chenin in the Aude at Limoux and in the Bouches-du-Rhône at the giant Listel winery, all the rest of France's Chenin is grown in the Loire valley, where it is also known as Pineau de la Loire. It provides the base for the Loire's sparkling wine industry, centred on Saumur, but is also evident at Vouvray and elsewhere in Anjou and Touraine. Chenin's unrelenting high acidity makes it good for fizz but, frankly, that acid bite can be a killer on the gums and all the best sparklers now have some Chardonnay or Cabernet Franc included as softener.

Chenin Blanc makes dry or off-dry wines in Anjou and Touraine. In poor years these can be raspingly austere, but increasingly the better winemakers are creating dry, appley wines very similar to good Sauvignon. The co-operative at Saumur is a leader here. Dry Vouvray and Jasnières can be remarkably nutty wines – if you allow them the five to ten years they need to soften. And some growers – like Monsieur Girault in Touraine-Mesland – are producing marvellous apricot-scented fruity wines by steeping the skins with the juice for up to a day before the fermentation starts (although the acid is in the flesh of the grape, the perfumes are under the skin, and a few hours steeping can extract wonderful flavours).

Sweet wines are the speciality of Anjou – though in sunny years there are some from Vouvray and Montlouis. The Coteaux de l'Aubance makes mildly sweet whites, whereas the Coteaux du Layon produces quite rich, nuts-and-honey-flavoured wines. However, the stars are two tiny areas in the Layon valley – Quarts de Chaume and Bonnezeaux. Here the Chenin is attacked by noble rot and can give tiny amounts of intensely sweet juice. Because the acidity is so high these wines seem dull and indistinct when they are young, but the best age brilliantly, building up to a most exciting peach, apricot and quince flavour at anything between 10 and 30 years of age.

CHEVALIER-MONTRACHET AC
grand cru
CÔTE DE BEAUNE, BURGUNDY
Chardonnay

They say that after Le Montrachet, Chevalier's next-door neighbour, this is the greatest white wine in the world. Well, never having possessed enough money to indulge in a bottle – its price is astronomical – I can't really. . . But hang on. . . Chevalier-Montrachet. . . Think, think. A limpid golden colour, a heavenly aroma of roasted hazelnuts and fresh-ground coffee and new bread new-toasted from the grate. And a flavour of honey and of cream, of nuts now smoking from the fire, and the waft of coffee just brewed late on a Sunday morning. So rich, coating my mouth with ripeness, luscious enough to be sweet as syrup, yet dry – amazingly, totally, dry. And I was in a garden in Hampshire, many summers ago, with my closest friends. And it was *my* bottle. 1966. Domaine Leflaive. Part of my first-ever wine-tasting prize. Yes. That summer's day at least, the greatest, the happiest bottle of white wine in the world. And what else? It's an 18-acre (7-hectare) *grand cru* in Puligny-Montrachet, just above Le Montrachet on the south-east facing slope. Best years: 1986, '85, '84, '83, '82. Best producers: Leflaive, followed by Bouchard Père & Fils, Jadot, Latour.

CHEVERNY VDQS
CENTRAL LOIRE
Sauvignon Blanc, Romorantin, Chenin Blanc, Chardonnay

Grapes like the Romorantin of Cheverny and the Savagnin of the Jura must survive simply because of the locals' stubbornness in preserving their traditions – it *can't* be because of the nice flavour of the wine. The Romorantin which grows *only* in Cheverny – a little-known area south-west of Blois covering 1250 acres (500 hectares) – gives an unremittingly harsh wine, bone dry, almost bitter in its acidity, and smelling suspiciously like a farmyard in need of a good hose down. It's another of those occasions when I say – yes, I support this wine's existence, but I just hope to goodness I never have to drink the stuff. As it is, Cheverny can make some very attractive light, nutty Chardonnay, and the fizz they create using the Champagne method is sharp, clean and 'bracing'. Oh dear. I wish I could bring myself to say – forget that old Romorantin rubbish and let's have another supply of good Chardonnay and decent fizz. But I can't. So I'll just say – let's see more of their Chenin, Sauvignon and Chardonnay as well. Best producers: Cheverny co-operative, Gendrier, Gueritte, Puzelat, Tessier.

CLAIRETTE DE BELLEGARDE AC
LANGUEDOC-ROUSSILLON
Clairette

This is one of those dull old workhorse whites you try out when you're sweltering away in the Mediterranean sun, but that is so unrefreshing you end up having a beer – which at least is fizzy and cold. Well, maybe that's unfair, but whenever *I* try the wine it's July or August and the stuff's been around for nearly a year, and that's well past retirement age for most Clairette. At a few months old it is supposed to have a lovely floral aroma of violets and honeysuckle and if I'm ever between Arles and Nîmes in the *département* of the Gard – where the half million or so bottles of this wine are made – around Christmas and New Year, I'll check that theory out on the new vintage and let you know.

CLAIRETTE DE DIE TRADITION AC
CENTRAL RHÔNE
Muscat, Clairette

Thinking man's Asti Spumante! This is one of the most deliciously enjoyable sparkling wines in the world. It's made from at least 50 per cent Muscat mixed in with Clairette and the result is a relatively dry, light wine with a lovely creamy bubble and the most orchard-fresh fragrance of ripe grapes and springtime flowers. In fact, why am I saying it's 'thinking man's Asti Spumante'? That sounds like an apology and this mouth-watering delight needs no apology from me – or from anyone.

Die is one of those lost areas of France on the road to nowhere and ringed round with hills. It's a very relaxing place to visit, with the river Drôme meandering through its centre. The 'Tradition' wine is made to sparkle by the *méthode Dioise*. This involves fermentation in bottle, but the process (unlike in Champagne) is arrested before all the grape sugar has been used up, and the wine is then filtered and re-bottled under pressure. As a result, the wine retains the flavour of the grape sugars and that heavenly Muscat scent. There is a Clairette de Die (*not* Tradition) from 100 per cent Clairette grapes and made by the Champagne method – but it isn't nearly so good. Best producers: Clairette de Die co-operative; also Achard-Vincent, Andrieux, Magord, Raspail.

CLAIRETTE DU LANGUEDOC AC
LANGUEDOC-ROUSSILLON
Clairette

What you want in the searing heat of the Languedoc down on the Mediterranean coast is cooling draughts of fresh, dry, white wine – which is exactly the kind of wine the locals find most difficult to make. I can only presume that the very fact that 11 communes in the river Hérault valley between Montpellier and Béziers made white wine at all was enough to earn them their AC, which was until 1985 the only all-white AC in the Hérault *département*. But you're never going to make anything exciting out of the Clairette grape, indeed a lot of the local white used to go to the vermouth factories, which says something pretty negative about quality. The 1·2 million bottles can be dry or semi-sweet – but either way the result is usually heavy and dull. My advice would be to catch it as young as possible and drink it ice cold on the spot – but I'd drink rosé if I had a choice. Best producers: Condamine Bertrand, St-André.

CLIMENS, CH.
Barsac AC, *premier cru classé*
BORDEAUX
Sémillon, Sauvignon Blanc

This is Barsac's leading property, a position which used to be shared with Château Coutet, but in recent vintages Climens has pulled away from its rival in the quality stakes. The 75-acre (30-hectare) vineyard lies on the highest ground in the AC to the south-west of the village of Barsac, its vines coming to rather an abrupt end when they meet the A62 autoroute that runs between Bordeaux and Toulouse. This height gives Climens a particularly well-drained vineyard and helps to account for its reputation as the most elegant and refined of all Barsac properties. It is a deserved reputation, as I have never had a Climens which was sticky or cloying. But it's also only half the story, because these wines are rich, luscious and exotic, not bursting with the peach and pineapple fruit of some 'sweeties', but having an exciting syrupy sweetness, a most appetizing, toasty, nutty, dry edge and a light, clear streak of lemon acidity to keep the wine fresh and long-lasting. Easy to drink at five years old, a good vintage will be much richer and more satisfying after 10 to 15 years. Best years: 1986, '83, '81, '80, '76, '75.

CONDRIEU AC
NORTHERN RHONE
Viognier

I made a little pilgrimage in 1986. Although I was racing down the Rhône valley to keep an appointment at Avignon, I turned off the motorway at Vienne, and drove six miles along the river's precipitous right bank to the village of Condrieu. It's not a pretty place: the houses are modern and functional, and the busy road barely squeezes through, but it is the unlikely birthplace of one of the world's great white wines.

To the west of the town, stark, forbidding cliffs rear towards the clouds; from the road you can see rows of vineyard terraces – many abandoned and rotting – and, on the first plateau, the roofs of modern villas poking above the ridge. Where are all the vines then? Well, there are *very* few and, since you can make more money by selling your Rhône-side plot – with a highly desirable view of the river – to a property-developer than you can by growing grapes, the rest of the vines are mostly in the nooks and crannies with less good vistas. Under 50 acres (20 hectares) of vineyard cling to the daunting rockface, although the AC covers a protected 500 acres (200 hectares).

But what a wine these straggly patches of struggling vines produce! The Viognier is the grape variety – a disease-prone, shy-yielding vine found only here, at the tiny neighbouring Château Grillet, at Côte-Rôtie (where it can be mixed with the red Syrah) and, in minute amounts, in the southern Rhône. A

grand total of 75 acres (30 hectares) for one of France's greatest grapes! The pathetic yield – rarely more than 20 hectolitres per hectare – and the proneness to rot and 'floral abortion' (when no grapes develop from the flowers) are the reasons for this scarcity: an entire Condrieu vintage has been known to give only 19 hectolitres!

But the flavour. Mmm! You think it must be sweet, as a fragrance of ripe apricots and juicy William pears floods the room, freshened by spicy flower perfumes. Yet the wine is dry. Full in your mouth, yes, almost thick and viscous – juicy apricot skins and ripe golden peaches, coated with a perilous richness like double cream about to turn sour. These remarkable wines fade with age, and are horrifyingly expensive – as expensive as a top white Burgundy – but at one to three years old they are a sensation everyone should try just once. Best producers: Delas, Dezormeaux, Dumazet, Guigal, Jurie des Camiers, Pinchon, Rozay, Vernay.

CORBIÈRES AC
LANGUEDOC-ROUSSILLON
Bourboulenc, Clairette, Macabeo and others

White is very much the minor partner in this wonderfully wild, aggressively mountainous region of the Aude, stretching from Narbonne to Carcassonne and south to the Pyrénées-Orientales. Less than ten per cent of Corbières wine is white and little of that is more than adequate with the reputation of this large AC being built on good gutsy reds.

About seven million bottles of white are normally produced, using the Clairette and Bourboulenc grapes. However, there is now a move towards producing *vin vert* or green wine. For this, the grapes are picked early, when they are not quite ripe. They are then fermented cold to a strength of only 10 degrees or so. The effect is light, sharp, lemony and, yes, green! Not memorable, but ice cold it's a pretty decent thirst-quencher after a dusty hike in 'them thar' hills. Drink the wine as young as possible. Best producers: Baronne, Bouîs, Étang des Colombes, Lastours; also Camplong d'Aude, Embrès-et-Castelmaure, Mont Tauch co-operatives.

CORTON AC
grand cru
CÔTE DE BEAUNE, BURGUNDY
Chardonnay, Pinot Blanc, Pinot Beurot

White wine from the great hill of Corton. But while *red* Corton is the greatest red wine from these vineyards, *white* Corton is not – the Corton-Charlemagne *grand cru* has that distinction. In fact very little white Corton is grown, some in the commune of Aloxe-Corton but more in Ladoix-Serrigny, at the north-east end of the hill. The best example is the Corton from the Vergennes vineyard which the Hospices de Beaune sell each year. The Domaine Chandon de Briailles also make white Corton in their Bressandes vineyard (a tip-top red site) from half-and-half Chardonnay and Pinot Blanc. There is even some Pinot Beurot (Alsace's Pinot Gris) grown! All in all a typically quirky example of Burgundy's *appellation* intricacies.

CORTON-CHARLEMAGNE AC
grand cru
CÔTE DE BEAUNE, BURGUNDY
Chardonnay

Perhaps it's because I've always drunk these wines young, and have never possessed a bottle on which I could lavish care and attention for the ten years or more Burgundy buffs say is necessary. Perhaps it's because most of the examples I've had have been bottled by merchants not growers, and their individuality has been lost. Or is the wine just not what it was?

In the early '70s I enjoyed young bottles of '71, '70 and '68 – yes, *'68*, a horrid year. They were inspiring and memorable. From a grower? No, from Bouchard Père & Fils, one of Burgundy's biggest merchants. But then in the early '70s *red* Burgundy was the more sought-after, more expensive wine. There was no great pressure on white production and no dollar-laden Americans intent on lapping up the great labels regardless of the wine's actual flavour. In these white-crazy days there certainly *is* pressure, but Corton-Charlemagne, the largest of the white *grands crus* with a production of about 150,000 bottles, should be able to produce enough to cope. Ah well.

So, where is it? And why Charlemagne? *It* is a wide strip of vineyard at the top of the hill of Corton, part south-facing in the commune of Aloxe-Corton, but veering round to the west in Pernand-Vergelesses. And the name? Well it really does stem from the Emperor Charlemagne whose favourite vineyard this was – though in those days, the wine was red, which left an awful mess on his flowing white beard. After a fair bit of nagging from his wife, he ripped up the red wines and planted white – the inferior Aligoté, not the delicious Chardonnay.

Nowadays it's all Chardonnay and *can* produce the most bluntly impressive of all white Burgundies – rich, buttery, nutty, a blast of splendid golden flavours, not as perfumed or thrilling as Montrachet – more like a kind of super-Meursault. Yet it is more than that, because if it does only show its true splendour at ten years old and more, which I can well believe, that slow revelation of unsuspected depths and nuances is the mark of a great wine. Best years: 1987, '86, '85, '83, '82. Best producers: Bonneau du Martray, Bouchard Père & Fils, Dubreuil-Fontaine, Hospices de Beaune, Jadot, Laleure-Piot, Latour, Rapet.

▼ Wicker harvesting baskets, traditional to Burgundy, piled high with Chardonnay grapes in Corton-Charlemagne.

COSTIÈRES DU GARD AC
LANGUEDOC-ROUSSILLON
Clairette, Bourboulenc, Grenache
Blanc and others

This large AC of 10,000 acres (4000 hectares) lies between Nîmes and Arles, close to the Rhône delta in the *département* of the Gard. There are 20 million bottles produced annually; only one million of these are white, although the trend is towards a higher white production. At present Clairette, Ugni Blanc and Bourboulenc are used – and at best they can produce light, appley, quick-drinking wines from careful cool fermentation.

COTEAUX CHAMPENOIS AC
CHAMPAGNE
Chardonnay

I don't know what possessed me, but I drank Coteaux Champenois on Easter Day this year. Strange choice? You're telling me! But I *thought* I'd be getting a really nutty mature Chardonnay because it was a 1976 – really hot year – from the good firm of Chaudron. I'd got this wine in 1978 from a Thames-side warehouse, long-since defunct. Then, it was tart, lemony, raspingly chalky and dry. Ten years on, had it changed? Not a bit. Pale gold, shockingly dry and with that chalky austerity like the lick of a cat's tongue on your cheek. What I'm saying is, no wonder they turn 99 per cent of the region's wine into fizz. I'd be quite happy if they made it 100 per cent!

This AC, which covers still wines – mostly Chardonnay – from the whole Champagne area, was only granted in 1974. Before then the wines could only be *vin de table*. I'm terribly tempted to say, repeal the AC, but I mustn't must I? After all, somebody, somewhere quite likes this lean, overpriced, ultra-dry white. Somewhere. Best years: 1986, '85, '83, '82. Best producers: Château de Saran (Moët & Chandon), Laurent-Perrier, Ruinart.

COTEAUX D'AIX-EN-PROVENCE AC
PROVENCE
Ugni Blanc, Grenache Blanc,
Sémillon, Sauvignon Blanc

▶ Provence – a characteristic vista of vines and olives and cypresses that has changed little since Roman times.

Coteaux d'Aix-en-Provence, covering a large area around Aix-en-Provence in the Bouches-du-Rhône *département* was only made AC in 1985 – long overdue when one considers that the sprawling Côtes de Provence region next door had been granted AC in 1977 despite a pretty frightful track record on quality. Ninety-five per cent of the AC's production of 14 million bottles is red or rosé and traditionally-made whites, based on Ugni Blanc are pretty flabby mouthfuls. But cool fermentation in, where possible, stainless-steel tanks, early bottling and, very importantly, an increased use of Grenache Blanc, Sémillon and especially Sauvignon Blanc are now producing some pleasant, but hardly rivetting, dry whites – to knock back sharpish. Best producers: Beaupré, Fonscolombe, Seuil.

COTEAUX D'ANCENIS VDQS
LOWER LOIRE
Chenin Blanc, Pinot Gris

The old fortress town of Ancenis, guarding the Loire upstream from Nantes, is most famous now for its pig market and giant food-processing plant. Uninspiring neighbours for quality-first wine growers. Not surprisingly, a good deal of unmemorable Muscadet is made in the surrounding vineyards, but Ancenis itself has kept alive a non-Muscadet tradition – Coteaux d'Ancenis VDQS. The 750 acres (300 hectares) of vines are more than 80 per cent Gamay and Cabernet Franc making fairly raw red and rosé, but there is a fair amount of Chenin. This too, I'm afraid, is pretty sharp stuff. The one joy of white Ancenis is the Malvoisie – alias Pinot Gris of Alsace. Only three growers even attempt it, but the wine has a delicious, gently honeyed, rather smoky flavour, vaguely sweet – and just right for a welcome draught of fruit after wading through the ocean of bone-dry Muscadet and Gros Plant which otherwise dominates the area. Drink it young. Best producer: Guindon.

COTEAUX DE L'ARDÈCHE, VIN DE PAYS
SOUTHERN RHÔNE
Chardonnay, Aligoté, Sauvignon
Blanc, Ugni Blanc

White wines only account for about three per cent of the 20 million bottles the Coteaux de l'Ardèche produces annually, yet it was white wine from the Chardonnay grape which first drew attention to this wild, upland area to the east of the southern Rhône valley. Louis Latour, a leading Burgundy merchant, saw that the world was developing a thirst for dry white wine from the

Chardonnay grape (which produces white Burgundy). Yet he also saw that there was no room for expansion in Burgundy itself. So he looked south and found the unexploited, disorganized backwoods of the Ardèche, and in its jumble of gorges and hillsides he saw tremendous potential for good vineyards.

Luckily, the co-operative movement there also saw that 'quality first' was the only route out of the poverty trap and they made an arrangement to produce Chardonnay for Louis Latour. When the foreseen world shortage of Chardonnay did develop, Louis Latour wheeled out his new baby, Chardonnay *vin de pays* from Ardèche. It was delicious, and I'm sure Monsieur Latour laughed all the way to the bank.

There are now several Chardonnays produced here, and Sauvignon, Aligoté and, unfortunately, the boring Ugni Blanc make up the rest of the white plantings. There are plans to increase Coteaux de l'Ardèche production from 20 million to 30 million bottles a year, and much of this increase will be from the new plantings of white grape varieties. Drink the whites as young as possible. Best producers: Latour, Ucova.

COTEAUX DE L'AUBANCE AC
CENTRAL LOIRE
Chenin Blanc

Gentle, charming, mildly sweet wine from a wide area centred on the Aubance river south of Angers. However, it isn't a popular AC, probably because it is neither fish nor fowl – neither sweet nor dry – in a wine world which likes to define flavours more exactly. So although ten different communes each produce a little Aubance, the total crop rarely amounts to more than 250,000 bottles. Many vineyards which could make Coteaux de l'Aubance prefer to produce red, rosé or dry white Anjou AC – easier to sell, though at a lower price. Drink Aubance young, though as with most Chenin wine, you can age it. Best years: 1988, '86, '85, '83. Best producers: Chauvin, Richou.

COTEAUX DES BAUX-EN-PROVENCE
Coteaux d'Aix-en-Provence AC
PROVENCE
Ugni Blanc, Clairette, Grenache Blanc, Sauvignon Blanc

There is a desolate moonscape of tumbled rocks and gaunt, skull-like cliffs dominating the scenery between Cavaillon and Arles in the foothills of the Alpilles in the Bouches-du-Rhône. It seems inconceivable that anything could grow here, but in the last few years the Coteaux des Baux-en-Provence, as part of Coteaux d'Aix-en-Provence, has proved to be one of the most exciting new wine areas in France, in particular showing that organic farming methods can produce spectacular results. But I'm afraid that virtually all of the wine so far is red. The quality of the fruit – and the inspiration in the wine-making – is so good here, that we are sure to see good whites soon, so watch this space. Estates like Mas de Gourgonnier, using 40 per cent Sauvignon Blanc in its fresh, snappy white, and Terres Blanches are showing the way.

COTEAUX DU GIENNOIS VDQS
UPPER LOIRE
Sauvignon Blanc, Chenin Blanc

There's a sign in the town of Cosne – just north of the Loire superstars Sancerre and Pouilly – which declaims, 'Taste here the *excellent* wine of Cosne, Coteaux du Giennois'. Methinks the lady doth protest too much – perhaps in jealousy of her chic neighbours – but the Giennois wines, based on the towns of Gien and Cosne, are *not* excellent. There's a little delicious rosé, but the white is merely dry, sharp – and welcome after a long thirsty drive. No more than that!

COTEAUX DU LAYON AC
CENTRAL LOIRE
Chenin Blanc

It's a terrible mixed blessing being a winegrower in one of those rare microclimates of the world where the noble rot fungus decides to claim its victims. This rot clings to the grape skins in warm, moist autumns and sucks out only the water, leaving the sugar and acids to concentrate almost to treacle. If the rot strikes all your vines and you carefully pick only the most syrupy, mushy grapes, then you have the chance of making great, intensely sweet, wines.

COTEAUX DU LAYON

Ackerman Laurance

MAISON FONDÉE EN 1811

Sémis très frais

PRODUCE OF FRANCE

APPELLATION COTEAUX DU LAYON CONTROLÉE

MIS EN BOUTEILLE DANS LE VAL DE LOIRE PAR

ACKERMAN-LAURANCE ST HILAIRE ST FLORENT MAINE ET LOIRE (FRANCE)

e 75cl

Well, the Layon valley, running south of the Loire just west of Angers, does get noble rot – and the Chenin grape reacts well to it. But it is incredibly expensive and risky to wait way into the autumn for the fungus to develop – some years it never does – and then to make several sorties through your vines selecting only the most-rotted grapes. If you get Sauternes prices, maybe it's worth it, but, except for its two *grands crus* – Quarts de Chaume and Bonnezeaux – prices for Coteaux du Layon are not high enough. Each bottle of Coteaux du Layon is certainly going to be sweet, perhaps with a very attractive peach or apricot flavour developing after three to five years, but it is unlikely to be intensely rich – though it isn't going to be very expensive either. A Coteaux du Layon makes a lovely, fresh, sweetish aperitif at a very fair price. If we want it to be a rich and rare dessert wine – we'll have to pay more for it. Best years: 1985, '83, '82, '76, '75. Best producers: Fresne, Rochettes, Soucherie.

COTEAUX DU LAYON-VILLAGES AC
CENTRAL LOIRE
Chenin Blanc

Seven villages in the Coteaux du Layon AC have, since 1955, been allowed to use their own name on their labels. These are Beaulieu-sur-Layon, Chaume, Faye-d'Anjou, Rablay-sur-Layon, Rochefort-sur-Loire, St-Aubin-de-Luigné and St-Lambert-du-Lattay. To qualify for this superior AC the wines must have at least one degree more alcohol than straight Coteaux du Layon – 12 degrees rather than 11. These wines can be extremely attractive – peachy-sweet after five to six years' ageing – and they are definitely underpriced for the quality. Best years: 1985, '83, '82, '76, '75. Best producers: Breuil, Clos de Ste-Catherine, Guimonière, la Motte, Rochettes, Soucherie.

COTEAUX DU LYONNAIS VDQS
NORTHERN RHÔNE
Chardonnay, Aligoté, Melon de Bourgogne

This is the Beaujolais understudy, and consequently it specializes in pleasant, gluggable reds. But these rather haphazard vineyards, appearing sporadically between Villefranche and Lyon, do produce a little white – from Chardonnay, Aligoté and even Melon de Bourgogne. It is mostly fresh and snappy, to be drunk at six months rather than a year.

COTEAUX DU TRICASTIN AC
SOUTHERN RHÔNE
Marsanne, Bourboulenc

This is the fastest-growing vineyard area in the southern Rhône, largely because it was settled by a number of extremely ambitious displaced wine-growers fleeing from North Africa after Morocco, Tunisia and Algeria gained their independence from France, the first two in 1956 and Algeria in 1962. The available area for the AC is pretty spread out in the southern part of the Drôme – between Montélimar, the nougat capital of France, and Bollène. Only a tiny amount of white wine is made, but if you do see some, it's worth trying for a fairly good, nutty, but fresh drink to consume within the year.

COTEAUX DU VENDÔMOIS VDQS
CENTRAL LOIRE
Chenin Blanc, Chardonnay

By the time you get to Vendôme, wine-growing is becoming a fairly marginal occupation. What vineyards there are are strung along the Loir (no 'e') valley which, 20 miles (32km) further north, shadows the far bigger Loire (with 'e'). The VDQS covers about 150 acres (60 hectares) and has to cope with the late-ripening Chenin as its main white grape, but at least they do allow 20 per cent Chardonnay in the blend – so there is a little softness in what is otherwise an extremely dry white. Best producer: Minier.

CÔTE CHALONNAISE
BURGUNDY

The vineyards of the Côte Chalonnaise have gained enormously in importance in the last few years, as a result of the spiralling price of white Burgundy from famous villages like Meursault and Puligny-Montrachet in the Côte d'Or. The Côte Chalonnaise vineyards could almost be thought of as an extension of the Côte d'Or, since they are directly to the south, but they are far less cohesive being a haphazard grouping of hills, only some of which are suitable for vines.

There are five ACs in the region. The best white wine vineyards are in the north. Bouzeron has its own AC for Aligoté, and Rully, once only famous for its sparkling wine, is now making very fine Chardonnay whites with excellent fruit and a hint of oak – Meursault flavours at half the price. Mercurey is the major *appellation* but is basically a red wine village as is Givry to the south, although bottles of white Givry occasionally surface. Montagny, the southern AC of the Côte Chalonnaise is entirely white, and though there are now signs of improvement, in particular the use of oak barrels to age the wine, these Chardonnay whites can seem a little lean and chalky,

CÔTE DE NUITS-VILLAGES AC
CÔTE DE NUITS, BURGUNDY
Chardonnay, Pinot Blanc

I'd always thought that the Côte de Nuits-Villages label applied solely to *red* wines from the villages of Brochon, Fixin, Comblanchien, Corgoloin and Prissey. Well, you live and learn! Out of the total production, which veers between 400,000 and one million bottles depending on the vintage, there are up to 25,000 bottles of white. Do I think they're worth seeking out? Well, no, not really. As with the rest of the Côte de Nuits, the reds are far better than the whites which tend to be earthy and unmemorable – welcome enough on a picnic in the vineyards, but not good enough to chase up and cart home.

CÔTES DE BERGERAC AC
SOUTH-WEST
Sémillon, Sauvignon Blanc, Muscadelle

The straight Côtes de Bergerac AC is for good quality reds. However, there are two subdivisions which apply to whites. One is Côtes de Bergerac Moelleux for sweet whites; the other is Côtes de Bergerac–Côtes de Saussignac – a superior *appellation* for dry Bergerac whites, using Sauvignon, Sémillon and sometimes Muscadelle. The minimum alcohol is 12·5 degrees as against the usual 11 degrees for Bergerac Sec, and consequently the wine is fairly big and broad, rather than the usual sharp, zesty Sauvignon-style now popular in Bergerac. This may explain why, although five communes grouped round Saussignac to the south-west of the town of Bergerac are allowed the AC, it is rarely used, and total production is only around 300,000 bottles. One of the few producers to utilize it is Château Court-les-Mûts, whose red and rosé are some of the best in the region, but whose white is merely good.

CÔTE D'OR

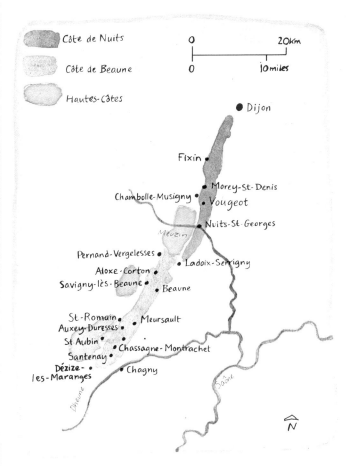

Côte de Nuits
Côte de Beaune
Hautes-Côtes

0   20km
0   10 miles

Dijon
Fixin
Morey-St-Denis
Chambolle-Musigny
Vougeot
Nuits-St-Georges
Meuzin
Pernand-Vergelesses
Ladoix-Serrigny
Aloxe-Corton
Savigny-lès-Beaune
Beaune
St-Romain
Meursault
Auxey-Duresses
St-Aubin
Chassagne-Montrachet
Santenay
Dézize-les-Maranges
Chagny
Dheune
Saône
N

MAIN WINES
Aloxe-Corton
Auxey-Duresses
Bâtard-Montrachet
Beaune
Chassagne-Montrachet
Chevalier-Montrachet
Corton
Corton-Charlemagne
Côte de Nuits-Villages
Criots-Bâtard-Montrachet
Fixin
Hautes-Côtes de Beaune
Hautes-Côtes de Nuits
Ladoix-Serrigny
Meursault
Monthelie
Montrachet
Morey-St-Denis
Musigny
Nuits-St-Georges
Pernand-Vergelesses
Puligny-Montrachet
St-Aubin
St-Romain
Santenay
Savigny-lès-Beaune
Vougeot

MAIN GRAPES
Chardonnay

The Côte d'Or – one tiny little sliver of land, never so wide that you can't easily see the other side, and sometimes so narrow that it wouldn't take you more than a couple of minutes to walk across it.

The suitability of land for vineyards is one of the frustrations yet fascinations of wine. Why can't there be more Côte d'Or wine made when there is so much demand? What's wrong with all those vineless acres, on the other side of the road, stretching out towards the Saône? Well, they *do* grow some vines there, and the wine is *never* anything like as good as even the most basic wine of Puligny-Montrachet. The soil is wrong – damp and clay-heavy – making it difficult for Chardonnay to ripen. And the aspect to the sun is wrong. Burgundy is a northerly wine-growing region, and every ray of sunlight and warmth counts. The best vineyards are gently angled towards the south-east and south, on quick-draining limestone slopes. You only have to experience a Montrachet or Corton-Charlemagne at its brilliant best to realize there is a logic behind the laws which, for instance, restrict the perfectly-sited Montrachet vineyard to precisely 18½ acres (7·5 hectares). There is a difference; those 18½ acres hold a magic something that no other vineyard does.

The Côte d'Or divides into two halves. The Côte de Nuits, south of Dijon, and extending to below Nuits-St-Georges is almost entirely red wine country. There are, literally, the occasional single hectares of white in villages like Fixin, Chambolle-Musigny, Vougeot, Morey-St-Denis and Nuits-St-Georges, but the wines have an almost red wine power to them, and are often made from Pinot Blanc rather than Chardonnay.

The village of Puligny-Montrachet has four *grands crus* and several *premiers crus*, including Clos de la Pucelle.

The Côte de Beaune, however – although white wines comprise a mere 25 per cent of the crop – shows the true brilliance of which Chardonnay is capable. Ladoix-Serrigny grows attractive white, but this is immediately superseded by Corton-Charlemagne, one of the majestic *grands crus* which have made white Burgundy famous worldwide. The villages of Pernand-Vergelesses, Savigny and Beaune itself all produce a little delicious white but the world's greatest concentration of top quality dry white wine is in the villages of Meursault, Puligny-Montrachet and Chassagne-Montrachet. The wines are never cheap – and can be exorbitant – but they are also an unforgettable experience. And if you want an experience almost as good – and a good deal cheaper – the lesser-known villages of Auxey-Duresses and St-Aubin can offer you just that.

CÔTES DE BERGERAC MOELLEUX AC
SOUTH-WEST
Sémillon, Sauvignon Blanc, Muscadelle and others

The AC for sweet wines from the whole Bergerac region. It can cover a multitude of sins, but the wines should be pleasant, fruity, easily sweet but not exactly rich. As such they seem to be tremendously popular in Texas. No, don't ask me why – they seem a very unlikely accompaniment to man-sized slabs of steak fresh from the ranch.

CÔTES DE BLAYE AC
BORDEAUX
Sémillon, Sauvignon Blanc, Colombard

The AC for whites from the Côtes de Blaye vineyards on the right bank of the Gironde. The wines can be dry, medium or even sweet, but almost all of the best whites of the area are now dry Blaye AC. A few sweetish wines remain, none very good, and these may be seen under the Premières Côtes de Blaye label. The chief grapes are Sauvignon and Sémillon, but the most interesting wines include a fair percentage of the Colombard grape, which has far more character here than the more renowned Sauvignon and Sémillon. Don't go out of your way to try these, but if you find one, drink it as young as possible.

CÔTES DE BOURG AC
BORDEAUX
Sémillon, Sauvignon Blanc, Muscadelle and others

Côtes de Bourg is very much a red wine district and only three per cent of the production is white. Coming from three shallow valleys north of the town of Bourg and running parallel to the wide Dordogne river where it joins the Gironde, the red wines have proved themselves time and again as high-quality, bargain-priced wines, but the whites, mostly using Sémillon with a little Sauvignon Blanc, are bone dry, rather lifeless and flat. If you find a white wine with a bit of fruit and zip the grower has probably sneaked in some Colombard – an excellent, but underrated grape quite widely grown in the northern reaches of the Bordeaux region.

CÔTES DE DURAS AC
SOUTH-WEST
Sauvignon Blanc, Sémillon, Muscadelle

A highly successful white Bordeaux look-alike. In fact, Bordeaux itself could learn a thing or two from Côtes de Duras, which uses the same grapes but places particular emphasis on Sauvignon Blanc. The Duras vineyards are on the north side of the Dropt river, between Entre-Deux-Mers and Bergerac, and produce up to seven million bottles a year; 4½ million of them are white. There is some sweet white but dry white, often labelled Sauvignon Blanc, is now far more important – it has a strong, grassy green fruit, but a surprisingly soft, gentle texture. So you can drink fashionably dry, yet it doesn't feel too much of an ordeal. Sounds like perfect '80s dry white – yes, that's exactly what it is! Drink the wines young, preferably at around a year old. Best producers: Duras and Landerrouat co-operatives.

CÔTES DE FRANCS
Bordeaux–Côtes de Francs AC
BORDEAUX
Sémillon, Sauvignon Blanc, Muscadelle

Côtes de Francs is one of the rapidly rising stars of the Bordeaux wine scene. For red wines, though, not for white. The investment in this lovely, hilly little enclave to the east of the St-Émilion-satellite ACs, has been made primarily by families from Pomerol and St-Émilion whose expertise is in red wine and whose ambitions are to produce Classed Growth standard reds. Even so, about ten per cent of the million or so bottles a year are white. Most of it is dry, though sweet is permitted under the Côtes de Francs Liquoreux AC; none of the leading properties makes white wine, so the quality is less than memorable. Best years: 1988, '87, '86.

CÔTES DE GASCOGNE, VIN DE PAYS
SOUTH-WEST
Ugni Blanc, Colombard, Gros Manseng, Sauvignon Blanc

A most unlikely superstar of the '80s. The wine that out-Sauvignons Sauvignon, out-Bordeauxs Bordeaux, yet is made from two grapes generally dismissed with contempt as inferior and gutless. Côtes de Gascogne covers the Armagnac region in the Gers *département* and the best whites come from the chalky soils of Haut-Armagnac to the north and south of the town of Auch. The wines are fabulous, usually very dry (though sometimes quite unnecessarily sweetened a bit for export), with high acidity, but a startling array of flavours – peach, pear, apple slashed with the tang of lemon and a whiff of liquorice and tobacco – and they're tremendous value. It makes me think: if they can do such exciting things with the supposedly unexciting Ugni Blanc and Colombard – why on earth can't the growers of Entre-Deux-Mers and Bordeaux do twice as well with their supposedly superior grapes? Drink young. Some wines are now being aged in new oak and these are delicious creamy soft whites. Best producers: Cassagnoles, Jalousie, Meste Duran, Planterieu, Tariquet.

CÔTES DE PROVENCE AC
PROVENCE
Ugni Blanc, Rolle, Sémillon, Clairette

Pêche au Coup
COTES DE PROVENCE

I suppose it's too much to hope that Provence – the area of France most capable of besotting and beguiling normally level-headed Englishmen – should have the perfect white wine to sip on the perfect beach, the perfect terrace or the perfect hill top. To be honest, *in* Provence it doesn't matter. The scenery, the wafting scents of thyme and rosemary, the clear warm air and the company – they're what matter. And I have to admit it, Côtes de Provence white wine is mostly pretty duff stuff. For a start, the AC granted in 1977 is almost completely indiscriminate, and covers 45,000 acres (18,000 hectares) of every possible sort of terrain in the Var *département*. There are three main vineyard areas: the coastal strip between Ste-Maxime and Toulon, providing most of the quaffing wine for the fashionable watering holes of the Riviera; the coastal vineyards between Toulon and Marseille, where most of the best sites qualify for the Bandol or Cassis ACs; and the vast sprawling hinterland north of the Massif des Maures, where quality is rarely even considered, and only the most committed winemaker is going to rise above the stewpot of fruitless hooch.

Over 90 per cent of the enormous production is red or rosé, and most of the whites suffer from the usual southern French grape varieties of Ugni Blanc and Clairette, though these can be improved by Sémillon or, unofficially, by Sauvignon Blanc. Domaine Gavoty is creating waves by using the Rolle grape to make a delicious fruity wine – and a few producers are following suit. But in general, unless you pick the grapes early, ferment them cold, and drink the wines as young as possible, they really don't have a lot to say for themselves. And me? I'd drink ice-cold rosé on *my* terrace. Best producers: Commanderie de Peyrassol, Curebéasse, l'Estandon (a surprisingly good branded wine), Féraud, Gavoty, Hauts de St-Jean, Ott (de Selle and Clos Mireille), les Maîtres Vignerons de St-Tropez, Richeaume.

CÔTES DU JURA AC
JURA
Chardonnay, Savagnin, Pinot Blanc

This is the regional AC for Jura and covers a wide variety of wines, including still dry white, Champagne-method sparklers, *vins jaunes* and *vins de paille*. Most of the vineyards lie in the south of the region between Poligny and Lons-le-Saunier. The Jura is a lovely region of peaceful woods and hills with vineyards spreading up the mountain sides, or nuzzling into the thick forests which carpet the slopes. But I'm afraid the flavours of the wine aren't of the delicate sylvan sort at all. The reason for this is the Savagnin grape – a strange, sour creature – which admittedly does come into its own with the dark yellow, sherry-like *vin jaune*.

However, there is respite in the friendly form of the Chardonnay and, more rarely, the Pinot Blanc which both perform well in the Jura. Although they are usually blended, some unblended Chardonnay is now coming on to the market. It can still be infected with the strange, resiny Savagnin character, especially when not vinified in a separate cellar; but at its best, especially from the vineyards betwen Poligny and Arbois, it is mountain-fresh Chardonnay of a particularly thirst-quenching sort. There is a little Champagne-method Côtes du Jura *mousseux* made from Chardonnay and Pinot Blanc, and the one from the co-operative at Pupillin is outstanding. Drink Côtes du Jura at one to two years old, although the Chardonnay and the fizz can age. Best producers: Arlay, Bourdy, Gréa, Pupillin co-operative.

CÔTES DU LUBÉRON AC
PROVENCE
Ugni Blanc, Clairette, Bourboulenc

The thing which used to strike me most often about the Côtes du Lubéron was that, strangely, the white was always being offered for sale a year older than the red. Since the white is at best a light, fresh-faced quaffer whose only virtue is its youth, this didn't go down too well with me and I stuck to the red. But things are changing as the co-operatives, who completely dominate the region, eventually react to the consumer's wishes rather than to their members' indolence, and the area was promoted to AC in 1988. The vines are mostly spread along the north banks of the Durance in the Vaucluse *département*, which is also a prime asparagus area – but this doesn't seem to permeate the wine flavours! The wines are not exactly long on complexity and perfume, but between six and nine months old they are bright, refreshing and very enjoyable. The one exception to this rule is Domaine Val Joanis – a vast new plantation wrested from the wild scrubland whose white, though still at its best within the year, can develop a full, soft peachy warmth, spiced with a hint of aniseed, if you leave it for longer. Best producers: Canorgue, Mille, Val Joanis, the co-operative at La Tour-d'Aigues.

CÔTES DU MARMANDAIS VDQS
SOUTH-WEST
Sémillon, Sauvignon Blanc, Muscadelle, Ugni Blanc

You need to have the nose of a bloodhound to track down white Marmandais – because there is very little of it and what there is won't get more than a mile or two from the winery before it is hijacked by locals and consumed: I don't know why they guard it so jealously because it isn't terribly exciting. Of course the wine *ought* to be a cheaper version of Bordeaux Blanc – since it's produced a little way up the Garonne from Entre-Deux-Mers. But the Marmandais have always set out to make *red* Bordeaux look-alikes – with a fair amount of success. Efforts at white are hampered by including the desperately feeble Ugni Blanc in their brew. Best producer: Cocumont co-operative.

CÔTES DU RHÔNE AC, CÔTES DU RHÔNE-VILLAGES AC
SOUTHERN RHÔNE
Clairette, Roussanne, Marsanne and others

Some of the best white Côtes du Rhône comes, incongruously, from a Beaujolais producer – Georges Duboeuf. The reason is that he makes it taste like a white Burgundy! Until recently this was a fitting comment: ordinary white Côtes du Rhône was normally so flat and lifeless that the more you could change its personality the better. Duboeuf created his 'Rhône-Mâcon-Villages' flavour by getting hold of early-picked grapes and then fermenting them really cool in stainless steel tanks. The result? Fresh, appley, dry whites, lovely to quaff and, yes, distinctly Burgundian. They almost taste as though they are made from Chardonnay – yet that grape's not allowed in the AC. Instead, there's the fairly interesting Marsanne and Roussanne, and the less electrifying Clairette, Bourboulenc, Grenache Blanc and, sometimes, a little Ugni Blanc; the mix for Côtes du Rhône-Villages is more selective – Clairette, Roussanne and Bourboulenc.

To be honest, there isn't much white Côtes du Rhône – about three million bottles out of a total of 200 million, most of this being made in co-ops and sold under various merchants' labels. And among the 17 'villages', only Chusclan and Laudun have any reputation for white. But as the price of white Burgundy shoots up, white Côtes du Rhône is sure to be more in demand – not the heavy, flat, nutty stuff of a few years' ago, but the fresh appley creations of non-locals like Georges Duboeuf. Drink as young as possible. Best producers: Bruthel, Chambovet, Duboeuf, Garrigon, Pelaquié, Rabasse-Charavin, Ste-Anne; co-operatives at Chusclan and Laudun.

CÔTES DU ROUSSILLON AC
LANGUEDOC-ROUSSILLON
Maċabeo, Malvoisie

Roussillon is the frontier area where France melts imperceptibly into Catalonia and Spain, somewhere high among the Pyrenean peaks. It was also one of the first areas of France where the co-operative movement geared itself towards quality, and although this has stamped the wines with a certain uniformity, it is a small price to pay for consistency and an immediately attractive wine style based solely on current drinkability rather than on traditional preferences. As usual in the far south, the Côtes du Roussillon AC – which spreads south of Perpignan to the foothills of the Pyrenees, as well as taking in a good deal of the flatter land to the north along the Agly river valley, and the most suitable vineyard sites to the west – is primarily red wine land. Out of the 25 million bottles produced annually only about four per cent are white. These come from the Macabeo grape, a variety which rivals Ugni Blanc for being unmemorable; but – in the hands of the modern co-operatives – if picked very early (almost unripe in fact) and fermented at low temperature, it makes bone-dry, lemon and *anis*-scented white wine for very early drinking, which isn't half bad at *less* than a year old. Taichat is the brand name for a heavier, deeper style which I find just a bit solid. Best producers: Cazès Frères, Jaubert-Noury, Sarda-Malet, Vignerons Catalans.

▼Spring in a Roussillon vineyard: the vines are bursting back to life, sprouting leaves, tendrils and then flower buds.

CÔTES DU VENTOUX AC
SOUTHERN RHÔNE
Clairette, Bourboulenc, Grenache
Blanc and others

Côtes du Ventoux is one of those ACs which has still not found its own identity. It quite surprised me to realize that these lovely vineyards, tumbling down the sides of Mont Ventoux, which towers above the eastern side of the Rhône valley, had enjoyed their own AC since 1973, because I had become so used to seeing them listed next to the cheaper Côtes du Rhône as a kind of Rhône substitute. With the exception of a couple of single estates making good *red*, not white wine, this is still the case, because 99 per cent of the 18 million bottles produced annually are made by the local co-operatives and sold off anonymously to merchants. The white production is insignificant but, interestingly, the area was making fresh, breezy whites *before* Big Brother Côtes du Rhône cottoned on to the fact and I wish there were more of them.

CÔTES DU VIVARAIS VDQS
SOUTHERN RHÔNE
Clairette, Marsanne, Bourboulenc
and others

As I gaze at the name of yet another virtually red-only southern French wine area and search both my mind and my tasting files for the slightest sign that I've ever experienced the rarefied joys of their *white* wines, the one thing that spurs me on is that the quality of the *reds* is modern, enjoyable and cheap – and hopefully the whites can start on that same path, even if they're not there yet. The Vivarais is an area just to the west of the Rhône, between Viviers and Pont-St-Esprit, in the Ardèche and northern Gard *départements*. The basic grape varieties are the same as those used for Côtes du Rhône wines – but as in the Vin de Pays de Coteaux de l'Ardèche, with which it shares common boundaries, there are signs of classier grapes such as Sauvignon Blanc and Chardonnay creeping in. If the success of the Ardèche wines is anything to go by, the results could be exciting – but as currently only 30,000 bottles out of the three million annual production are white, I just hope I'm lucky enough to find a bottle to witness the improvements.

COUTET, CH.
Barsac AC, *premier cru classé*
BORDEAUX
Sémillon, Sauvignon Blanc,
Muscadelle

I thought I should check – and anyway, I felt in the need of a bit of a treat – so I opened a half bottle of Coutet 1979 to write this entry. I was checking out the rumours that Coutet, Barsac's largest Classed Growth property at 100 acres (40 hectares), was no longer making the quality of wine which had traditionally linked it with Climens as the co-leaders of the Barsac AC. Coutet and Climens are the only two Barsac First Growths and are equally famous.

Well, was my 'treat' a treat? Only sort of – the wine was quite rich, vaguely unctuous, or sumptuous, or one of those other words which are all suggestion, yet have no real meaning. But was it First Growth Barsac? No, not really, and looking back at my tasting notes I haven't really got excited about Château Coutet since 1971. Well, that's not quite true. In exceptional years a wine called Cuvée Madame is made from the sweetest grapes on the oldest vines. I've managed to taste it a couple of times and it is stupendously rich and, well, sumptuous. But only a few barrels are made and I've never seen it in a shop. And I do think the wine that we can actually buy is the important one for judging the property, so I'd say – good, yes, but really should try harder. Best years: 1986, '83, '76, '75, '71.

CRÉMANT D'ALSACE AC
ALSACE
Pinot Blanc, Pinot Auxerrois,
Riesling and others

This Champagne-method sparkling wine from Alsace shot to fame a few years ago. An AC had been granted in 1976, but nothing much happened until the price of Champagne rocketed in the early 1980s. From a pretty docile start, with only eight registered producers, the numbers went up to 200! Five per cent of the Alsace crop was being processed as Crémant. All looked set fair – until Champagne had two whopping harvests in 1982 and '83. The price of Alsace Crémant plummeted and the producers were left with large amounts of froth on their faces.

Enthusiasm has since waned for this pretty tasty sparkler, but, paradoxically, the quality is better now that the opportunists have departed the fray, and

▲The grey skies are misleading. Alsace, protected by the Vosges mountains, has a warm, dry climate ideal for grape-growing.

someone must be drinking it, because production has gone from half a million bottles to 13 million in the last ten years. The only trouble is the price – higher than sparkling Saumur, Blanquette de Limoux and Crémant de Bourgogne – and not that much cheaper than Champagne. Best producers: Cattin, Dopff au Moulin, Dopff & Irion, Ginglinger, Willy Gisselbrecht, Kuentz-Bas, Muré, Ostertag, Willm, Wolfberger from the Éguisheim co-operative.

CRÉMANT DE BOURGOGNE AC
BURGUNDY
Chardonnay, Aligoté, Pinot Blanc, Pinot Noir

I don't go out on a limb and state categorically in my pre-Christmas newspaper articles, 'Forget cheap Champagne this year, Crémant de Bourgogne is better – and less pricy,' unless I really believe what I'm saying. Well, a few years ago Crémant de Bourgogne – then called Bourgogne Mousseux – was dismissed as raw and reedy fizz, only fit for the desperate. And I sort of agreed. To be honest, I could never understand why it was such a feeble fizz – after all didn't it come from Burgundy and have a good dose of Chardonnay in it? Well, I rather think that then, any left-over grapes from anywhere between Chablis and Beaujolais were pressed into service, but in the '80s things have taken a dramatic turn for the better.

Now, Chardonnay is the base grape – and is often used 100 per cent – and in the 1983, '85 and '86 vintages the full, soft, almost honeyed flavour of ripe Chardonnay made far more attractive drinking than the green, tart, bargain-basement Champagne produced further north. Cheap Champagne is now back on track, but I have to admit – I'm still buying Crémant de Bourgogne. It ages well for two to three years, but is usually good to drink when released. Best producers: Delorme, Lucius-Gregoire, Simmonet-Febvre; co-operatives at Bailly, Lugny, St-Gengoux-de-Scissé and Viré.

CRÉMANT DE LOIRE AC
CENTRAL LOIRE
Chenin Blanc, Chardonnay, Cabernet Franc

The Crémant de Loire AC was created in 1975 in an effort to improve the quality of Loire sparkling wines. It hasn't taken off, but not because the quality isn't good. In fact, although the grapes can come from anywhere in Anjou or Touraine, the required lower yield and the longer period the wine must remain on its yeast sediments to gain a soft, creamy flavour, mean that much Crémant de Loire – always made by the Champagne method – actually outclasses supposedly superior sparkling Saumur and Vouvray. The lack of precise geographical definition on the label is one reason for its lack of popularity, and certainly most of the Saumur and Vouvray firms – having spent years building up the reputation of their particular ACs – aren't likely to get enthusiastic about promoting a potential rival. Since Crémant de Loire is generally a softer wine than Saumur, it is usually good to drink as soon as it is released, but a bit of extra time doesn't do any harm. Best producers: Ackerman-Laurance, Berger, Gabillière, Vincent Girault, Gratien & Meyer, Liards.

CRÉPY AC
SAVOIE
Chasselas

I'm always reminded of lace curtains when I think of Crépy. That, and streamers at Christmas time. Which is just as well, because there's not a lot else to remember about Crépy – definitely a front-runner for the title 'white AC with the least discernible taste'. The problem is its grape, the Chasselas, which is fine for eating but produces wines which are water-white and water-light. It has a low alcoholic strength – only nine degrees – with a relatively noticeable acidity of the 'neutral lemon' sort. The only examples with any zip are those bottled off their own lees (*sur lie*, like the best Muscadets). This traps a little carbon dioxide in the wine and may also leave the slightest hint of yeast. The AC's 800,000 bottles are grown on 200 acres (80 hectares) of hillside vineyard just south of Lake Geneva. Some people age them, but I've never seen the point and would drink them as young as possible. Best producers: Goy, Mercier.

CRIOTS-BÂTARD-MONTRACHET AC
grand cru
CÔTE DE BEAUNE, BURGUNDY
Chardonnay

Criots-Bâtard-Montrachet is the only white *grand cru* entirely in the Chassagne-Montrachet commune. It occupies just 4 acres (1·6 hectares) of stony slope (*criots* is dialect for pebbles), facing due south towards the N6 road. To all intents and purposes the wine is the same as that of its neighbour Bâtard-Montrachet – rich, savoury, full of nuts and honey and spice – but since there is so little of it and it is fiendishly expensive, such a direct comparison is not easily made! There are only about 7000 bottles produced in an average year. Best years: 1986, '85, '84, '83, '82. Best producers: Bachelet, Blain-Gagnard, Delagrange, Marcilly.

CROZES-HERMITAGE AC
NORTHERN RHÔNE
Marsanne, Roussanne

Crozes-Hermitage is the largest of the northern Rhône ACs, 2000 acres (800 hectares) of vines spreading over the hillocks and plains behind the great hill of Hermitage, which towers above the little town of Tain. Crozes-Hermitage whites are almost never as exciting as Hermitage whites, even though the same grapes are used – the Marsanne and the Roussanne. This is because, except on the hilly slopes at Mercurol, most of the wine is grown on fairly flat, productive land and so the fruit lacks the astonishing concentration which marks out Hermitage.

There is another reason – modern wine-making techniques! While most white Hermitage is still produced in the traditional manner, which results in thick, gluey wines which may take ten years to open out properly, Crozes-Hermitage is almost always now made by careful cool fermentation to draw out the fruit and perfume at the expense of the weight. Although Desmeure still makes a highly successful old-style Crozes – thick with the flavour of buttered almonds and bruised apples – the best Crozes is now extremely fresh, with a lovely flavour of raw nuts and apple blossom, sometimes licked with aniseed and smartened up by a gentle but clean acidity.

But there is still a lot of dullish white about which lacks the splendour of the old style and the breeziness of the new. In general, drink white Crozes young, since the floral perfume will be the first thing to go. Best years: 1988, '85, '83. Best producers: Desmeure, Fayolle, Jaboulet, Pradelle.

DOISY-DAËNE, CH.
Barsac AC, *2ème cru classé*
BORDEAUX
Sémillon

This is a consistently good Barsac sweet wine and unusual in that the 35-acre (14-hectare) vineyard next to Château Climens is planted 100 per cent in Sémillon. Since Sémillon provides the fatness in Sauternes and Barsac wines this would lead me to expect Doisy-Daëne to be one of the richest examples around, but Pierre Dubourdieu ferments his wine in stainless steel and ages it for only one year in new oak barrels (as against two or three years in many other properties). The result is a wine which is certainly extremely sweet, but which has an almost lemony acidity clinging to the richness that not only stops it from cloying, but allows it to age well for ten years and more. Best (sweet) years: 1986, '83, '82, '80, '79.

There is also a highly successful dry white wine – Doisy-Daëne Sec, AC, which is full of perfume and fruit and far in excess of that achieved by any other Barsac property. How? Well, by not taking too much notice of the local AC laws, that's how. Monsieur Dubourdieu uses Sauvignon Blanc, Sémillon and Muscadelle for his dry white wine, which is fair enough – but then adds in both Chardonnay and Riesling, two grapes which *definitely* don't figure in the Bordeaux regulations. The wine is so good I suspect no-one from the local *appellation* authority has ever dared question the Bordeaux AC he sticks on the label! Best years (dry): 1988, '87, '86.

DOISY-VÉDRINES, CH.
Barsac AC, *2ème cru classé*
BORDEAUX
Sémillon, Sauvignon Blanc

This is a completely different style of wine to its neighbour Doisy-Daëne (they used to be the same estate until split in the nineteenth century). The wine is both fermented and aged in barrel and the result is *very* rich wine, fatter and stronger, more syrupy even than most Barsacs, but at the same time lacking a little of the perfumed charm of Climens or Doisy-Daëne which is such a mark of the best Barsac wines. Even so, I must say that if I'm paying high prices for my Barsac I want it to be *sweet* – so I'll stick by Doisy-Védrines without complaint.

Although 50 acres (20 hectares) of vineyard are planted with white grapes – 80 per cent Sémillon and 20 per cent Sauvignon Blanc – the total production of Barsac wine on the property is only 30,000 bottles (as against 48,000 from the smaller Doisy-Daëne). This is because much of the production is vinified dry and sold as Bordeaux AC. There are, in fact, a further 25 acres (10 hectares) of vineyard in *red* grapes – simply because during the 1960s no-one wanted to buy sweet wines and the owners had to develop a red and dry white wine brand in order to survive. Nowadays most Sauternes and Barsac châteaux make some dry white, though not many also make red! Best years: 1986, '85, '83, '82, '80, '76, '75.

DOMAINE DE CHEVALIER
Pessac-Léognan AC, *cru classé*
de Graves
BORDEAUX
Sauvignon Blanc, Sémillon

If there's ever going to be a white wine from Bordeaux to challenge the great *grands crus* of Puligny-Montrachet, I'll put my money on Domaine de Chevalier. Some of the Burgundians might too. At the VinExpo world wine fair in Bordeaux one of Burgundy's most famous winemakers was offered a glass of Domaine de Chevalier to taste blind. 'Mmm, lovely, nutty, intense, exciting *grand cru* Burgundy,' he thought. He said he liked it very much indeed and probably thought he'd made it. 'But it's a Bordeaux,' his host finally blurted out. The Burgundian's eyes narrowed, his lips pursed, and suddenly this 'nectar' was merely 'curious', the glass was set down and we heard no more from him for quite a while. But the point of the story is – Burgundians are notorious for liking only their own wines, and one of their luminaries was quite convinced Domaine de Chevalier was a top Burgundy. Well, it's not – although it's made with more care and devotion than most Burgundy winemakers would ever dream of.

This lovely wine comes from Pessac-Léognan, the new AC within Graves. The whole vineyard is only 37 acres (15 hectares), tucked into the forest just west of Léognan, and the white grapes occupy just 5 acres (2 hectares), producing at best 7000 bottles as against 60,000 bottles of red. The wine is both fermented and aged in oak barrels and, if anything, acquires more power and structure than most top white Burgundies. At first the Sauvignon greenness is very marked in the wine, but after three to four years this fades and the increasingly creamy, nutty warmth takes over, building at ten years old to a deep, honeyed, smoky richness, just touched with resin. In the best vintages the wine will still be improving at 15–20 years old, but with only 7000 bottles made each year, I don't know anyone who'd have the patience to wait that long – if they could get hold of a bottle in the first place, that is. Best years: 1986, '85, '84, '83, '82, '81, '79, '78, '75.

ENTRE-DEUX-MERS AC
BORDEAUX
Sémillon, Sauvignon Blanc, Muscadelle

▶ The clay-gravel soil of Entre-Deux-Mers in the Château Thieuley vineyards.

The phoenix rises from the ashes. Ten years ago Entre-Deux-Mers was a byword for boring, fruitless, vaguely sweet white wines of the sort that could put you off drinking for life. But in the 1980s there has been a dramatic about-turn, and Entre-Deux-Mers is increasingly coming to stand for some of the freshest, brightest, snappiest dry white in the whole of France.

The name means 'between two seas' – in this case the Garonne and the Dordogne rivers, which form a triangular wedge until they converge just north of the city of Bordeaux. The hinterland, east to the boundary of the Gironde *département*, contains over 6250 acres (2500 hectares) of vines – intensely cultivated in the north-west of the region, but gradually becoming interspersed with other crops as you head east. The AC only covers dry white wines, on average 13 million bottles annually. Red wines are produced extensively but they can only use the Bordeaux or Bordeaux Supérieur AC.

The technique behind the Entre-Deux-Mers revival is cold fermentation, and the flavours are totally dry, grassy, appley, often with a little more weight than straight Bordeaux Blanc AC. A few properties use new wooden barrels for ageing and this adds a creamy, apricoty flavour which can be delicious. Although there are still some dull, stale-nutty tasting wines, they are determinedly being squeezed out by the good guys. In general, drink the wine of the latest vintage, though the better wines will last a year or two. Much of the wine is made by modern co-operatives, but there are some excellent private producers. Best producers: Bonnet, Canet, les Gauthiers, Launay, Laurétan, Moulin-de-Launay, Thieuley, Toutigeac.

L'ÉTOILE AC
JURA
Savagnin, Chardonnay, Poulsard

L'Étoile – the star – is a lovely name for a tiny little area in the centre of the Côtes du Jura which has its own AC for white wines and *vin jaune* only. The Savagnin grape is much in evidence, though less violently so than further north in the region, and there is a good deal of Chardonnay, either unblended – when it is light and fresh, but creamy – or blended with Savagnin, when it does succeed in soothing the savage and dissuading it from its worst excesses. The red Poulsard grape can also be part of the white wine blend.

In general the wines are cleaner and fruitier than most Côtes du Jura or Arbois whites, and Champagne-method fizz can be as good as that of Pupillin in Arbois. There is also the daunting *vin jaune* and even the very rare sweet *vin de paille* (straw wine) – so beware! The best place to taste is the local co-operative in L'Étoile – it's the only place I've found inhabited whenever I've visited. But don't expect some efficient-looking concrete monstrosity – this co-operative is more like the ante-room of some half-forgotten monastery, and even then I met more chickens than humans. Best producers: Château d'Étoile, the l'Étoile co-operative, Domaine de Montbourgeau.

DE FARGUES, CH.
Sauternes AC, cru bourgeois
BORDEAUX
Sémillon, Sauvignon Blanc

The most remarkable thing about Château de Fargues is that, even though it is a mere Bourgeois Growth, not even considered when the Sauternes properties were classified in 1855, it regularly sells for more than any other wine in the AC save the great Château d'Yquem. Well, it does help if you're owned by the Lur-Saluces family who also own d'Yquem, I have to admit. Indeed they've owned de Fargues for 500 years – 300 years longer than they've owned the legendary d'Yquem!

The vineyard – only 30 acres (12 hectares) and right on the edge of the Sauternes AC in the village of Fargues – is by no means ideal, which presumably explains its exclusion from the Classed Growths, and the quality of the wine is more a tribute to the commitment of the Lur-Saluces family and their winemaker, Pierre Meslier, than it is to the inherent quality of the estate. The vines ripen ten days later than at d'Yquem, and the selection of grapes is so strict that each vine only yields two-thirds of a glass of wine! Even at d'Yquem they get one glass per vine. The result is that the total production rarely exceeds 10,000 bottles.

De Fargues is generally a rich, reasonably exotic wine, very honeyed, indeed almost syrupy, with something of the taste of pineapples and peaches, and a viscous feel, like lanolin, which coats your mouth. Fine, rich wine, but there are several Classed Growths which are better, and less expensive. Best years: 1986, '83, '81, '80, '76, '75.

FAUGÈRES AC
LANGUEDOC-ROUSSILLON
Clairette, Bourboulenc, Grenache
Blanc, Marsanne

Faugères, with its valleys stretching up into the mountains north of Béziers, in the Hérault, away from the suffocating heart of the Mediterranean plains, certainly has the terrain to make good white wine, but so far, while the red wine quality has steamed ahead, nothing much has happened with the white. Of course, if your only white grape is the dullish Clairette there's not an awful lot you can do and the best results so far have been from winemakers who have picked the grapes early, fermented the juice cold and then sold the wines for drinking as young as possible. These show a quite attractive, full, liquorice and apple softness for a few months, but it has long gone by the time they are 12 months old. As yet there is very little white made, but one or two more progressive growers have now planted Bourboulenc, Grenache Blanc and Marsanne, which, while still not the most exciting grapes in the world, should add a bit more character to the wine. Best producers: Fraïsse.

DE FIEUZAL, CH.
Pessac-Léognan AC
BORDEAUX
Sauvignon Blanc, Sémillon

The first time I ever tasted apricots in a dry white Bordeaux was at Château de Fieuzal. A neighbour nodded sagely as I waxed lyrical about this wonderful discovery, then took me outside and pointed to the right-hand side of the vineyard. 'That used to be an apricot grove,' he said, 'before they extended the vineyard.' Well, I was really chuffed, but for all the wrong reasons. I hadn't really pulled off some wonderful wine-tasting coup. It was just that de Fieuzal was the first property I had come across which was using cold fermentation, followed by maturation in new oak barrels – and this combined with ripe Sauvignon Blanc and Sémillon grapes does produce a wonderful taste of apricots! Since then I've found it more frequently every year, and I love it – but de Fieuzal led the way, and the wine is still outstandingly good, whether drunk young, or aged.

Yet the strange thing is that only the red wine is a Classed Growth. The little white plot does admittedly produce less than 10,000 bottles a year out of a total of over 100,000 bottles, but the quality should put it at the top of the white Classed Growths. Perhaps when the Graves classification was revised in 1959 to include white wines, the patch of white vines was still apricot trees. Best years: 1986, '85 '84, '83, '82, '81.

FIXIN AC
CÔTE DE NUITS, BURGUNDY
Pinot Blanc

Whenever you find that the AC regulations for a totally red wine area include the permission to make white wine, you presume that someone, sometime made a bit of it, don't you? Or do you just presume – as happened at Musigny a few miles further south – that the local grandee's wife was partial to a drop and so allowance was made for white. Well, Fixin is the first major Côte de Nuits village south of Dijon, with 370 acres (150 hectares) devoted to Pinot Noir red wines. Or should I say 369 acres because I have managed to winkle out *one* grower of white Fixin – Bruno Clair, who has planted a few rows of Pinot Blanc (rather than Burgundy's more normal Chardonnay). So I have discovered white Fixin exists. I haven't yet managed to taste it, but I'll report when I do.

GAILLAC AC
SOUTH-WEST
Mauzac Blanc, L'En de l'El, Ondenc
and others

There are a few encouraging signs that the tide of staggeringly dull Gaillac which has been siphoned off to us over the years has been at least halted, and that the true potential of a vineyard area which dates from pre-Christian times will increasingly be realized. Altogether about seven million bottles of wine are produced from vineyards spread quite widely between Albi and St-Sulpice in the Tarn *département*, and about half these are white.

The Mauzac, with its sharp, but attractive, green apple bite, is the main grape, abetted by the local l'En de l'El (which seems to mean 'out of sight' in their dialect), Ondenc, Muscadelle, Sauvignon and Sémillon. Mauzac has a very 'direct' line of taste, so even the best whites are rather stern, but from a decent grower there is a refreshing sharp apple and liquorice fruit.

The star of Gaillac, however, is the fizz – made by the Champagne method, or by the *méthode rurale* in which the fermentation is arrested, then finished off in bottle, to create the bubbles. This Gaillac Mousseux AC can be fabulous – full of apricots and apples, honey and peaches and a sting of tobacco and pepper too. Not quite dry, it's outstanding sparkling wine. The local co-ops make a *pétillant* (a sort of demi-semi-sparkler), Gaillac Perlé AC, which is not the same thing by any means. In fact it's usually so feeble you'd need a microscope to know it was sparkling at all. In general, drink all the Gaillacs as young as possible. Best producers: Albert, Boissel-Rhodes, Bosc Long, Jean Cros, Labarthe, Larroze.

▼The Gaillac AC takes its name from a small town on the river Tarn but includes some 75 communes. Over half the vineyards are planted with white grapes.

GARD

GARD
LANGUEDOC-ROUSSILLON

Gard could consider itself a bit unlucky, because of all the southern *départements* it has the least coastline and what it has is merely a sliver of unprepossessing marshland just east of Montpellier. It's a little unlucky in its wines, too, because although there is a decent chunk of the Côtes du Rhône in the Gard, with Tavel and Lirac inside its borders, the real Rhône fireworks are to the east and the north. To the south and west of the Gard, the Languedoc is taking off as a wine producer, with increasing amounts of exciting gutsy wines – and yet the Gard can't quite get in on that act either. Lirac apart, its only white AC of any renown is the flat, dull Clairette de Bellegarde, although one or two fresh whites are beginning to appear from good, young, Costières du Gard producers. Otherwise, the only bright signs are the experimental plots of Chardonnay and Sauvignon Blanc and the occasional Grenache Blanc under the Vin de Pays du Gard banner, mostly from those same unprepossessing marshes near Montpellier.

GEWÜRZTRAMINER

Although the Gewürztraminer is a popular grape throughout the wine-making world, in France, the country where it most easily reaches its peak, the variety is found in only one place, Alsace. Alsace's proximity to Germany, and its Germanic dialect, explain the long, very German name. *Gewürz* means 'spicy', and *Traminer* means 'from Tramin' – actually a German-speaking town in the Tyrolean region of northern Italy, the Alto Adige, and the presumed birthplace of this variety.

It is the 'spice' which has made Gewürztraminer famous, but the intense, often overpowering smell and taste isn't so much spicy as exotically perfumed, muskily floral and tropically fruity! It's Nìvea Creme, flowers – full, blowsy roses, just losing their petals but still exuding heady perfumes in a last ditch effort to seduce – and tropical fruits – especially lychees, mangoes and maybe peaches, often flecked with fresh ground pepper.

Sometimes, on the down side, there's a rather oily tackiness and consequent lack of refreshing acidity – but if the pungency is there I can cope with that. Of course, the shock after all those purple epithets is that Alsace Gewürztraminer is almost always dry! Seems impossible, but it is. And the fact that it covers 6250 acres (2500 hectares) in Alsace, which makes it Alsace's most widely planted grape, does mean that styles can vary considerably, but even the lightest ought to have a few of these marvellous self-indulgent flavours in there somewhere.

GILETTE, CH.
Sauternes AC
BORDEAUX
Sémillon, Sauvignon Blanc, Muscadelle

A tasting to display the new vintage from Château Gilette was held a couple of years ago. It was delicious wine: deep and honeyed with a fabulous gooey richness, like toffee and butter melted over squashy banana. In fact, it was holding up very well for a 1955. Yes. I really mean it, 1955! This astonishing Sauternes property of a mere 8·6 acres (3·5 hectares), huddled down near the Garonne river in the village of Preignac, releases its vintage wine at anything between 20 and 30 years old – when even the best of its neighbours are beginning to taste distinctly wobbly at the knees.

Production is tiny – perhaps 500 cases, sometimes more. Gilette's method is to pick the grapes in their full flood of overripeness, seething with the richness-concentrating noble rot; to ferment the wines very gently, and then to store them in little concrete vats for a decade or two. Whereas wooden barrels add flavour and allow oxygen to speed up the maturation of the wine, concrete is inert. Almost nothing happens for year after year, but the wine imperceptibly deepens and gains character. If I have to be absolutely honest I think the top Sauternes made in the traditional way are a tiny bit more exciting, their intense sweetness a little more unnervingly exotic – but Gilette is a great original and I wouldn't have it 'wise up' to boring things like economic necessity for anything. Best years: 1959, '55, '53, '49.

GIVRY AC
CÔTE CHALONNAISE, BURGUNDY
Chardonnay

There was a time when the wines of Givry were reckoned to be as fine as those of the famous Gevrey-Chambertin and Nuits St-Georges; Henri IV was said to regard Givry as his favourite wine (but his mistress did have a vineyard there) . . . Even so, I'm afraid these historic Givrys were red, and frequently the fact that Givry produces a small amount of white – about 65,000 bottles out of 600,000 – is easily overlooked. The number of Burgundy tastings I've been to which featured a white Givry can be counted on the fingers of one hand. They've usually veered towards the sharp and neutral (not at all like Chardonnay should be in Burgundy) but in recent years the wines seem to be a little fuller and nuttier – which is much more attractive. Best years: 1986, 85. Best producers: Derain, Joblot, Ragot, Thénard.

ALFRED GRATIEN
Champagne AC
CHAMPAGNE
Pinot Noir, Chardonnay, Pinot Meunier

If I have to own up to having a favourite Champagne, I must admit it'll have to be Alfred Gratien. Alfred who? Well, this isn't a big company – producing only 200,000 bottles in its backstreet cellars in Épernay (the giant Moët & Chandon, for instance, produces 18 million) but whoever said you had to be big to be good? No, the reason I love Gratien is because in the modern world of Champagne where many companies are more concerned about their international brand image than they are about the quality of their wines, Gratien declares that its image *is* the quality of the wine and nothing else. The wines are made in wooden casks – *very* rare nowadays, only moved by gravity since pumping is thought to bruise the wine, kept on their lees under a real cork – most other houses use crown corks similar to those on a Coca-Cola bottle – and stored appreciably longer than usual before release. The non-vintage blend is usually four years old when sold; many other companies sell their wine aged for little more than two years. The vintage wine is deliciously ripe and toasty when released but can age for another ten years, and is usually in the slightly less fizzy Crémant style.

GRAVES AC
BORDEAUX
Sémillon, Sauvignon Blanc

The Graves has always relied for its good reputation on the efforts of a small number of famous properties situated just to the south and west of the city of Bordeaux. Here the soil was extremely gravelly – which is how the area came to be called 'Graves' – and the climate was slightly warmer than the Médoc to the north, excellent conditions for producing high-quality wine. Well, it can't rely on the efforts of these favoured few any longer, because the villages in the north of the Graves region, clustered close to Bordeaux, have broken away and formed their own AC – Pessac-Léognan – to emphasize what they see, quite rightly, as their historic superiority over the southern Graves. So they form a kind of 'super-Graves' and the less-favoured area – increasingly clay and sand – is left with the straight Graves AC.

It is not an AC I would particularly want to be lumbered with since Graves for too long has been a byword for vaguely medium, fairly fruitless, murky-tasting wine of no style. However, there is a new wave of wine-making sweeping through the Graves which is producing bone-dry wines, with lots of snappy freshness and a lovely, rather apricoty flavour. Add to this a touch of spice from a few new oak barrels, and Graves AC doesn't really have any reason to be sorry for itself at all. The grapes used are Sémillon and Sauvignon Blanc: the former gives weight, the latter, a grassy tang.

The soil is similar in the south towards Langon and there are several villages to the south of the Garonne river, like Portets, Arbanats and Illats (in the sweet white Cérons AC but allowed the Graves AC for its dry wines) which are already making a name for themselves and their fresh, fruity whites. In general, drink within two years, but the wines which have been given some oak maturity can age much longer. Best properties: Cabannieux, Clos Floridène, Constantin, Domaine de la Grave, la Garence, Magence, Rahoul, Respide-Médeville, Roquetaillade-la-Grange, St-Pierre.

GRAVES AND PESSAC-LÉOGNAN

The world of Graves was thrown into turmoil in 1987 when the northern part of the area, closest to the city of Bordeaux, and containing all the most famous properties, declared independence, and announced that from henceforth it would be called Pessac-Léognan, after its two leading communes. So now, although the whole region is still known as the Graves, it has two ACs: Pessac-Léognan for the area closest to Bordeaux, and Graves for the rest, primarily to the south and encircling Cérons, Sauternes and Barsac.

The name 'Graves' means gravel, and the vineyards which now make up Pessac-Léognan are notable for their gravelly soil. Gravelly soil is heat-retaining and quick-draining, and this, allied to a warmer climate than that of the Médoc further north, and a close proximity to the city of Bordeaux, meant that the 'Graves', as the area became known, was for a long time the leading Bordeaux wine area. And until *very* recently the bulk of the wine made was white. However, the majority of this was extremely *bad* white wine, so it is hardly surprising that almost two-thirds of the wine now is red.

However, the world is thirsty for good white wine, and while some proprietors were busy replacing white vines with red, others were revolutionizing the way white wine was made and in so doing were creating one of France's most exciting white wine regions. The major grapes are the Sémillon and the Sauvignon Blanc, abetted by a little Muscadelle.

Sémillon by itself can be a little flabby, while Sauvignon Blanc can be rather earthy and raw. However, if the juice is vinified carefully at a low

►Château la Louvière, a non-classified property near Léognan, makes its white wine from 85% Sauvignon and 15% Sémillon.

temperature in stainless steel, delicious clean fruit flavours immediately become apparent. If the fermentation takes place in a small barrel and if the wine is then aged in new oak barrels, the result is a wine of rich apricot fruit and an exciting creamy vanilla spice which immediately puts it in the top quality league for white wine worldwide.

Pessac-Léognan encompasses ten communes. Although its supremely gravelly soil does favour red wines over the rest of the Graves, whites can be grown successfully on the sandier, and less well-exposed areas further south towards Langon. The Graves AC only applies to dry whites, but there is a little-known Graves Supérieures AC, which can be applied to sweet wines, and which sometimes comes up with super sweet wines at a very low price. However, if the Graves is to be encouraged to produce world-class wine, we mustn't try to force the price too low — or it won't be worth the winemakers' while.

MAIN ACs
Graves
Graves Supérieures
Pessac-Léognan

MAIN CHÂTEAUX
Carbonnieux
Domaine de Chevalier
de Fieuzal
Haut-Brion
Malartic-Lagravière
Rahoul
Smith-Haut-Lafitte
La Tour-Martillac

MAIN GRAPES
Sauvignon Blanc
Sémillon

GRAVES DE VAYRES AC
BORDEAUX
Sémillon, Sauvignon Blanc,
Muscadelle

A small enclave in the north of the Entre-Deux-Mers region, running down to the Dordogne river and looking across to Libourne and the red wine paradise of Pomerol and St-Émilion. It's one of those ACs which is rapidly becoming irrelevant, because its most important product was a reasonably good version of the medium-sweet whites which used to swamp Entre-Deux-Mers, and for which there is now very little market at anything but subsistence level prices. So most of the whites are now made dry, to be drunk at one to two years old, and as such they are perfectly pleasant mainstream white Bordeaux wines. I've never come across a bottle which actually excited me. Total production of white is about 19·7 million bottles. Best years: 1987, '86, '85.

GRAVES SUPÉRIEURES AC
BORDEAUX
Sémillon, Sauvignon Blanc,
Muscadelle

This is an *appellation* in decline, covering the whole Graves region south of Bordeaux. The intention was to use it for dry, medium and sweet white Graves of at least 12 degrees alcohol, which in the case of the dry wines would ensure only the ripest grapes would be used (straight Graves has a minimum strength of 11 degrees). But the AC never caught on, especially since the producers of dry wines found no benefit at all in tacking Graves Supérieures after their name – in fact, since the most successful producers using the AC come from the southern Graves around the Sauternes area, and *they* apply it to sweet wines, it became positively confusing for the dry producers' customers, so they dropped it altogether. There are some fair wines from the villages of Portets and Langon in the south, and the AC of Cérons can also label its sweet wines Graves Supérieures. The sweet wines can, in decent years, have a good lanolin richness to them and quite a sweet, buttery taste, making not bad Sauternes substitutes – at a lot less money. In general, drink these wines young. Best years: 1986, '83. Best producer: Clos St-Georges.

GROS PLANT DU PAYS NANTAIS VDQS
LOWER LOIRE
Gros Plant

1987 wasn't a vintage which won widespread acclaim in France. But in the damp, marshy, salt-flats round Nantes, at the mouth of the Loire, they were rejoicing: they had finally made wine which a foreigner not brought up on draughts of battery acid and spirit vinegar might possibly enjoy – because the vineyards around Nantes are the home of the Gros Plant du Pays Nantais, one of the fiercest, sourest, most gum-numbing white wines the world has yet invented. And in 1987, somehow, the acid just wasn't there.

But, traditionally, Gros Plant is searing stuff – one of the grape's other names is Picpoul which roughly translates as 'lipstinger' and it is also grown in the Cognac and Armagnac regions because its high acid wine is perfect for distilling. Yet strangely, if you have a great plateful of seafood plonked down in front of you – wreathed in seaweed and still heaving with the motion of the ocean and the crunching of Atlantic rollers against the battered Brittany coast – you'll find the barefaced, eye-watering tartness of Gros Plant is surprisingly well-suited to oysters, mussels, crab and the rest. Since they eat seafood by the bucketful around Nantes I can only presume that explains the survival of Gros Plant as the local white. But, except in 1987, I'd pay a few francs more and drink the other equally dry, and – in comparison – positively sumptuous local wine: Muscadet. Best year: 1987. Best producers: Bois-Bruley, Clos des Rosiers, Cuvée du Marquisat, Guindon, Hallereau, Métaireau, Sauvion.

GUIRAUD, CH.
Sauternes AC, *premier cru
classé*
BORDEAUX
Sémillon, Sauvignon Blanc,
Muscadelle

Guiraud was just about the first Sauternes I ever drank. A local off-licence had loads of the stuff on a top shelf; its label was dusty with neglect, but you couldn't help noticing the sultry, burnished gold colour of the wine, challenging the world to get those bottles down and drink up. I don't know what the shopkeeper thought of this strange troupe of supposedly impoverished students filing in and cleaning him out of those hoary has-beens from the top shelf. But that wine was so rich it flowed as slow as honey from the bottle, the colour was turning the unquenchable, raging gold of a dying sun, and the flavour was burnt syrup, nuts boiled in caramel, orange peel from the Christmas pudding, honey and cream and crystallized pineapple chunks.

Well, that was the 1961 and '62. We'd never had anything like it, and once we'd polished off our hoard – that was it. Guiraud went into decline – we ran out of money – and the property was heading for oblivion until 1981, when it was bought by an obsessively determined Canadian, bent on making great Sauternes. He's managed it. His 1983 was exceptional. His '86 is quite possibly the richest young Sauternes I have ever tasted. The vineyard is a good one, classified as a First Growth, and big – 185 acres (75 hectares) of vines in the south of the AC, just by the village of Sauternes. The owner, Hamilton Narby, ruthlessly selects only the best grapes, uses at least 50 per cent new oak each year to age the wine, and charges a very high price – quite rightly since it is clearly one of Sauternes' most exciting wines. The wine needs at least ten years to reach its peak – and good years may need 15–20. Best years: 1986, '83, '82, '81.

HAUT-BRION, CH.
Pessac-Léognan AC, *premier cru classé de Graves*
BORDEAUX
Sémillon, Sauvignon Blanc

Haut-Brion is certainly Pessac-Léognan's greatest red wine property, and its owners would like to claim the same quality achievement for their white wine – 12,000 bottles a year from 7 acres (3 hectares). The inconsistency which can plague the red wine also affects the white, and since the price of the latter is an arm and both legs I'm not so keen to risk a disappointing bottle. But, at its best, Haut-Brion is fabulous wine, perfectly marrying the vanilla and spice of new oak barrels with a fruit which seems almost neutral at first – just a sensation rather than a taste – but which over five to ten years blossoms out in to a wonderfully lush flavour of nuts and spice, cream and a hint of apricots, sometimes a hint of pine resin too. The wine is bought almost entirely by very rich people who certainly don't invite *me* to dinner. . . Best years: 1986, '85, '84, '83, '82, '81, '79, '76.

HAUTES-CÔTES DE BEAUNE AC
CÔTE D'OR, BURGUNDY
Chardonnay

These wines come from vineyards set back in the hills behind the great Côte de Beaune slopes. If scenery could influence what went into the bottle, this lost little region of twisting country lanes, ancient trees and purest sylvan peace would surely produce ecstatic wines. As it is, the very beauty of the land is the wine's undoing. For, in this higgledy-piggledy landscape, the aspect of the sun is rarely ideal and the altitude, at 1150–1300 feet (350–400 metres), is also a handicap; all the best vineyard sites on the Côte de Beaune itself are below 1000 feet (300 metres). So don't expect very ripe flavours from the Hautes-Côtes de Beaune.

That said, the 20 villages with the right to AC can produce pleasant, slightly sharp Chardonnay and, under the Bourgogne Aligoté AC, some good, spirited, ultra-dry Aligoté. In really hot years, like 1982, '83 and '85, the Chardonnay can even get a dry, but discernibly nutty, taste after a couple of years which slightly – ever so slightly – might remind you of a wispy Chassagne-Montrachet. Whites account for about 40,000 bottles in a total of two million. Best years: 1986, '85, '83, '82. Best producers: Caves des Hautes-Côtes, Cornu, Jacob, Joliet, Marcilly, Château de Mercey.

HAUTES-CÔTES DE NUITS AC
CÔTE D'OR, BURGUNDY
Chardonnay

The relatively compact Hautes-Côtes de Nuits vineyards belong to 14 villages directly behind the Côte de Nuits. Inevitably, altitude, averaging out at 1300 feet (400 metres), is a problem. It isn't for nothing that the steep slopes on the Côte de Nuits proper are mostly left unplanted at more than 1050 feet (325 metres), and frequently the land is just scrub at anything over this height. So ripening is by no means guaranteed. As the vineyards mature this is less serious, and attractive lightweight wines can be made, but so far the best are red. The whites from Chardonnay and Aligoté (not covered by the Hautes-Côtes AC) tend to be rather dry and flinty. Interestingly, one of the fuller whites I've tried was not Chardonnay at all but its less good look-alike, Pinot Blanc. Production of white is only 50,000 bottles out of a total of over one million. In general drink young – although they will age. Best years: 1986, '85, '83, '82. Best producers: Caves des Hautes-Côtes, Chaley, Dufouleur, Hudelot, Thévenot-le-Brun, Verdet.

L'HÉRAULT
LANGUEDOC-ROUSSILLON

The Hérault *département* is the fountainhead of France's infamous contribution to the EEC wine lake – *and* the heart of the Brave New World of wine-making which could yet transform the Midi into a high-tech, California-style provider of cheap, attractive, everyday table wines. This dull, tired land centred on Béziers and Montpellier is the most densely planted *département* in France – and until recently had the fewest ACs. But there is now a good deal of interesting wine coming from the hills to the north of Béziers, most of it as yet red, but as methods of cool-fermentation in stainless steel take hold, and as new grape varieties are planted, the whites are improving too. The only white AC in the Hérault used to be the fairly dull Clairette du Languedoc, though several villages in the new Côteaux du Languedoc AC have a reputation for white – notably La Clape and Pinet.

However, Languedoc-Roussillon's leading fortified Muscat is made at Frontignan, on the coast near Sète, and the 27 *vins de pays de zone* in the Hérault, which now produce 200 million bottles a year, are encouraging wine merchants to be innovative and to aim for quality. Chardonnay, Sauvignon Blanc, Sémillon and Marsanne are appearing as well as attractively aromatic versions of Grenache Blanc, Bourboulenc, Macabeo and dry Muscat. The steps are still faltering ones, but the Hérault *is* taking the first steps on the long path back to quality. Some good Vin de Pays de l'Hérault producers are Bosc/Cante Cigale (the best), Lenthéric, Prieuré d'Amilhac.

HERMITAGE AC
NORTHERN RHÔNE
Marsanne, Roussanne

Chante-Alouette
APPELLATION HERMITAGE CONTRÔLÉE
BOTTLED BY
M. CHAPOUTIER S.A.
NÉGOCIANTS-ÉLEVEURS A TAIN L'HERMITAGE (DRÔME) FRANCE
e 75cl

▶Dawn light over Tain l'Hermitage picks out the chapel which gives Hermitage hill and its vineyards their name. Below, in the morning mist, lies the river Rhône.

I did a tasting of Hermitage reds and whites from Gérard Chave (reckoned by many Hermitage fans to be the best producer). The reds were tremendous, though they were clearly getting tired at the 20-year-old mark and distinctly fading long before they hit 40. But those whites! I mean, for the first five or ten years I thought – what's so special about these dull, heavy, lumpish things? And then they just got better and better. They had to drag me away from the simply sensational 1929 *white*!

Later I went round to Chapoutier's, one of the most important Hermitage merchants. I wasn't enjoying the reds that much, and I think Monsieur Chapoutier noticed because he disappeared for a moment and came bouncing back with – a 1942 white. Fantastic stuff. Unbelievably deep and rich, alive and kicking long after the reds had given up the ghost. Yet it is *red* Hermitage which has the reputation for ageing. Well! Some winemakers, like Jaboulet, are making modern, fruity, fragrant whites – with an exciting floral, lemon peel, liquorice and apple flavour. Lovely at one to two years old but I can't see how they'll improve.

But there are others – from grisly-minded traditionalists who won't be swayed by fashion and the chance of an easy sale. They've been growing the Marsanne and Roussanne grapes on the dizzy slopes of the giant hill of Hermitage for generations, and they don't care if their wine then takes generations to mature so long as it is the 'real thing'. The flavour of Hermitage from someone like Gray, Chave, Grippat or Chapoutier will seem fat and oily at first, reeking of bruised apples, soured peaches and unswept farmyard rubbish; but give it ten years, 20, maybe twice as long, and a remarkable transformation takes place – apples and pears blend with fresh-roasted nuts, toffee, liquorice, pine resin, herbs from the wild Rhône hills, mint and peaches and cream. From such sullen beginnings the glory of white Hermitage finally blazes forth – for you if you can wait, for your children if you can't. About 30 per cent of the vineyard is white, producing some 200,000 bottles a year. Best years: 1987, '85, '83, '82, '78, '76, '71, '70, '69. Best producers: Chapoutier, Chave, Desmeure, Gray, Grippat, Guigal, Jaboulet.

JASNIERES AC
CENTRAL LOIRE
Chenin Blanc

I didn't think I'd ever be able to look a Jasnières producer in the eye and say, 'I would like to try your wine'. All my attempts to enjoy it have found me reeling and gasping for breath as it confirmed its reputation as the Loire's most uncompromising, bone-dry Chenin wine. But last December, at a Wine Fair in Paris, I got caught by a most disarming, unthreatening lady who, I discovered too late, owned a largish vineyard – in Jasnières. Without breaching the most basic rules of good manners, I didn't have a lot of choice really but to taste it. So there I was, shifting from foot to foot and wondering if my travel insurance covered dissolved teeth as she wrested the cork from the bottle with some difficulty (if I'd been a cork in a Jasnières bottle I'd have been out quicker than a rat up a drain-pipe).

Well, it was delicious. This young, 1986, Domaine de la Chanière white Jasnières was very dry but full of lovely apricot, honey and even sultana overtones which were already attractive but would be fabulous in five years' time. It was simply a case of modern wine-making. The skins of the grapes were steeped in the juice before fermentation to extract the perfume which the skins possess – but which is usually lost in the crushing and running-off of juice. And the fermentation had been careful, clean and cold. So this tiny, 47-acre (19-hectare) AC, 25 miles (40km) north of Tours on the little Loir river (Tours is on the big Loire river) still makes bone-dry Chenin white – but it *can* be delicious rather than a heavy-duty gum scourer. Best years: 1986, 1985, 1983, 1982. Best producers: Chanière, Fresneau, Pinon.

JURANÇON AC
SOUTH-WEST
Petit Manseng, Gros Manseng,
Courbu

'I was a girl when I met this prince; aroused, imperious, treacherous as all great seducers are – Jurançon.' It's not my quote, but I wish it were (though I'd have to do something about the 'girl' bit). It's the great French novelist Colette, and the confident power of suggestion – unhindered by the requirements of accurate description, or grape types, or even taste – puts us wine-writers to shame. So. Back to my humble task. What is Jurançon? Well, it's the historic white wine of the western Pyrenees. It's made mostly from the excellent Petit Manseng and the not quite so good Gros Manseng, and is dry or sweet. Dry, labelled Jurançon Sec, the wine is rather dull and flat – especially as made by the rather too-powerful local co-operative, though a new oenologist is rapidly raising standards. But sweet, from one of the few independent growers, it can be heavenly. They let the grapes hang late into November – shrivelled and thick with sugar – then slowly ferment the juice and leave the wine for a couple of years, till it develops a lusciousness of honey, nuts and mangoes, strongly spiced with cinnamon, cloves and ginger, and always held back from cloying by a pure laser streak of lemon acidity. Rare, special and almost worthy of Colette's immortal prose. Best producers: Cauhapé, Clos Cancaillaü, Clos Uroulat, Cru Lamouroux, Guirouilh.

KRUG
Champagne AC
CHAMPAGNE
Pinot Noir, Chardonnay, Pinot Meunier

If Bollinger has cornered the image of high society's favourite fizz for whooping it up, Krug has always had a much more demure reputation. Partly this is because the cheapest bottle of Krug costs more than most companies' most expensive cuvées. The Krug non-vintage is called Grande Cuvée and actually knocks spots off the general run of De Luxe brands which one sometimes suspects were merely developed for the night club trade rather than anything more salubrious. It comes in a supremely elegant wide-based bottle and although splendid on release, gets much more exciting with a year or two's extra ageing. The blend is made up of as many as 50 different wines from up to 25 different villages and utilizing perhaps eight different vintages going back ten years or more. The result is perfect, contemplative harmony in a sparkling wine. Sheer pleasure. Krug also do an excellent vintage wine and a single vineyard Clos du Mesnil Blanc de Blancs.

LADOIX-SERRIGNY AC
CÔTE DE BEAUNE, BURGUNDY
Chardonnay

I have actually got a bottle of Ladoix white. It was given to me by a contralto who had it given to her by a bass. I'm a baritone, waiting for a soprano to share it with, perhaps. Well, I can think of worse offers. After all, white wine from Ladoix-Serrigny, the northernmost village in the Côte de Beaune, is very rare – they only produce 15,000 bottles each year. And the wine *is* good – a light, clean Chardonnay flavour, softened to nuttiness with a little oak ageing and two or three years' maturity. I just wish I had another bottle in case the soprano and I get on. Best years: 1985, '83, '82. Best producer: Cornu.

LAFAURIE-PEYRAGUEY, CH.
Sauternes AC, *premier cru classé*
BORDEAUX
Sémillon, Sauvignon Blanc, Muscadelle

It's fashionable to criticize the detrimental effect on quality following the takeover of a property by a large merchant. Often the criticism is justified, as organization becomes centralized in some distant head office, traditions are lost and loyalty undermined – but the large Cordier company has always taken great care of its properties (they bought this one in 1913). In the 1980s their investment and commitment in this 50-acre (20-hectare) *premier cru* near the hamlet of Bommes have made Lafaurie-Peyraguey one of the most improved Sauternes properties in recent vintages. They made outstanding wines in the great '86 and '83 vintages, but also were very successful in lesser years like '85, '84 and '82. Lafaurie-Peyraguey isn't the most exotically rich of the *premier cru* wines, but it does have a deep apricot and pineapple syrup sweetness, a cream and nuts softness and a good, clear, lemony acidity – wonderful for long ageing. Best years: 1986, '85, '83, '82, '81, '80, '79.

LIRAC AC
SOUTHERN RHÔNE
Clairette, Bourboulenc, Picpoul and others

▲ At work in the Lirac vineyards. This small AC makes a little white wine but hardly any of it is exported.

I wish there were more white Lirac because decent dry whites are at a premium in the southern Rhône, and white Lirac can be as good as white Châteauneuf-du-Pape when it's on form. There are 2200 acres (875 hectares) of Lirac, directly west of Châteauneuf-du-Pape, producing 2½ million bottles of wine – but so far only about 100,000 of these are white, though the total is increasing. Clairette is the chief grape, with other local varieties added. Despite this typical southern hotchpotch, the flavour of white Lirac is extremely fresh, with a simple apple and aniseed fruit that is quite delicious. You must drink it young though, preferably before it's a year old, because the perfume goes and what's left is nice, soft Rhône white – which tastes OK, but not a patch on what was there before. Best producer: Maby.

LOUPIAC AC
BORDEAUX
Sémillon, Muscadelle, Sauvignon Blanc

A sweet wine area directly across the Garonne from Barsac. The few remaining owners who still try to make sweet wine must gaze gloomily across the river and long for the renown of Barsac, and its prices – at least twice the level of a Loupiac. But the Loupiac growers, despite using the same grapes, can't persuade noble rot to affect their vines nearly so frequently as it does in Barsac, and they do have a far higher permitted yield – 40 hectolitres per hectare as against Barsac's 25 hectolitres per hectare. So they almost never achieve the concentrated richness needed to command top prices. Despite this, there are some good estates producing wine which is attractively sweet, if not really gooey. Drink young, though it can age. Best years: 1986, '85, '83. Best producers: du Cros, Loupiac-Gaudiet, Mazarin, de Ricaud.

LOIRE

The Loire river cuts right through the heart of France, east to west. It rises a mere 30 miles (50km) from the Rhône valley and, after surging northwards, executes a graceful arc up to Orléans and then unhurriedly sets its course for the sea.

Along the way the Loire manages to encompass some of France's best-known wines – Sancerre, Anjou, Muscadet – with some of its most obscure – Jasnières, Bonnezeaux, Vin de l'Orléanais. In all there are about a hundred wines made in the Loire valley – reds, rosés, sparkling, and the entire gamut of whites from searingly dry to unctuously sweet.

The upper reaches of the Loire don't produce a great quantity of wine, but what there is has become world-famous, because this is the home of Sancerre and Pouilly-Fumé – the snappy green-tinged Sauvignon wines.

The province of Touraine is a positive market garden, with vines taking their place alongside a host of other crops, but the Sauvignon grape excels here too, and at Vouvray and Montlouis, the Chenin makes pretty good fizz and still whites ranging from sweet to very dry.

Anjou is most famous for rosé, but the best wines are white, either sweet from the Layon valley or very dry Chenin from Savennières. Saumur's sparklers are well-known and good in their biting way.

Finally, in the low flatland around Nantes they grow Muscadet which is rapidly becoming the most famous of all French white wines on the export market, due to its uncomplicated style – and its friendly price.

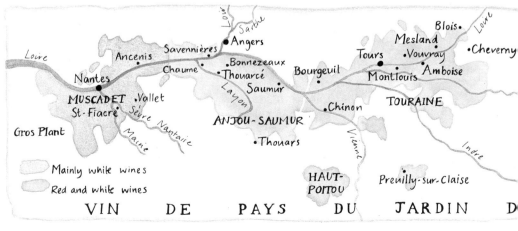

Mainly white wines

Red and white wines

VIN DE PAYS DU JARDIN D

MAIN WINES	Pouilly-sur-Loire
Anjou	Quarts de Chaume
Bonnezeaux	Quincy
Cheverny	Reuilly
Coteaux d'Ancenis	St-Pourçain
Coteaux de l'Aubance	Sancerre
Coteaux du Giennois	Saumur
Coteaux du Layon	Saumur Mousseux
Coteaux du Layon-Villages	Savennières
Coteaux du Vendômois	Touraine
Crémant de Loire	Vin de l'Orléanais
Gros Plant du Pays Nantais	Vin de Pays du Jardin de la France
Jasnières	Vin du Haut-Poitou
Menetou-Salon	Vouvray
Montlouis	
Muscadet	MAIN GRAPES
Muscadet de Sèvre-et-Maine	Chardonnay
Muscadet des Coteaux de la Loire	Chenin Blanc
Pouilly-Fumé	Sauvignon Blanc

◄Sancerre, in the Upper Loire, produces one of France's trendiest white wines – from the super-tangy Sauvignon Blanc.

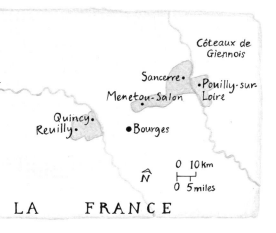

MÂCON AC
MÂCONNAIS, BURGUNDY
Chardonnay

The most basic AC in the Mâconnais – increasingly used for red wines, but usurped by the superior Mâcon-Villages for whites. Of the 14 million or so bottles produced, only three million are now sold under the simple name Mâcon Blanc, or Mâcon Supérieur (rarely a quality indicator, merely a sign that the wine has reached a minimum of 11 degrees alcohol as against the 10 degree minimum for straight Mâcon). This used to be a cheap, bland quaffer – probably the least impressive wine made from Chardonnay in all France. Now it is a rather expensive basic quaffer, since the magic name Chardonnay has allowed prices to boom. Quality has rarely kept pace with price inflation, and it is generally worth moving up to Mâcon-Villages. Occasionally, good wines will appear from quality-conscious shippers like Duboeuf, but in any case the wine should be drunk for its simple lemony zing – and as young as possible. Best years: 1987, '86.

MÂCON-VILLAGES AC
MÂCONNAIS, BURGUNDY
Chardonnay

I used to wax and wane, enthusiastic or despairing, about Mâcon-Villages in fairly equal proportions, but I must admit that recently there's been a lot more waning than waxing. This is chiefly because in the period 1981–87 there have been a series of good to excellent vintages. There has been no excuse whatsoever for us not to see a steady stream of enjoyable, fruity, fresh, creamy Mâcon-Villages Chardonnay wines flowing out of the region at a fair price. Maybe it's their bad luck down in the Mâconnais, but this period has also seen the revival of Bordeaux as a producer of attractive whites – at half the price of Mâcon-Villages. And we've also been regaled and seduced by the Chardonnays of Australia and New Zealand – twice the flavour and cheaper every time.

Even so, I would still enjoy much Mâcon-Villages if it was presented as a soft, appley – slightly grapy even – Chardonnay wine to be enjoyed and not made a fuss of. But that magic Chardonnay variety can be a blessing and a curse. It is a marvellous, easy-growing grape producing lots of good wine at not too great a cost – that's the blessing. The curse is the name: 'Chardonnay' has a magic ring. White Burgundy is Chardonnay's most sought-after manifestation, so if the Mâconnais can dub itself 'white Burgundy' (as it obviously can) then the chance exists for exploitation of its 'white Burgundy' wine. Which is what has happened. Mâcon-Villages can be very attractive, direct wine – appley, with a touch of honey warmth, usually made without oak, but occasionally with – and as such it deserves a fair price, not a grand one. At the moment it can be more expensive than a Sancerre or a Graves, and that doesn't make sense.

Altogether there are 43 villages which can either call their wine Mâcon-Villages or else append their own name – as in Mâcon-Viré for the village of Viré. The bulk of the best 'Villages' wine comes from the northern Mâconnais; Mâcon-Lugny, Mâcon-Viré and Mâcon-Clessé are the most frequently seen labels. Other good villages include Uchizy, Chardonnay (probable birthplace of the vine), Igé, St-Gengoux-de-Scissé and, in the south, Prissé and Charnay. Eighty-five per cent of Mâconnais wines are made by co-ops who are as strong here as anywhere in France and who have done much to promote the wines and raise prices. Best years: 1987, '86, '85. Best producers: Bonhomme, de Chervin, Clos de Condemine, Guichard, Pierre Mahuet, Manciat-Poncet, de Roally, Jean Thévenet, Tissier, co-operatives at Chardonnay, Clessé, Lugny, Prissé, St-Gengoux de Scissé, Viré.

MALARTIC-LAGRAVIÈRE, CH.
Pessac-Léognan AC, *cru classé de Graves*
BORDEAUX
Sauvignon Blanc

One of the few Pessac-Léognan Classed Growths whose reputation has been upheld by its white rather than its red wine (though the red is also good). The property is quite small – 35 acres (14 hectares), out towards the woods just south of Léognan – near de Fieuzal and not far from Domaine de Chevalier. It is worth noting that these three close neighbours all make outstanding whites. But Malartic-Lagravière differs from the other two in that there is no Sémillon: its little block of white vines – just under 5 acres (2 hectares) – is planted 100 per cent with Sauvignon Blanc. The wine is given new oak ageing, but still has a startling nettle green fruit at first, which then warms and softens over three to four years into a really lovely nutty Graves – disproving the theory that Sauvignon without Sémillon can't age well. It all depends how you handle it! Best years: 1986, '85, '84, '83, '82, '81.

DE MALLE, CH.
Sauternes AC, *2ème cru classé*
BORDEAUX
Sémillon, Sauvignon Blanc,
Muscadelle

Even if you don't taste the wine, Château de Malle is one of Bordeaux's loveliest estates. The de Bournazel family have owned it for more than 500 years, and the present château – shown on the label of the wine, with the wrought iron gates making an elegant frame – was designed in the seventeenth century and set in the midst of lawns and an Italian garden. That all this survives – and didn't go under the hammer during the Sauternes slump of the '50s to '70s – is because Comte de Bournazel was one of the first to see the slackening demand for fine sweet wine and to diversify into dry red and dry white. The wine itself is more like a Barsac than a Sauternes, with a soft, brazil-nuts-in-caramel sweetness and light, lemon peel acidity. You can drink – and enjoy – it at five years old but good vintages will be better at ten. Best years: 1986, '83, '80.

MENETOU-SALON AC
UPPER LOIRE
Sauvignon Blanc

Although the village of Menetou-Salon is virtually the neighbour of the grander and far more famous Sancerre, it's a devil of a place to find. You spend an eternity poring over your increasingly grubby Michelin map totally bemused or – even worse – you ask the locals the way. Since there are more sheep and pigs in these mellow rolling grasslands of central France than people, and since a mixture of mild amusement and impenetrable dialect has never been a recipe for succinct directions, progress is, well, erratic. It's worth making the effort, though, if only to build up a thirst for the extremely attractive Sauvignon whites the AC makes. There are only 250 acres (100 hectares) so far – although several growers are planting more as they realize that their chalky clay is the same as the best soil in Sancerre and Chablis, and that the ever-increasing prices of Sancerre must give them a chance to score with similar wine at lower prices. And this is exactly what they're doing. They make very dry, but soft Sauvignon, with a nice hint of gooseberry and blackcurrant leaves in the taste and a pleasant chalky-clean feel. So far they don't equal the best Sancerre, but they are cheaper – and often much more refreshing. Total production is about 450,000 bottles, with 300,000 plus being white. Drink within two years of vintage. Best years: 1987, '86, '85. Best producers: Chatenoy, Chavet, Denis, Mellot, Pellé, Teiller.

MERCUREY AC
CÔTE CHALONNAISE, BURGUNDY
Chardonnay

The white wine of Mercurey, the leading village of the Côte Chalonnaise, has never had a very good press. It's always accused of being heavy, lifeless, cloddish, lardy – making it sound more like a pile of potato pancakes than a white Burgundy made from the world-famous Chardonnay grape. Well, I'll try to redress the balance. There isn't a lot of the white – only 130,000 bottles from a total of over three million, and the locals rather dismissively whisper that they only plant Chardonnay on ground which is unsuitable for the red Pinot Noir – but the wine can be as good as many far more expensive offerings from the more fashionable Côte d'Or further north. It *is* quite full – but then so is Meursault – and it *does* have a very attractive buttery, nutty, even spicy taste – and so, often, does Meursault! Hmm. I think I'd give it a try, at three to four years old – but not any older, because until the last three or four vintages I would have agreed with the critics and labelled it lumpish and not worth the drinking. But recent results are more promising. Best years: 1986, '85, '84. Best producers: Chartron & Trébuchet, Faiveley (Clos Rochette), Genot-Boulanger, Juillot, Rodet (Chamirey).

MEURSAULT AC
CÔTE DE BEAUNE, BURGUNDY
Chardonnay

▲ Wintertime – and a sprinkling of snow lies on the vines in Meursault, one of Burgundy's most famous white wine villages.

I'm thinking of a pale golden wine glinting in the cool, bright winter sunlight. The powerful scent catches the aroma of spring blossoms in the courtyard and mingles tantalizingly with the sweet perfume of fresh-hewn oak casks. I'm tasting Meursault from the latest vintage, still raw and bony, but already promising the smooth-sided succulence which will make the wine cling to my palate – and to my memory in years to come.

I'm thinking of a wine, straw-gold but cut with green, the emptiest bottle in the tasting room as taster after taster has reached for it and poured a measure just a mite more generous than judicious. The smell is buttery, peachy too, cream coating the fruit, with honey and hazelnuts hiding behind the richness and the distant breakfast smells of coffee and buttered toast. The spittoon is dry. Not even the professionals will spit out this Meursault, now perhaps two years old, already so lovely, yet still only hinting at what's to come.

And I'm thinking of sitting with my friends, conversation strangely muted, but the room suffused with beaming pleasures as the deep golden wine weaves its magic. Almost savoury – the rich smoke of toast and roasted almonds and a flash of cinnamon spice, the cream and melted butter of its youth now gone golden, half-way to brown – less luscious but deeper, richer. A conversation, a dream, an ideal, all in itself; Meursault-Charmes, or Meursault-Perrières maybe, the 1978 perhaps or even the '73. White wine perfection.

Ah, if it were all like this – but Burgundy being Burgundy, for every grower striving to excel there's another with his eye on the cash-register, because Meursault, at 1030 acres (417 hectares) the biggest white wine village on the Côte d'Or, is also the most popular. Some of its vineyards are a little flat and less well drained, but the general standard of wine *is* high. Meursault pays for this high average by not having any *grands crus*, but has a whole cluster of *premiers crus* which are almost as good. The tiny hamlet of Blagny on the slopes south of Meursault is allowed to sell its lean but classy whites as Meursault-Blagny. Altogether Meursault produces perhaps 2½ million bottles of wine that is lovely to drink young, but better aged for six to ten years. There are many growers bottling their own wine but the better merchants also make good stuff. And the less than exceptional vintages – like '82 and '84 – are often great successes in Meursault; they haven't had a disaster for 20 years! Best years: 1986, '85, '84, '83, '82. Best producers: Boisson-Vadot, Coche-Debord, Coche-Dury, Jobard, Lafon, Matrot, Michelot-Buisson, Millot-Battault, Pierre Morey, Pitoiset-Urena, Prieur, Roulot.

MOËT ET CHANDON
Champagne AC
CHAMPAGNE
Pinot Noir, Chardonnay, Pinot Meunier

If there is one company which rules our perception of Champagne as a drink, it has to be Moët & Chandon, with its enormous production of 18 million bottles a year, and its domination of so many of the export markets. People seem to be shooting the corks out of gigantic bottles of Moët at every first night, every film award, every Grand Prix victory or glossy showbiz wedding, in fact, anywhere there is likely to be a photographer who is likely to get a picture of the event – and a bottle of Moët – into the newspapers. The result is that Moët is the most famous Champagne in the world yet you hardly ever see an advert – you just see lots of famous people spraying each other with it.

With all this notoriety comes inconsistency – which is a great pity, because when you get a good bottle of Moët non-vintage it is soft, creamy, a little spicy. . . and absolutely delightful to drink. The vintage is more consistent, and usually has a good strong style to it, though Moët is one of those houses which are apt to release a vintage virtually every year, when some might suggest the quality of the harvest left a bit to be desired. Dom Pérignon is their De Luxe cuvée, famous throughout the night spots of the world. It can be one of the greatest of Champagnes, but it must be given several years age, even after release, for the flavours to develop, otherwise all you're paying for is an elegant bottle and a pretty label.

MONBAZILLAC AC
SOUTH-WEST
Sémillon, Sauvignon Blanc, Muscadelle

The leading sweet wine of the Bergerac region, and the only one which is likely to be truly sweet in the style of Sauternes, rather than mildly sweet in a light and unmemorable way. But, actually, most Monbazillac nowadays is just that – light, vaguely sweet and entirely forgettable – largely because the noble rot fungus, needed on the overripe grapes to suck out water and concentrate sweetness, doesn't always appear here. Since Monbazillac can't command anything like the price of Sauternes or Barsac, few growers are going to risk losing their crop in the autumn storms simply on the off-chance that noble rot might turn up sometime in November.

In fact, only a mere handful of properties even consider making traditional rich Monbazillac – most of the eight million bottles produced each year come from the good but unadventurous co-operative. At its best the wine is full and honeyed, with a sweetness of peaches and barley sugar. Lighter versions are likely to be very pale and resemble pleasantly drinkable sweet apples with just a touch of honey. The vineyards, south of Bergerac town, run up a north-facing slope to the impressive Château de Monbazillac (the wine's not as exciting as the architecture). In general drink young, but a real late-harvested example could last ten years. Best years: 1986, '85, '83. Best producers: la Borderie, le Fagé, la Jaubertie, Château de Monbazillac, Septy, Treuil-de-Nailhac.

MONTAGNY AC
CÔTE CHALONNAISE, BURGUNDY
Chardonnay

▲ Montagny is the southernmost of the five ACs on the Côte Chalonnaise. Its vineyards, on limestone soil, produce mostly white wine; any red has to be labelled Bourgogne Rouge, not Montagny.

Montagny is a white-only AC at the southern end of the Côte Chalonnaise. Since I love white Burgundy, and enthusiastically champion the Côte Chalonnaise as providing decent white Burgundy at a reasonable price, I was always desperately disappointed that Montagny wines had such a dull flavour – bone dry, chalky, lean beyond belief, and showing none of the fullness and ripeness I want from the Chardonnay grape in Burgundy. But then Montagny discovered the 'new barrel'! Just a few months' ageing in a new, or relatively new, oak barrel adds the nuttiness and soft spice which have been conspicuously lacking up until now. And suddenly, I'm getting excited about the wines for the first time.

Montagny has some 750 acres (300 hectares) of vines and an annual production of 400,000 bottles. If you see a wine labelled Montagny *premier cru* don't be fooled into thinking it comes from a superior vineyard site – as you'd assume in the rest of Burgundy. No. Somehow the Montagny growers wangled it that any white wine which reaches 11·5 degrees of alcohol – half a degree more than usual – can call itself *premier cru*. And even worse, though all the rest of us have been complaining for years, the local AC authorities blithely continue to allow it. In general, drink Montagny one to three years after the vintage. Best years: 1986, '85. Best producers: Buxy co-operative, Latour, Martial de Laboulaye, Michel, Roy, Steinmaier, Vachet.

MONTHELIE AC
CÔTE DE BEAUNE, BURGUNDY
Chardonnay

Monthelie is an attractive village, with 250 acres (100 hectares) of vines, looking down on Meursault from the north. Its steep streets and huddled houses give some clue to the wine's character, which is generally of the strong, herby, rustic, but satisfying type. That's fine for reds and obviously the growers think so too because, of the 460,000 or so bottles produced each year, more than 450,000 are red! The few rows of white Chardonnay vines produce a wine which has tasted rather dry and lean when I've tried it from the barrel – but I have to admit I haven't tracked down a single *bottle* yet so can't comment on its ageing potential (*not* supposed to be its strong point, by the way). Best years: 1986, '85.

MONTLOUIS AC
CENTRAL LOIRE
Chenin Blanc

Montlouis is the southern neighbour of Vouvray, within a stone's throw across the river Loire. But not within a short drive or stroll, because the only bridge between them carries the railway line, and you have to detour several miles westwards to find a bridge which will take you and your car. Certainly Montlouis doesn't share the fame of Vouvray and you can sense the growers' resentment at Vouvray's greater renown and higher prices. But the grape is the same – Chenin Blanc; the chalk, limestone, gravel and clay mix of the soil are the same; and the styles of wine are the same – dry, medium and sweet whites, and Champagne-method fizz.

Yet the style is a *little* different – the dry wines leaner, the sweet wines developing quite an attractive flavour of nuts and honey, but rarely subduing the high Chenin acidity. Only the sparkling wines – whose production makes up 80 per cent of the four million plus bottles – match Vouvray and, with their cleaner apple fruit sometimes touched by honey, they can improve upon the slighter sterner style of the Vouvray sparklers. The still wines age extremely well – in fact they need ageing – for five maybe ten years, but sparkling Montlouis should be drunk young and snappy. Best years: 1986, '85, '83, '82, '78, '76, '70. Best producers: Berger, Deletang, Levasseur, Moyer.

LE MONTRACHET AC
CÔTE DE BEAUNE, BURGUNDY
Chardonnay

Given the incredibly meagre amount of Montrachet made – a good year may produce 30,000 bottles – and given the extreme unlikelihood that most wine writers have ever possessed a bottle, or drunk it in its mature state more than once in a blue moon, there must have been more adjectives expended per mouthful swallowed on this than on any other wine in the world. Those who love white Burgundy dream of Montrachet as the pinnacle of their wine-drinking life and, OK, I do too.

I've tasted it so new that it flowed milky-white from the barrel and stung my mouth with a piercing richness far beyond youthful flavours of fruit – more like an essence coaxed, in minute allowance, deep from the vineyard's earth. I've been faced with it at tastings, so thick in the glass it seemed like syrup, and so coarse and bloated in the mouth – like an elixir of buttered orchard fruit – that I started back with shock only to find some wiser head than mine nodding sagely and saying, 'Don't worry, it needs ten years to sort itself out'. And, just once or twice, I have experienced it at ten and more years old. The sheer concentration of the wine is unchanged. But all the coarseness is gone, and there seems to be a richness which owes nothing to sugar, but everything to the ripest of fruits, the most tantalizing of scents, and the most fragrant of drifting woodsmoke wrapped in a cocoon of triple-thick cream. Dry-sweet, luscious-lean – the most perfect binding together of opposites in the world of wine.

Montrachet comes from an 18½-acre (7·5-hectare) vineyard, 10 acres (4 hectares) in Puligny-Montrachet and 8½ (3·5) in Chassagne-Montrachet. The land seems nothing to look at – poor, stony – but there's a thick vein of limestone just below the surface, the drainage is exceptional, and the perfect south to south-east exposure soaks up the sun from dawn to dusk. Couldn't you say all that about lots of other vineyards? Perhaps. But stand among the vines of Montrachet at sunset, and a dip in the hills to the west is still allowing the sun's rays to warm Montrachet while all the great surrounding vineyards are in shadow. There's one reason at least why their wines for hundreds of years have never *quite* reached the peaks of brilliance of Montrachet. But the world of wine is changing. Someone, somewhere in the world – Australia, California, Italy – will stumble on a magic piece of dirt, and more by intuition than design, will unlock the secrets of its soil. Best years: 1986, '85, '84, '83, '82, '78, '76, '73, '71, '70. Best producers: Bouchard Père & Fils, Lafon, Laguiche, Pierre Morey, Prieur, Domaine de la Romanée-Conti, Thénard.

MONTRAVEL AC, CÔTES DE MONTRAVEL AC, HAUT-MONTRAVEL AC
SOUTH-WEST
Sémillon, Sauvignon Blanc, Muscadelle

White wines from the western fringe of the Bergerac region. Basic Montravel is dryish, while Côtes de Montravel and Haut-Montravel – both from hillside vineyards – are certainly sweeter but lack real richness. The Montravel wines, falling uneasily between proper sweet and proper dry, are not much in fashion and so production – already low at 300,000 bottles a year – looks likely to decline further.

MOREY-ST-DENIS AC
CÔTE DE NUITS, BURGUNDY
Pinot Noir

Another of these strange anomalies when one single Côte de Nuits grower, with a considerable reputation for red wine, indulges his whim by making a tiny amount of white. In the Monts-Luisants vineyard to the north of the village, Monsieur Ponsot uses a weird white mutation of Pinot Noir to produce about 3000 bottles of white wine. It can be rather hard and empty to start with, but in hot years it gains a tremendous, deep, almost overpowering, honeyed nutty weight, which is certainly impressive – but the last time I started on a bottle, none of us could finish it! Best years: 1986, '85, '83, '82.

MUSCADET AC
LOWER LOIRE
Muscadet

Muscadet is now so popular that its name has become a kind of generic term for cheap, dry, French white wine. But in reality, Muscadet can only come from a legally defined area at the mouth of the Loire near Nantes. There isn't an actual town of Muscadet – this is one of the rare occasions in France that a wine takes its name from its grape.

The Melon de Bourgogne grape migrated from Burgundy during the seventeenth century and, en route, changed its name to Muscadet. It became very popular with growers all over the Nantes area and they simply called their wine after the grape – Muscadet. In fact, we don't see much wine just labelled as Muscadet because the bulk of production (85 per cent) comes from the best area, to the south of the Loire, and so qualifies for the Muscadet de Sèvre-et-Maine AC. Only wine from less suitable vineyards, mostly closer to the sea, carries the plain Muscadet AC. This is usually pretty dull, bland wine, but does have one thing in its favour – a *maximum* alcoholic strength of 12·3 degrees. Since the Muscadet is an early-ripening, low acid grape – though you'd never know it to taste some of the cheaper export versions – this legal maximum is imposed to preserve at least a modicum of freshness in the wine. With that in mind, always drink straight Muscadet very young – even as Muscadet Nouveau, since some firms release a 'new vintage' wine as early as November – certainly within twelve months.

▶Atlantic weather – damp and mild – characterizes the Muscadet region and helps give the wine its low-acid, light, dry style.

MUSCADET DE SÈVRE-ET-MAINE AC
LOWER LOIRE
Muscadet

The Maine and the Sèvre rivers converge south-east of Nantes before flowing into the Loire and on to the Atlantic ocean, and give their names to the mild, gently hilly region where 85 per cent of Muscadet is made. There's no doubt that the best Muscadet comes from here – but that 85 per cent also includes a lot of wine of no discernible personality except that it is sharply dry and acid.

Well, certainly Muscadet is dry, but in fact the grape is a low-acid variety and because of its pretty neutral taste, the traditional method of bottling gives the

wine quite a full, soft feel which is a revelation to anyone who has always just bought the cheapest bottle available. This method entails bottling the wine directly off its sediment, its lees – and is shown on the label with the words *mise en bouteille sur lie*. When the fermentation is over, the wine is put into a barrel and, instead of being drained off periodically, it just waits, gaining a creamy, yeasty flavour and a slight prickle of carbon dioxide. What *should* then happen is that the wine is drawn off, extremely carefully, into the bottle, without filtering, leaving a layer of sediment in the bottom of the barrel. But one expert says that not more than two per cent of supposed *sur lie* Muscadet *is* made like this – and, from some of the lifeless examples available, I'm inclined to agree.

Just occasionally, you find a wine with a creamy softness, livened up with a sharp edge of grapefruit, pepper and lemon – and with just enough prickle to make your tongue tingle. That's true Muscadet and it's delightful wine, on its own or with the seafood of the region. And although you should really drink Muscadet within the year, these 'true' Muscadets can age for several years, going quite full and nutty with time. Best years: 1987, '86. Best producers: estate bottlings from Michel Bahuaud, Bossard, Chasseloir, Chéreau-Carré, Clos des Roches-Gaudinières, Dimerie, Donatien-Bahuaud, Dorices, Marquis de Goulaine, Métaireau, Sauvion, Touche, Tourmaline.

MUSCADET DES COTEAUX DE LA LOIRE AC
LOWER LOIRE
Muscadet

Quite a large area stretching up both banks of the Loire from Nantes towards Angers, but not specially packed with vines, since only five per cent of Muscadet comes from these vineyards. You hardly ever see the wine labelled as such since most exporters find it easier to use the simple Muscadet AC. But if Coteaux de la Loire Muscadet *does* have a special character, it is perhaps a little fuller, and flatter, lacking the fresh zip of the better Sèvre-et-Maine wines.

MUSCAT

It's highly likely that the Muscat is the original wine grape, and that all other varieties descend from this one vine, so it should be treated with great respect by connoisseurs the world over. But sadly it isn't. Muscat suffers from a single fault – its wines are too easy to enjoy: the wine buff can claim no superiority over the ordinary mortal when it comes to drinking Muscat because the delicious grapy, honeyed taste is obvious, delightful and without hidden complexities. To me that makes it very special, particularly when I want to drink a wine for sheer pleasure and not have to whip out my notebook and spend 15 minutes jotting down the slightest nuance of flavour I think I may spy there.

There are three main sorts of Muscat grown in France (though since it makes wonderful eating there are more like 200 members of the Muscat family worldwide). By far the finest is Muscat Blanc à Petits Grains or 'white Muscat with little berries'. In Alsace this used to be the sole Muscat variety, producing pale, fragile but headily perfumed dry white wines like no other in the world. Because of susceptibility to disease so far north, its place in Alsace was largely taken by Muscat Ottonel, but plantings are now on the increase again as the Petits Grains' superior quality is acknowledged. In the northern Rhône it is grown at Die and gives the sublime grapy perfume to the lovely Clairette de Die Tradition sparkling wine, while further south at Beaumes-de-Venise it is responsible for the wonderful rush of grapy, peachy, apples and honey fruit, made more exciting by a whiff of roses, which makes such a perfect after-dinner drink. Although also called Muscat de Frontignan, the position of Muscat Blanc à Petits Grains as the leading grape in the fortified wines of the Mediterranean coast is being usurped, but it will predominate in good examples of these *vins doux naturels*.

Muscat Ottonel is a crossbreed created in 1852. It doesn't have quite the perfume of the 'Petits Grains' Muscat, but is more reliable in Alsace where thankfully it doesn't overripen and produce the strangely meaty aroma it does in hotter climes.

Muscat of Alexandria is a big, chubby eating grape which I've seen growing in English glasshouses and happily guzzled numerous times. But the wine doesn't manage to capture that warm clinging scent of the hothouse vine. It does give a high, healthy yield and in the far south it is now three times as heavily planted as Petits Grains in the fortified Muscat centres around Rivesaltes. The heavy, orange marmalade and raisin richness of most of these wines is evidence of this.

The Muscadelle is related to the Muscat family, as its name implies. Some 5000 acres (2000 hectares) are planted in Bordeaux, and can give a pleasant, honeyed aroma to the rather neutral dry white of the Entre-Deux-Mers as well as adding spice to a Sauternes.

MUSCAT DE BEAUMES-DE-VENISE AC
SOUTHERN RHÔNE
Muscat Blanc à Petits Grains

This is the most delicious manifestation of sweet Muscat in France, and consequently the most expensive. But that's fair enough because the wine is a beauty and in a period in the late 1970s when sweet wines looked to be in terminal decline, the phenomenal success of Muscat de Beaumes-de-Venise gave other sweeties the breathing space they needed to wait for the world's attention to turn their way once more – as it now has.

Beaumes-de-Venise itself is an attractive little village huddled up against the crags of the Dentelles de Montmirail in the southern Rhône and they've been making Muscat wine there since the Middle Ages. It's what is called a *vin doux naturel* – a fortified wine where the fermentation is arrested by the addition of a slug of high-strength spirit. This preserves the flavour of the unfermented grape juice and accounts for the wine's sweet, grapy taste. In the local bars they throw back shots of their Muscat on the way home from work in the same way as we might stop off at the pub for a beer. They are continually amazed at how their everyday happy-juice has become a revered sweet wine to drink at the end of sophisticated urban dinner parties. Well, I'm not, because the wine is certainly rich, often very rich, full of the flavour of peach and grapes, orange peel, apples and honey, and with a wisp of the scent of roses left hanging in the air. But the secret is that the wine doesn't cloy; it has a fruit acidity and a bright fresh feel which satisfies your thirst as well as stimulates your after-dinner wit. Presumably *that's* why it's so popular with Beaumes-de-Venise workers on their way home! The wine can age, but is best drunk young to get all that lovely grapy perfume at its peak. Best producers: Bernardins, Coyeux, Durban, Guigal, Jaboulet and the Beaumes-de-Venise co-operative.

MUSCAT DE FRONTIGNAN AC
LANGUEDOC-ROUSSILLON
Muscat Blanc à Petits Grains

This is the leading Muscat *vin doux naturel* on the Mediterranean coast and comes from Frontignan, a small town south-west of Montpellier in the Hérault. At one time it was so well-known that the Muscat à Petits Grains grape took the name Muscat de Frontignan when it migrated to new wine-making areas of the world such as Australia and California in the nineteenth century.

Muscat de Frontignan is supposed to be made 100 per cent from superior Muscat à Petits Grains, but my palate tells me there *must* be an increasing amount of the coarser Muscat of Alexandria being planted in the vineyards. This would go some way to explaining why much Muscat de Frontignan, though sweet and quite impressive, has a slightly cloying taste, like cooked marmalade, militating against the fresh grapy sweetness. Muscat de Beaumes-de-Venise from the southern Rhône, which is made predominantly of Muscat Blanc à Petits Grains, is equally rich, but beautifully fresh, and scented with honey and flowers. Both wines are *vins doux naturels* – which means that the grapes are harvested as ripe as possible, partially fermented and then 'muted' by the addition of high-strength spirit. This stops the fermentation and leaves a substantial amount of the grape sweetness still in the wines. Varying between bright gold and a deep orange gold, Muscat de Frontignan is certainly good, but definitely short of the top class. Production is about two million bottles annually. Best producers: la Peyrade, Robiscau.

MUSCAT DE LUNEL AC
LANGUEDOC-ROUSSILLON
Muscat à Petits Grains

Although the little town of Lunel, north-east of Montpellier, boastfully gives itself the title of 'La Cité de Muscat' (the city of Muscat), few people who didn't actually live there would agree. Muscat de Lunel is not well-known – with both Muscat de Frontignan west of Montpellier, and Muscat de Rivesaltes down towards the Pyrenees, having far higher reputations. That said, however, the fairly small amounts of Muscat de Lunel aren't bad with a very good raisiny flavour and less of the flat marmalady character than the better-known ones exhibit. So perhaps they aren't being so boastful after all. Best producers: Belle-Côte, Cave Co-operative.

MUSCAT DE MIREVAL AC
LANGUEDOC-ROUSSILLON
Muscat à Petits Grains

Almost never seen outside its own locality, this is one of several fortified Muscat wines (called *vins doux naturels* – natural sweet wines) which pepper the Mediterranean coast between the mouth of the Rhône and Perpignan at the base of the Pyrenees. Mireval is a neighbour of the much better-known Frontignan, but is just a little further inland and the wines, while still sweet and ripe, can have a little more acid freshness, and quite an alcoholic kick as well!

MUSCAT DE RIVESALTES AC
LANGUEDOC-ROUSSILLON
Muscat of Alexandria, Muscat à Petits Grains

Rivesaltes, a small town just north of Perpignan, makes good Côtes du Roussillon but its reputation is based on *vin doux naturel* – the traditional fortified wine style of the south of France. The best of these is Muscat de Rivesaltes, made primarily from the Muscat of Alexandria grape, which gives a big, rather thick, deep coloured wine, not as aromatic as the best Muscats, and with a sweetness veering between raisins, honey and cooked orange marmalade. Good, but not inspiring. Most other Rivesaltes *vin doux naturel* is based on the red Grenache Noir, but there is a little made from the white Malvoisie, Grenache Blanc and Macabeo which, while not as sweet as the Muscat wines, can be fresher and more appetizing. Best producers: Cazès Frères, Corneilla, Sarda-Malet.

MUSIGNY AC
CÔTE DE NUITS, BURGUNDY
Chardonnay

There shouldn't really be dry white Musigny at all – Musigny is a red wine *grand cru* in the Côte de Nuits village of Chambolle-Musigny which has been red right through since the fourteenth century. Ah yes, but since when have a few silly things like regulations stopped a determined Frenchwoman from having her way? The Comte de Vogüé owns most of the Musigny vines, and makes a famous Musigny red. But what do you do if your wife prefers white? You rip up a few precious Pinot Noir vines and replant with Chardonnay – *et voilà* – you can make white wine – just for your own consumption mind. But you serve it at dinner, your friends plead with you for a bottle or two to buy, and, well, why not? So now there's three-quarters of an acre (0·3 hectare) planted with Chardonnay, producing between 1000 and 2000 bottles a year. The wine *is* good, dry, soft and nutty, and sells for a whopping price – if you can ever find it.

NAIRAC, CH.
Barsac AC, *2ème cru classé*
BORDEAUX
Sémillon, Sauvignon Blanc, Muscadelle

A rising star in Barsac which by dint of enormous effort and considerable investment is now producing a wine reckoned to be on a level with the First Growths – not as intensely perfumed, not as exotically rich, but proudly concentrated, with a fine lanolin richness and buttery honey coating the mouth, and with more spice from new oak barrels than many properties have. Production is rarely more than 24,000 bottles – sometimes a lot less! The quality-obsessed proprietors ditched all their 1977 and '78 wine as not being good enough and only released 40 per cent of their '79! The influence of ageing in new oak casks, adding spice and even a little tough tannin, makes Nairac a good candidate for ageing 10–15 years. Best years: 1986, '83, '82, '81, '80, '76, '74.

NUITS-ST-GEORGES AC
CÔTE DE NUITS, BURGUNDY
Pinot Noir

The few precious bottles of white Nuits-St-Georges made by Domaine Henri Gouges are the most famous whites made in the Côte de Nuits where the red Pinot Noir is so completely dominant that Monsieur Gouges doesn't even grow Chardonnay and Pinot Blanc but a strange white mutation of Pinot Noir. When he bought the *premier cru* Clos de Poirets vineyard in 1934 he noted with alarm that some of the red Pinot Noir vines were sprouting white grapes. So he took grafts and planted them in the neighbouring Perrière vineyard higher up the slope just below the treeline. Ever since then he has made exceptional white wine, very dry, with a savoury, almost Pinot Noir perfume but then growing richer and fatter in your mouth – more like a top wine from the northern Rhône. Strange, but delicious, and hardly like white Burgundy at all. The production is never more than 2500 bottles and often considerably less. There is also a little Chardonnay planted in Clos Arlots, a mile further south, but I've never seen it away from the vineyard itself. Best years: 1986, '85, '84, '83, '82.

PACHERENC DU VIC BILH AC
SOUTH-WEST
Gros Manseng, Petit Manseng, Ruffiac and others

What a name – hardly the most come-hither of titles for a white wine! At the end of World War Two there was scarcely anything left of this ancient vineyard, but luckily it is grown inside the same wine boundaries as Madiran. And as Madiran, also virtually extinct at the end of the war, got its act together and expanded, so Pacherenc clawed its way back from the brink. But that name! Well, Pacherenc is local dialect for *piquets en rang* – posts in a line, and Vic Bilh are the local hills. So the name literally translates as 'posts in a line from the Vic Bilh hills' – a reference to the local habit of training vines very high on two-metre posts. Whatever the explanation it still does not do much for my thirst! But actually the wine, sometimes sweetish but usually dry, can have an exciting flavour of pears and apricots – especially if bottled straight off its lees. Only the best estates achieve this and even they make very little, because the total crop is only 90,000 bottles. If you find one, drink it as young as possible. Best producers: Aydie, Crampilh.

PALETTE AC
PROVENCE
Clairette, Grenache Blanc, Ugni Blanc and others

Pines and herb shrubs surround the tiny vineyards of Palette, only 37 acres (15 hectares) to the south-east of Aix-en-Provence, and I'm afraid pine resin and the rather bitter chewy bits from a herb like thyme are the only kind of memorable flavours I've got from tasting white Palette. But Palette can be proud of one achievement. Given the basic neutral bunch of southern white grapes – Clairette, Grenache Blanc and Ugni Blanc – Château Simone, the only producer of white Palette, has managed to squeeze more flavour out of this trio than any other AC. It must be due to the limestone soil and two years' sojourn in oak barrels. Certainly, there are experts who think Palette is fantastic, but I'm content to admire it from a safe distance and advise people not to smoke when there's an open bottle around. The total production is 85,000 bottles, with some 25,000 of these being white.

▼Preparing grapes for pressing prior to fermentation at Château Simone.

PAVILLON BLANC DU CHÂTEAU MARGAUX
Bordeaux AC
BORDEAUX
Sauvignon Blanc

You can't claim the Margaux AC for a white wine, or even the lesser Haut-Médoc AC. But Château Margaux does make some white wine. The grapes don't come from the precious Margaux vineyards round the neo-Palladian château buildings, but from an entirely separate holding in Soussans, a mile or so to the north-west and outside the best red wine area. There are 25 acres (10 hectares) planted exclusively with Sauvignon Blanc, which is vinified at the château, but in a separate cellar so that the great red wine is not in any way affected. The result is delicious. A good stint in oak barrels adds a rich creaminess to the dry, flinty Sauvignon fruit, and after two to three years it gains all the nutty intensity and dry honey fullness of a good Graves. They produce over 40,000 bottles a year and charge a fiendish price for it – making it the most expensive Bordeaux AC by a country mile. Best years: 1986, '85, '83.

PERNAND-VERGELESSES AC
CÔTE DE BEAUNE, BURGUNDY
Chardonnay, Aligoté

One of Burgundy's forgotten villages – which at least gets in on some of the action because a sizeable chunk of the white *grand cru* Corton-Charlemagne lies within its parish boundaries. But since the name Pernand-Vergelesses never appears on the label (*grand cru* vineyards don't have to use their village name) no one ever links poor old Pernand with the heady heights of Corton-Charlemagne. And whereas Aloxe-Corton wines are frequently overpriced; Pernand-Vergelesses can actually be a bargain – and *that*, for Burgundy, is a very rare phenomenon.

Most of the 50,000 bottles of white come from Chardonnay, and although they're a bit lean and dry to start with, they fatten up beautifully after two to four years in bottle. But there are also some very old plantings of Aligoté (some even used to be in the Corton-Charlemagne vineyards till the authorities found out), and the wine is super – dry, deep, snappy, almost peppery and scoured with lemon peel. *And* they have a vineyard cryptically named 'Under the Wood of Noel and the Pretty Girls', or somesuch! I think there's more to Pernand-Vergelesses than meets the eye! Best years: 1986, '85, '84, '83, '82. Best producers: Bonneau du Martray, Dubreuil-Fontaine, Germain, Guyon, Laleure-Piot, Pavelot, Rapet, Rollin.

PESSAC-LÉOGNAN AC
BORDEAUX
Sémillon, Sauvignon Blanc,
Muscadelle

The recent (1987) revision of the AC system in the Graves area to the south of Bordeaux hived off the area immediately to the south of the city – centred on the villages of Pessac and Léognan, but also including the communes of Talence, Cadaujac, Villenave d'Ornon and Martillac as well as four others. In effect, this is the area of Graves which includes all the Classed Growths, and has the highest proportion of the classic gravelly soil which gives the Graves its name. Although there is now an exciting quality movement in the southern Graves, there is no doubt that the soil there is far less gravelly, sand and clay become increasingly dominant and both drainage and a decent aspect to the sun become more of a problem. So it is reasonable that the estate owners in the favoured Pessac-Léognan area should want to distance themselves from the rest of the Graves, and they achieved this in 1987 with the new Pessac-Léognan AC.

Until recent years the standard of most whites in the region was depressingly poor – dull, sulphurous, lacking fruit and flavour – but with the advent of cool fermentation, controlled yeast selection and the use of new oak barrels for fermentation and ageing of the wines, this is now one of the most exciting areas of France for top class whites. Best years: 1986, '85, '84, '83, '82. Best producers: Domaine de Chevalier, Couhins-Lurton, de Fieuzal, Haut-Brion, Laville-Haut-Brion, La Louvière, Malartic-Lagravière, Pontac-Monplaisir, de Rochemorin, Smith-Haut-Lafitte.

PETIT CHABLIS AC
CHABLIS, BURGUNDY
Chardonnay

Petit Chablis means little Chablis – and that name fits the bill exactly. Uninspired, rather green, unripe Chardonnay wine from the least good nooks and crannies of the Chablis region. But Petit Chablis does sound demeaning doesn't it? Not good for the ego or the bank balance of the grower. So when there was a surge of interest in white Burgundy and Chablis in the late 1970s and early '80s one of the first things to happen was that a lot of Petit Chablis land, especially that owned by politically-minded growers, was magically deemed worthy of the full Chablis AC – and, quite coincidentally, of the increased price a Chablis got as against a Petit Chablis. Had the wine changed in taste? No, just in title. But 'Chablis' does look so much nicer on the label, doesn't it?

What's left of Petit Chablis is about 300 acres (120 hectares) – which *must* be pretty feeble if the crafty Chablis growers couldn't get them upgraded. The La Chablisienne co-operative is the best bet for an adequate light Chardonnay – but it's not even a bargain any more, so why bother?

PICPOUL DE PINET VDQS
LANGUEDOC-ROUSSILLON
Picpoul, Clairette, Terret

Here's our friend the 'lip-stinger' Picpoul again; in the salty, damp vineyards of the Loire estuary where it masquerades as Gros Plant and makes sensationally sour white, it fully deserves the nickname. But Picpoul de Pinet, a beleaguered little Coteaux du Languedoc˙ *cru* between Montpellier and Béziers, is soft and bland, dry, yes, but almost terminally lacking in acidity. What's the problem? Well, it *may* be that the extra sun of the Mediterranean coast ripens the grape well enough for it to *lose* all its acidity – this often happens with Ugni Blanc, which makes a very tart wine further north in Cognac. But it *could* be that this is an entirely different grape! So why would a different grape, producing soft, mild wine, be called 'lip-stinger'? All I can say is that the tracing and identifying of exactly what grape is what is a tortuous and exhausting academic exercise undertaken by about one demented botanist per generation. If *they* can't sort it out, I don't suppose I can either. Anyway, there are about one million bottles produced – and you have to drink it *really* young to get any buzz from it at all.

PINOT BLANC

Pinot Blanc is a chorus member rather than a solo artiste in the grape hierarchy of France. In Italy, however, exciting things are achieved with Pinot Blanc or Pinot Bianco, and in the Alto Adige it can outshine even the great Chardonnay. There is a great deal of similarity between the wines of these two varieties, but they are not related at all – Pinot Blanc is a mutation of the red Pinot Noir, Chardonnay is not. In Burgundy, particularly on the Côte d'Or in the *grand cru* vineyard of Corton where both varieties are planted, the Pinot Blanc produces round, fat, apple-creamy wine, positively rich in a warm year, but ultimately lacking the exciting balance of flavours which makes Chardonnay so special. However, Pinot Blanc's chief power-base in France is in Alsace where, with the similar-tasting Auxerrois, it is taking over the 'workhorse' role from Sylvaner and Chasselas. This is good news because not only does the wine have a clear, yeasty, appley taste, sometimes with a slight grapy 'spice' when young, which makes for refreshing drinking, but good examples can also age to a delicious, honeyed fullness after a couple of years. When picked early it is neutral and quite acid – the perfect base material for sparkling wine. Most of Alsace's expanding fizz production, Crémant d'Alsace, now uses Pinot Blanc.

PINOT GRIS

Pinot Gris, or Tokay d'Alsace, isn't a subtle grape, but the fat, broad, honey and raisin flavour of which it is capable is so compelling and indulgent that I'm really not bothered about subtlety. Alsace is where almost all the French plantings are, although its 1500 acres (600 hectares) only represent five per cent of Alsace's total. Almost all of these vines are on the steep slopes of the best wine villages, because the local winegrowers revere the variety as the best accompaniment for the region's richest dishes. Even a simple co-operative-produced Pinot Gris will have a lick of honey – not exotic Mount Hymmetus fit-for-the-gods-type honey but dead straight, cheap, supermarket runny honey. As I said, not subtle. The acidity is low and the colour deep, but for some reason this doesn't affect the wine's ability to mature. As the quality improves through Vendange Tardive (made from late-harvested overripe grapes) to Sélection de Grains Nobles (intensely sweet grapes affected by noble rot), the honey becomes more and more gooey – but it doesn't become classier or more perfumed. It picks up smoke, it packs in raisins, and overlays this with a thick fat coating like butter oozing through toast – but it never puts on airs. Pinot Gris at its best still has the common touch, rich, fat, intelligible – and irresistible.

The grape occasionally surfaces in Burgundy, where it still clings to its honeyed taste, making a deep, over-golden-coloured wine. In a very welcome survival from the nineteenth century, when the grape was much more widespread in France than it is today, it appears as Malvoisie at Ancenis, in the lower Loire, where it makes lovely, gentle, honeyed wine; and at Reuilly, west of Sancerre, it makes some extremely pleasant pale rosé.

POL ROGER
Champagne AC
CHAMPAGNE
Pinot Noir, Chardonnay, Pinot Meunier

If you look closely at the label of Pol Roger non-vintage you'll see that it is bordered in black. Why? As a mark of respect and mourning for Winston Churchill when he died! This may sound far-fetched, but Pol Roger is in fact the most anglophile of companies, and I rather think the current head, Christian de Billy, would take it as a great compliment if you mistook him for an Englishman! As for Winston Churchill, he was an avid, indeed voracious consumer of Pol Roger, and it was Pol Roger he was thinking of when he said, in the dark days of World War Two, 'In victory we deserve it, in defeat we need it'.

The Churchill connection has been enshrined by Pol Roger, who, in 1984, launched a Cuvée Sir Winston Churchill, which, in a period when many special De Luxe Champagnes are proving overpriced disappointments, is a delicious, refined drink worthy of the name. However, most of the production is of the non-vintage White Foil, which is gentle, light and consistently good. They also produce a Vintage, a Vintage Chardonnay, and a Vintage Reserve Special which are each among the best in their class.

POUILLY-FUISSÉ AC
MÂCONNAIS, BURGUNDY
Chardonnay

The wine I love to hate. There must be more examples of flagrantly over-priced, second-rate Pouilly-Fuissé on the market than any other wine. American demand is the problem. The name, pronounced, I suspect, 'Pooly Foos', caught on there in a most dramatic way, and what was admittedly the leading wine of the Mâconnais – but not a patch on a decent Meursault or Puligny-Montrachet – demanded, and obtained, a price higher than either. Well, a weaker dollar has put paid to that caper, and prices dropped 50 per cent in 1986 and even more drastically since 1987. So now the wine, although still expensive, is beginning to find a vaguely sensible price level.

Pouilly-Fuissé is a dry white wine from the vineyards of five villages – Pouilly, Fuissé (yes, you did see a comma, they're two different villages!), Vergisson, Chaintré and Solutré. The vineyards are beautiful – clustered under the startling rock outcrop of Solutré. Many are ideally situated to produce fine wine, but the overbearing importance of the Chaintré co-op, which processes over 95 per

▶The vineyards of Pouilly-Fuissé, in the Mâconnais, are dominated by the spectacular cliff of Solutré.

cent of the AC's crop, and the cynical disregard for quality by the merchants who buy three-quarters of the wine for their own-label requirements, has meant that most growers can see no benefit in trying to create something special when milking their vineyards of every last grape is giving them such a good living. This would explain why less than 1500 acres (600 hectares) of vines manage to produce 5·6 million bottles a year.

Luckily, two or three per cent of the AC is in the hands of committed growers who care passionately about the quality that can make Pouilly-Fuissé a great wine. They restrict their yields, use only ripe grapes, employ wooden barrels (almost unheard of at the Chaintré co-op) to ferment and mature their wines, and the result is great wine – buttery, nutty, the fruit full of peach and melon and banana, and all this enriched with the spice of cloves and cinnamon and a generous splash of honey. *This* is what Pouilly-Fuissé should be. *This* is what made it famous in the first place. These wines can be wonderful at two years old but often age beautifully for up to ten years. Best years: 1988, '87, '86, '85, '83. Best producers: Corsin, Feret, Château Fuissé (Vincent), Guffens-Heynen, Leger-Plumet, Luquet, Noblet.

POUILLY-FUMÉ AC
UPPER LOIRE
Sauvignon Blanc

That 'fumé' in the title means 'smoky', and there's no doubt that a good Pouilly-Fumé has a strong pungent smell. The old-time winewriters used to say it had a whiff of gunflint about it. But the smokiness which *I* find fits the bill best is that fabulous, fresh yet acrid stench of roasting coffee as the fumes billow through the extractor vents of a traditional coffee merchant.

The only grape allowed is the Sauvignon Blanc, which is famous for its gooseberry, grassy-green, even asparagus flavours, and what gives the extra smokiness in Pouilly is that many of its vineyards – covering 1500 acres (600 hectares) on slopes near the town of Pouilly-sur-Loire – are on a particularly flinty soil called silex. The wines produced on this silex soil are tremendously full and positively rich for the normally more biting Sauvignon, meaty even, and filled with the heady perfume of lychees and elderflower. As such the wines can age for five years or more, though they're a sensation at a year old.

However, by no means all Pouilly-Fumé wines are as exciting as this, and dramatic price rises in recent years – even for the most basic wines from the less good vineyards – have meant that this is an AC of great potential quality, but one whose ordinary wines are very over-priced; for half as much money, a good Sauvignon de Touraine can be just as tasty. The best wines come from the hamlets of Les Berthiers and Les Loges: look for these names, and the word 'silex' on the label. Pouilly-Fumé may also be labelled Pouilly-Blanc-Fumé or Blanc Fumé de Pouilly. Best years: 1988, '87, '86, '85. Best producers: Bailly, Didier Dagueneau (his 'silex' is superb), de Ladoucette (his Baron de L is a crazy price but very good), Redde, Saget, Tracy.

POUILLY-LOCHÉ AC, POUILLY-VINZELLES AC
MÂCONNAIS, BURGUNDY
Chardonnay

Loché and Vinzelles are two perfectly decent Mâconnais villages with vines on the flatter land just to the east of Fuissé. Funnily enough, the growers of Vinzelles tried to organize their own AC in 1922 – long before Pouilly-Fuissé – but as Pouilly-Fuissé's Midas touch turned every bottling run into a money-minting extravaganza, it seemed obvious that adding Pouilly to their own names might prove profitable. That's the angle. So does it work? Yes, Pouilly-Vinzelles and Pouilly-Loché are more expensive than equivalent wines like Mâcon-Viré. And no, the quality of the wine – largely processed by the Loché co-op, but sold as Pouilly-Vinzelles regardless of which village it came from – is not a patch on a good Pouilly-Fuissé, and indeed no better than the normal Mâcon-Clessé or whatever. Once again we're in the impasse of a highly efficient co-op doing a highly efficient processing job, but with everyone getting too greedy and not asking themselves – do I *really* deserve that price, shouldn't I try to make better wine first?

POUILLY-SUR-LOIRE AC
UPPER LOIRE
Chasselas

▲ Domaine de Ladoucette, the leading producer of Pouilly-Fumé. This stylish Sauvignon wine comes from vineyards around the town of Pouilly-sur-Loire which also has its own AC for Chasselas whites.

Pouilly-sur-Loire is the town which gives its name to the famous Pouilly-Fumé, one of the world's leading whites from the Sauvignon grape. However, 15 per cent of its vineyards are planted not with Sauvignon but with Chasselas – the area's traditional grape for hundreds of years – and these wines can only take the Pouilly-sur-Loire AC.

Chasselas is not much of a grape – giving light, frail, tasteless whites whose only worth lies in their youthfulness. The reason it still survives, despite being both less good and less popular than the Sauvignon, is that there is some Pouilly land not suitable for Sauvignon. But with rocketing prices for the Sauvignon-based Pouilly-Fumé tempting growers, irresistibly, to plant Sauvignon wherever remotely possible, it will soon only be the *totally* unsuitable land which grows Chasselas. Production of Pouilly-sur-Loire is about 300,000 bottles annually and falling. The declining production is no great loss to the wine world, because even now the only examples with any character are those from producers who pass the Chasselas wine over Sauvignon lees to try to pick up a bit of flavour! Drink as young as possible.

PREMIÈRES CÔTES DE BLAYE AC
BORDEAUX
Sémillon, Sauvignon Blanc, Muscadelle

The AC for Blaye whites made from only three grape varieties, as against a possible seven for Côtes de Blaye. The wines can be dry, medium or even sweet, but almost all of the best dry ones use the Côtes de Blaye AC. In fact, the Premières Côtes de Blaye AC is primarily for reds. Don't go out of your way to try these, but if you find one, drink it as young as possible.

PREMIÈRES CÔTES DE BORDEAUX AC
BORDEAUX
Sémillon, Sauvignon Blanc, Muscadelle

Premières Côtes de Bordeaux has some of the most captivating scenery in Bordeaux. This lovely hill-tousled AC stretches for 38 miles (60km) down the right bank of the Garonne river, from opposite the city of Bordeaux to opposite Sauternes and the southern Graves. Opposite. That says it all. Time and again as you breast a hill you find yourself at the top of steep slopes running down to the Garonne, and you have an unparalleled view across to the famous properties of Graves and Sauternes – on the opposite bank.

But what of the wines? Well, the Premières Côtes were always thought of as being best for medium sweet whites – there are even three sweet wine enclaves inside the AC, Loupiac, Ste-Croix du Mont and Cadillac. But as the fashion for sweet wines faded during the '70s, more and more growers turned to red wine with a good deal of success: and in the last ten years white plantations have dropped by over 20 per cent to about 1730 acres (700 hectares). Most of this white, however, is the fashionable super-dry type and as such only qualifies for Bordeaux Sec AC – since the Premières Côtes AC requires a minimum of four grams of sugar per litre of wine. This isn't a lot, but it *is* too much for growers who are trying to make the dry-as-a-bone whites which are popular right now. The result is that white Premières Côtes dwindles every year, while reds forge ahead. Best years: 1987, '86. Best producers: Birot, Grand Mouëys, du Juge (in the Premières Côtes, though they may release their wines as simple Bordeaux AC), Lamothe, Reynon, Tanesse.

PULIGNY-MONTRACHET AC
CÔTE DE BEAUNE, BURGUNDY
Chardonnay

If you feel a thirst coming on in Puligny-Montrachet, making a beeline for the Café du Centre won't do you much good. Although the sign is still there, the café has been closed for years. In fact all the cafés and bars in Puligny are shut. It's a strange feeling! Puligny-Montrachet – the home of what most people reckon is the greatest dry white wine in the world – and yet you can't get a drink there for love nor money! Maybe it's because prices for Puligny's superb whites have risen to such astronomical heights on the export market that growers jealously guard every single bottle to earn their dollars, pounds and Swiss francs. More likely, it is because this dull little village has been declining in population for years as the mighty merchants of neighbouring Beaune buy up the land to guarantee their supplies of wine, and families whose forebears have worked the vineyards for generations must now shuffle off townwards.

But the mediocrity of the village cannot dim the brilliance of its best vineyards. Altogether there are 580 acres (235 hectares) of vines – about 97 per cent white Chardonnay, producing 1·2 million bottles a year. The pinnacle is the *grand cru* Le Montrachet, an ordinary-looking 18½-acre (7·5-hectare) vineyard which manages to produce such a wine that Alexandre Dumas said it should only be drunk 'on one's knees with head uncovered', while its smell has been likened to 'a religious cantata resounding through the vaults of a Gothic cathedral'! Stirring stuff, eh!

There are three other *grands crus*, almost as good but less spiritual – Abide With Me at a Wembley Cup Final perhaps – and ten *premiers crus*, which are still among the most exciting wines in Burgundy. These take up all the best slopes above the village, and although the flatter land down by the houses is covered in vines, and allowed the Puligny-Montrachet AC, the result is less consistently thrilling. But the price is still formidable, and as always in Burgundy, the name of the producer is the most important thing on the label. Good vintages really need five years to show what all the fuss is about, while the *premiers crus* and *grands crus* wines may need ten years and can last for 20 or more. Best years: 1986, '85, '84, '83, '82, '79, '78. Best producers: Bachelet-Ramonet, Boisson-Vadot, Boyer-Devèze, Carillon, Chartron & Trebuchot, Drouhin, Jadot, Labouré-Roi, Laguiche, Leflaive, Château de Puligny-Montrachet, Ramonet-Prudhon, Rodet, Roux, Sauzet, Thénard.

PYRÉNÉES-ORIENTALES
LANGUEDOC-ROUSSILLON

Pyrénées-Orientales is the torrid, gale-scoured, southernmost French *départe-ment*, climbing up to the Spanish border in a succession of thin-aired high passes which start in alarming but visually exhilarating style on the sheer cliffs above the Mediterranean, and end shrouded in clouds near Andorra. The extreme climate is much better suited to red wine, but there is some quite attractive Côtes du Roussillon white from the Macabeo grape, occasionally improved by a little Malvoisie. There are also about 1½ million bottles of white Vin de Pays des Pyrénées-Orientales which aren't terribly exciting and *must* be drunk very young. The one white wine glory of the *département* is nearer a deep gold in colour – the Muscat de Rivesaltes, full, rich, gooey, winning no prizes for perfume, but thick and grapy nonetheless.

QUARTS DE CHAUME AC
grand cru
CENTRAL LOIRE
Chenin Blanc

Sample a young Quarts de Chaume, and you'd never know that you were experiencing one of the world's greatest sweet wines in its infancy. Whereas most dessert wines at least taste rich right from the start, Quarts de Chaume can be rather nuttily dull, vaguely sweet in a crisp apple kind of way and acidic – above all, acidic. This is thanks to the Chenin grape – the most fiercely, raspingly acidic of all France's great grapes. But on the 100 acres (40 hectares) of gentle slopes protected by a low horseshoe of hills around the village of Chaume, the Chenin finds one of its most special microclimates.

This is the *grand cru* Quarts de Chaume, a little enclave inside the larger Coteaux du Layon AC. (The *quarts* or 'quarters' refer to a medieval landlord's practice of claiming a quarter of the harvest every year.) The vineyards slope south to the little Layon river, and if the sun shines, the grapes – protected from northerly chill – ripen more than any others in the Loire. And as the mists of autumn begin to twine and curl off the river, the magic noble rot fungus – which attacks the grapes' moisture but has the good dietary sense to leave the sugar untouched – concentrates the richness to as great a degree as in Sauternes. And yet the acidity remains proud and unmoved. They have to make several passes through the vineyard to pick only the grapes affected by 'noble rot', and this contributes to Quarts de Chaume having the lowest maximum yield of any AC in France – 22 hectolitres per hectare; in many years they don't even achieve that. The winter often closes in as the pickers toil through the vineyard for a last time, and in the icy cold of the next few months the wine ferments quietly till the spring, when it is bottled.

The result is all fruit and no oak influence. And it lasts for as long as any sweet wine in the world – thanks to Chenin's acidity. It *may* seem dull for its first few years, but after ten the pale gold becomes tinged with orange, the apple sweetness blends with apricot and peach. . . and in the full sunset glow of 20 years' maturity, honey fills out the perfume of the peach – with a bitter twist of nut kernel roughness and the dark, fascinating intensity of quince jelly that herald the beginnings of decline. The wine may then stay in this happy state for another 20 years. Production of this classic is less than 100,000 bottles, and the price is now rising fast as it gains long-overdue recognition, but I reckon something this special is worth paying a decent price for. Best years: 1985, '83, '82, '81, '78, '76, '70, '69, '66, '64, '59, '47. Best producers: Baumard, Bellerive, Echarderie, Suronde.

QUINCY AC
UPPER LOIRE
Sauvignon Blanc

Sometimes Quincy seems to pack more unmistakable Sauvignon flavour into its bottles than any other French wine. I know we're supposed to find gooseberry and asparagus and nettles in Sancerre and Pouilly-Fumé – but those wines have become so popular and the vineyards so burdened with overproduction, that we rarely do. Yet Quincy always reeks of gooseberry and asparagus and nettles – and yes, you guessed, Quincy is *not* popular: in fact you hardly ever see it at all. But if you really want a nostril-full of unashamed Sauvignon, it's worth seeking out.

There isn't much of it, though. The vineyards – clustered along the left bank of the river Cher, just west of Bourges – produce only 450,000 bottles of this intensely flavoured dry white. You can age it for a year or two, but it won't improve, merely become slightly less outrageous. And if I buy Quincy I'm usually in the mood to be outraged! Best years: 1987, '86, '85. Best producers: Jaumier, Mardon, Pichard, Pipet.

RAHOUL, CH.
Graves AC
BORDEAUX
Sémillon

This tiny property at Portets – in the low-lying Graves vineyards next to the Garonne river, and well away from the best sites of Pessac-Léognan – has achieved remarkable renown, given that its 6 acres (2·5 hectares) of vines produce only about 12,000 bottles a year. The explanation lies in its erstwhile winemaker, Peter Vinding-Diers, a Dane who came to Bordeaux in 1978 and during the next ten years proceeded to turn white wine-making ideas upside down. By using stainless steel, cool fermentation, carefully selected yeast strains, and maturation in new oak barrels, he produced wines of such intense pineapple, coconut, apricot and vanilla flavours that the Classed Growth winemakers now look to him as an example of how *they* should be making their wine. And he achieved all this with 100 per cent Sémillon, disdaining the more trendy Sauvignon Blanc and showing that, given the right treatment, the Sémillon can actually make the deeper, more complex-flavoured wine. Rahoul is lovely young but ages beautifully. Best years: 1987, '86, '85, '84.

REUILLY AC
CENTRAL LOIRE
Sauvignon Blanc

I have to admit the reason I first became interested in the wines of Reuilly was because a friend of mine told me there was a grower in Reuilly called Oliver Cromwell. And there was! It took me ages to track down a bottle and when I finally got the cork out I'm afraid it was pretty unmemorable. Even so, at least it had made me find out where Reuilly was and what the wine was made from. Well Reuilly is really in the middle of nowhere – west of Bourges in the featureless but vaguely soothing agricultural land which is typical of the middle of France. The grape they grow is the Sauvignon, and since Sancerre is about 37 miles (60km) to the east, you'd expect a similarity. In fact the very high limestone element in the soil makes good Reuilly extremely dry, but with an attractive nettles, gooseberry nip to the fruit. The best Reuilly is never as good as the best Sancerre, but most Reuilly is better than poor Sancerre, so if you see a bottle do try it – it's cheaper than Sancerre too. Drink within two years. Best years: 1988, '87, '86. Best producers: Beurdin, Cordier, Lafond.

RHÔNE

The Rhône valley is a positively macho red wine region at heart – but here and there whites do pop up and they can be outstandingly good. In the north, on the startlingly steep slopes south of Vienne, the Viognier grape produces minute amounts of sublime wine at Condrieu and Château Grillet. Just south of Hermitage, the Marsanne and Rousanne grapes produce rather solid, still whites and pleasant but hardly frivolous fizz at St-Péray. Much more frivolous, thank goodness, is the Clairette de Die Tradition, grown to the east of the Rhône valley, which is a wonderful hothouse grape – a scented, fizzy mix of Clairette and Muscat. The best dry white of the southern part of the valley is Châteauneuf-du-Pape. Again, there's very little of it, but if drunk really young it can be an exciting zingy wine. White Côtes du Rhône is rarely as good, though the villages of Laudun and Chusclan produce attractive wines, and Châteauneuf-du-Pape's neighbour Lirac can produce lovely stuff. But I suspect the best-known white Rhône is the rich, luscious Muscat de Beaumes de Venise.

RIESLING

Riesling is a German grape and one does wonder whether France's long-standing historical mistrust of Germany has to answer for the Riesling's almost total absence from the French wine scene. It is an important grape in Alsace, a region bordering the Rhine which has twice been under German rule since 1870, and whose traditions in grape-growing are consequently intermingled with those of Germany. Elsewhere in France there is a tiny experimental patch at the Listel mega-winery near Montpellier in the Midi. There is also a technically outlawed plot at the Bordeaux château of Doisy-Daëne in Barsac that makes a floral contribution to the owner's excellent dry white.

Otherwise, nothing. The Riesling is proscribed, banned, beneath contempt and what a pity – it's a great grape variety. As its phenomenal success in the torrid plains of Australia shows, it could offer a tremendous boost in floral perfumes and grapy fruit flavours to many of the duller French whites. Indeed, the Californians often add Riesling to the less good Chardonnay to give it some personality. I've tasted a lot of Mâcon Blanc-Villages recently that couldn't but benefit from such 'outrageous' bending of the laws. So we're left with Alsace, where there are over 5000 acres (2000 hectares), 16 per cent of Alsace's total, and happily most of the best vineyard sites or *grands crus* are at least partially planted with Riesling.

The wine is almost always dry, with a strong lemon and lime acidity, and a green apple crispness when young, which fills out to a strange but exciting richness with a few years' age. The acidity starts to resemble a mixture of lime and the fumes from an open can of petrol, the fruit takes on the flavour of nuts flecked with drops of honey – not enough to make it seem rich, but just the right amount to smooth out its steely cutting edge. Occasionally, late-harvest Vendange Tardive or 'noble rot' Sélection de Grains Nobles wines are made from Riesling and these are bigger, broader, more intense but still not really sweet, and still streaked with the acidity of limes – and what I think of as the beautiful and characteristic pungency of petrol.

RIEUSSEC, CH.
Sauternes AC, *premier cru classé*
BORDEAUX
Sémillon, Sauvignon Blanc, Muscadelle

Apart from the peerless and scarcely affordable Château d'Yquem, Rieussec is often the richest, most succulently self-indulgent wine of Sauternes. If Rieussec has a fault it is that this gorgeous flowing tide of exotic sweet fruit is not always held in check by the stern hand of good acidity. Yet there is such a riot of pineapple and peach and honey to wallow in, that it is difficult not to say – oh, what the hell, maybe it won't last quite as long as d'Yquem or Guiraud or some other leading property, but it's so irresistible that I really couldn't care. In fact the 153 acres (62 hectares), situated on high ground just inside the parish boundary of Fargues, lie alongside d'Yquem and, since the property was bought in 1984 by the Rothschilds of Lafite-Rothschild (Pauillac), I wonder if they are going to try to challenge d'Yquem. In a way I hope not, because the wine is already wonderfully rich and satisfying – and I can just occasionally afford a bottle. I've never been able to afford a bottle of d'Yquem! There is a very rare special selection called Crême de Tête which is quite remarkable, and there is also a dry wine called 'R' which isn't. Best years: 1986, '85, '83, '81, '79, '76, '75.

LOUIS ROEDERER
Champagne AC
CHAMPAGNE
Pinot Noir, Chardonnay, Pinot Meunier

▶Cellars for reserve wine at the Champagne house of Louis Roederer. Reserve wines are wines from different years which are kept back for blending with young wines to make non-vintage Champagne.

This company has the reputation of having the best winemaker in Champagne. Obviously the word's got around, because the chief problem with Roederer is to try to find a bottle which is mature enough for you to experience its full splendour. The number of times I've had Roederer and said – yes, the quality is fabulous, but I wish it had just a little more age – doesn't bear thinking about. But despite that, the quality is extraordinarily good, and the green edges which afflict so much over-young Champagne are soothed and softened here by the spicy ripeness of the fruit. Too young or not, Louis Roederer is frequently my first choice when ordering Champagne.

They also make a big, exciting Vintage, and the famous Roederer Cristal, which comes in a clear bottle originally designed for the Russian tsar, and is usually delicious. Another strong point is that Louis Roederer make the best medium and sweet Champagnes on the market. They need ageing to show their class, but can be rich and honeyed and not at all cloying – quite unlike most sweet Champagnes, which are feeble stuff.

ROSETTE AC
SOUTH-WEST
Sémillon, Sauvignon Blanc, Muscadelle

Hurry, hurry, hurry! Rosette is fading fast. Well, don't give yourself a hernia in the rush, because Rosette isn't *that* splendid, but this tiny AC for semi-sweet wines from the hills just north and west of Bergerac is now down to 20,000 bottles. And each year local pundits predict that *this* is the year the AC will die out completely. Somehow it still hangs on, and the wine can be lightly sweet in a rather whimsical way – as befits an AC which is rapidly becoming a mere afterthought. Best years: 1986, '85. Best producer: Puypezat.

RULLY AC
CÔTE CHALONNAISE, BURGUNDY
Chardonnay

An example of a little-known village hauling itself up by the bootstraps. Rully is the northernmost of the Côte Chalonnaise ACs (though Bouzeron, with its special AC for Aligoté, is further north still), and its vines, covering 620 acres (250 hectares), formerly provided thin light base wine for the village's thriving fizz industry, which meant the village had no real reputation for its still wines.

This all changed in the '70s as the prices of both red and white Burgundy from the Côte d'Or, just a few miles to the north, began to go crazy – not only was there a lot of new planting in Rully, but the bubbly-makers began to bring in their wines from elsewhere, leaving Rully's own vineyards to capitalize on a sudden demand for good quality, reasonably-priced Burgundy. Rully has always made fairly light wines, due to its limestone-dominated soil, but in recent vintages the wines have become fuller, rather nutty, their appley acidity jazzed up by an attractive hint of honey. As some growers also begin to use oak barrels, we should start to see an increasing amount of exciting wine, at a price nearer a Mâcon Blanc-Villages than a Meursault. Some wines sport the name of a vineyard – probably one of the 19 *premiers crus*, but, as is usual in the Côte Chalonnaise, the term *premier cru* doesn't mean a lot. Best years: 1988, '86, '85, '83, '82. Best producers: Belleville, Bêtes, Brelière, Chanzy, Cogny, Delorme, Dury, Duvernay, Faiveley, Jaffelin, Noël-Bouton.

ST-AMAND, CH.
Sauternes AC, *cru bourgeois*
BORDEAUX
Sémillon, Sauvignon Blanc

One of the few non-Classed Growth properties which regularly manages to produce big, rich, classic Sauternes – *and* which doesn't charge the earth. The 54-acre (22-hectare) estate is in the commune of Preignac – right next to the little river Ciron, whose autumn mists have so much to do with the formation of noble rot on the grapes. This may explain why St-Amand consistently makes more exciting wines than several of its Classed Growth neighbours. Although drinkable young it ages well for ten years. It is sometimes sold under the label Château la Chartreuse. Best years: 1986, '83, '81, '80.

ST-AUBIN
CÔTE DE BEAUNE, BURGUNDY
Chardonnay

I sometimes wonder whether St-Aubin isn't in fact the patron saint of that hard-pressed species the white Burgundy lover with limited means, because the wines of St-Aubin – a little village with 300 acres (120 hectares) of vines set well back in the hills from Chassagne-Montrachet – are always delicious, and are never overpriced. It's a great pity that perhaps only one-third of the vineyard area is planted in white grapes – though the red St-Aubin is also very good – because the lean, racy fruit combined with a delicious toasty, biscuity perfume from a little oak ageing makes these wines as good as many Chassagne-Montrachets or Meursaults. Two-thirds of the vineyards are classified as *premiers crus* and they deserve it, with the best ones you're likely to see being Les Frionnes and Les Murgets des Dents de Chien. They're delicious young, but are better after five years' ageing. Best years: 1986, '85, '83, '82. Best producers: Bachelet, Clerget, Colin, Duvernay, Jadot, Jaffelin, Lamy, Lamy-Pillot, Albert Morey, Roux, Thomas.

STE-CROIX-DU-MONT AC
BORDEAUX
Sémillon, Sauvignon Blanc,
Muscadelle

▼Morning mists lift from
Ste-Croix-du-Mont. In autumn similar
mists encourage the growth of noble
rot – vital to the creation of the AC's
sweet wine.

The best of the three sweet wine ACs which gaze jealously across at Sauternes and Barsac from the other – wrong – side of the Garonne. It is directly south of Loupiac and Cadillac (the other two sweet ACs) and the views are magnificent as the vines tumble down what look to be perfectly sited, south-west-facing slopes. But to make great sweet wine, sunshine isn't enough: you must have the clammy, humid autumn days which encourage the noble rot to shrivel your grapes and concentrate their sugar. The little river Ciron running through Sauternes creates these conditions, but the wide Garonne is far less likely to waft morning mists towards Ste-Croix-du-Mont. Even so, the 1050 acres (425 hectares) of vines do occasionally produce splendidly rich wines, but more often the wine is mildly sweet – very good as an aperitif or with hors d'oeuvres, but not really luscious enough for the end of a meal. And those 1050 acres aren't all even trying to produce sweet wine – many growers have switched to dry whites to gain a more reliable income. Best years: 1986, '85, '83. Best producers: Loubens, Barbe-Maurin, Lousteau-Vieil, de Tastes.

ST-JOSEPH AC
NORTHERN RHÔNE
Marsanne, Roussanne

At its best St-Joseph has an astonishing flavour half-way between the peach and apricot headiness of a Condrieu and the buttery richness of a good Meursault. At its worst it is a flat, hollow wine with no fruit or acidity. And somewhere in between is a pleasant, flowery, apple-scented wine for chilling and drinking without too much ceremony at a year old or so.

The worst is simply the result of bad wine-making, and since this is very much a red wine area, only a few growers put much effort into white. The 'in-between' is the result of bang up-to-date wine-making – stainless steel tanks and cool, slow fermentation. Such wines are very good, though not identifiably from St-Joseph as against anywhere else in the Rhône valley.

But the best are the old-style wines, made from low-yielding vines round Tournon and Mauves, matured in old oak and capable of lasting 20 years. They are rich, heavy, scented with sandalwood, woodsmoke and peaches, and tasting of toast and brazil nuts draped in butter caramel – with a strong acidity gnawing at a central kernel of fruit that is as dry yet rich as preserved apricots. Sadly, there aren't many examples of these, especially since the St-Joseph AC – which is centred on the steep slopes of Mauves and Tournon – has been extended to take in flat, characterless riverside land right up to Condrieu, near Vienne. In all less than 100,000 bottles are produced. Best years: 1987, '86, '85, '83. Best producers: Courbis, Florentin, Grippat, Trollot.

ST-PÉRAY AC, ST-PÉRAY MOUSSEUX AC
NORTHERN RHÔNE
Marsanne, Roussanne

The community of St-Péray wears a rather smug, suburban air, and its spread of villas and bungalows identify it as a dormitory town for the city of Valence, directly across the Rhône. So it's a bit of a surprise to discover that a century ago St-Péray was the producer of France's most famous sparkling wine – after Champagne, of course. Sparkling wine is supposed to be lively, vivacious, witty stuff – but not only is St-Péray depressingly suburban, it is also in the hot Rhône valley, and it seems extremely unlikely that the 150 acres (60 hectares) of vineyards which remain can produce the light, acid wine flavoured by fizz-makers.

Well, they can't. The Marsanne and Roussanne grapes make big round wines which undergo the Champagne method of inducing sparkle and turn out as – big round wines with fizz in them! The whole production is only 260,000 bottles, and most of that goes no further than the bars and restaurants of St-Péray and Valence. There is a little still white, which is usually dry and stolid, but which can occasionally be altogether more exciting. Admittedly big and broad, the wine can have a lovely golden feel of nuts and honey, and fruit just touched with the spice of apricots and quince, with a flicker of orange peel at the end. This is Marsanne at its best, and it is too good to make into fizz – but such flavours, I'm afraid, are still very much the exception. Best years: 1987, '86, '85. Best producers: Chaboud, Clape, Juge, Thiers, Voge.

ST-POURÇAIN VDQS
UPPER LOIRE
Tressalier, Chardonnay, Sauvignon Blanc

If you've ever had the misfortune to sample Vichy-St-Yorre, you'll begin to understand the gastronomic distress inflicted upon health-fad tourists taking the waters at Vichy. And you'll agree that the local wine need not be measured against the highest international standards, since after a couple of days spent glugging Vichy water – overpoweringly salty and minerally – even the feeblest brew would be welcomed with open arms.

Well, feebleness isn't the problem at St-Pourçain-sur-Sioule, with about 1000 acres (400 hectares) of vines 15 miles north of Vichy. The wines, although very light, are not short of flavour: it's just that the flavour is generally sharp, rather acidic and infected with a deeply strange smokiness, rather like wet hay trying to catch fire. I can only presume this is due to the local Tressalier grape. I have had wine from 100 per cent Chardonnay which was light and clean and rather attractive, but I'm afraid I'll leave the bulk of St-Pourçain to speed the recovery of the inmates at Vichy. Best producers: Pétillat, Ray.

ST-ROMAIN AC
CÔTE DE BEAUNE, BURGUNDY
Chardonnay

St-Romain tastes more like a Chablis than a Meursault, although Meursault is only a few miles away. The wine is flinty dry, hinting at ripeness but held back by a rather herby, stony personality which can be quite refreshing but is unlikely to charm your socks off. St-Romain is huddled into the rocks at the head of a little valley which runs up, through Meursault and Auxey-Duresses, from the mainstream Côte de Beaune. There really isn't much suitable vineyard land – only 346 acres (140 hectares) out of a possible 5000 (2000) are cultivated, and there are no *premiers crus*. In fact, but for kind officialdom and a certain historical reputation for quality, St-Romain would have had to content itself with the lowly Hautes-Côtes de Beaune AC. As it happens St-Romain is better known for barrel-making than wine, but if you do see one of the 200,000 bottles of white around, it's worth a try – and will probably age well for a good five years or more. Best years: 1986, '85, '83, '82. Best producers: Bazenet, Buisson, Gras, Taupenot, Thévenin-Monthelie.

ST-VÉRAN AC
MÂCONNAIS, BURGUNDY
Chardonnay

Until 1971 the Mâconnais had one star white AC – Pouilly-Fuissé – and then merely a welter of Mâcon-Villages; in the south, there was also a certain amount of Beaujolais Blanc shared with the Beaujolais communes of Leynes, St-Vérand (yes, there *is* a 'd') and St-Amour. It was clear, however that these three villages – and five others tightly grouped round the Pouilly-Fuissé AC – were far better than the general run, more closely resembling the classier examples of Pouilly-Fuissé than the normally anonymous glut of Mâcon-Villages. So in 1971 they were given their own AC – St-Véran – and it immediately came to be thought of as a Pouilly-Fuissé understudy.

Often, however, it is much more than that, because while the best Pouilly-Fuissés are superb, the majority veer between adequate and disgraceful – whereas the overall quality of St-Véran is good and the price is fair. The United States has not caught on to St-Véran as a Pouilly-Fuissé look-alike so it's generally less than half the price. Oak is very rarely used in St-Véran, revealing the gentle Mâconnais Chardonnay at its clearest and best – gentle and very fresh, but with a richness combining bananas, apples, pineapples, peaches and even musky grapes, softened with a yeasty creaminess. All that appears during the first year of the wine's life, and though the wines will age they don't gain a great deal from extra maturity. Best years: 1988, '87, '86, '85. Best producers: Chagny, Corsin, Depardon, Duboeuf, Gregoire, Loron, Lycée Agricole de Davayé, Tissier, Vincent, and the co-operative at Prissé.

SANCERRE AC
UPPER LOIRE
Sauvignon Blanc

Sancerre is such a well-known name nowadays, that I find it difficult to accept that the first wine book I got hold of, less than 20 years ago – a famous and much respected discourse of 300 pages on the wines of France – accorded Sancerre precisely *five* lines. It didn't say what grapes were used, what colour the wines were, what they tasted like, whether they should be drunk young or old. . . Merely five lines to say Sancerre existed. Funny how fashion veers one way then the other!

The omni-thirsty Henry IV – who seems to have done little else but dash about tasting France's fruit of the vine – is on record as saying that Sancerre was the best wine he'd ever drunk and that if all his subjects were to drink it there'd be no more religious wars. Louis XVI said much the same thing a short while before the French Revolution proved otherwise. And then, about 20 years ago, some Paris journalists (always on the lookout for a new fad wine) noticed the high mound of Sancerre rising powerfully above the upper reaches of the Loire, tasted the wines from its steep chalk and flint vineyards, and tore back to Paris with the news – Sancerre was the tangiest, zippiest, super-freshest, ultra-modernest white wine in France and they were 'crazy' about it.

Sancerre mania broke out – firstly with the white, which can indeed be a wonderful refreshing drink, tasting of nettles, asparagus and gooseberries, and

a whiff of brewing coffee, and then with the far less exciting reds and rosés. This is all excellent news for the growers, but Sancerre is now *the* expense account white and consequently is *always* expensive. Since it can provide the perfect expression of the bright green tang of the Sauvignon grape, perhaps we shouldn't complain too much, except that all over France and in Italy, Spain, America, Australia and New Zealand, growers have shown that they too can produce the snappy, high-acid, thirst-quenching whites which Sancerre epitomizes. But even so, a Sancerre from a village like Bué, Chavignol, Verdigny or Ménétréol, made by a good grower in a vintage which wasn't too hot, and drunk before it is two years old, can be one of the most deliciously refreshing white wines of France. Best years: 1988, 87, '86, '85. Best producers: Bailly-Reverdy, Bourgeois, Francis Cotat, Paul Cotat, Daulny, Alain Dezat, Pierre Dezat, Dupuy-Chavignol, Lalone, Merlin, Migeon, Millérioux, Natter, Picard, Roger, Vacheron, Vatan.

SANTENAY AC
CÔTE DE BEAUNE, BURGUNDY
Chardonnay

Santenay produces over 1½ million bottles of wine a year – about 40,000 of them are white. Most of these are drunk locally, since Santenay has a casino – and a spa – to boost demand. The wine isn't bad but that rather earthy – even muddy – lack of definition which affects a lot of the red Santenay is also likely to be present in the white. The best results come from Les Gravières *premier cru* which borders Chassagne-Montrachet, one of Burgundy's top white wine villages. Best years: 1986, '85, '83. Best producers: Lequin-Roussot, Maufoux, Prieur-Brunet.

SAUMUR AC
CENTRAL LOIRE
Chenin Blanc, Chardonnay,
Sauvignon Blanc

You only have to taste the basic still white wine of Saumur to realize why most of it is rapidly transformed into fizz – it is thin, harsh, acid stuff, often showing off the Chenin grape at its graceless worst. The shining exception to this comes from the St-Cyr-en-Bourg co-operative, whose still Saumur Blanc is tart and crisp, but packed with fruit. The locals drink most of it – young and well chilled. Up to 20 per cent Chardonnay or Sauvignon can be blended in.

SAUMUR MOUSSEUX AC
CENTRAL LOIRE
Chenin Blanc, Chardonnay, Cabernet
Franc

For many years the sparkling wines of Saumur – made by the Champagne method since 1811, and for more than a century actually sold as Champagne – were regarded as the natural cheap alternative to Champagne. However, the Chenin base wine doesn't have the ability of Champagne's Chardonnay or Pinot Noir to start harsh and dry yet fill out, after a few years, to something gentle and honeyed. Nor does it pick up the creamy, toasty flavours of the yeast cells which lie in the bottle during the second fermentation, and which are a mark of true Champagne. So you could use it as a substitute for *cheap* Champagne (classy Champagne taste-alikes are Crémant de Bourgogne or Crémant d'Alsace).

Efforts are now being made to produce a rather more charming wine, and the addition of Chardonnay and Cabernet Franc (red but pressed as white) does make for softer, more interesting results. Saumur can be vintage, but is usually non-vintage and the title *Saumur d'origine* is generally used on the label. Best producers: Ackerman-Laurance, Bouvet-Ladubay, Gratien & Meyer, Langlois-Château, St-Cyr-en-Bourg co-operative.

SAUSSIGNAC AC
SOUTH-WEST
Sémillon, Sauvignon Blanc,
Muscadelle and others

Superior *appellation* for Bergerac whites made around the village of Saussignac. The minimum alcohol is 12·5 degrees as against 11 degrees for basic Bergerac Sec, and consequently the wine is richer and broader – and sometimes off-dry. Since most producers opt for the Bergerac Sec AC, Saussignac is relatively rare, with production averaging only 300,000 bottles. Best producer: Court-les-Mûts.

SAUTERNES AND OTHER SWEET BORDEAUX WINES

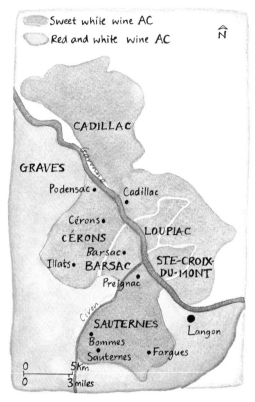

Sweet white wine AC

Red and white wine AC

N̂

CADILLAC

GRAVES

Podensac •

Cadillac

Cérons •

CÉRONS

Barsac •

Illats • BARSAC

LOUPIAC

STE-CROIX-DU-MONT

Preignac •

SAUTERNES

Langon

Bommes

Sauternes • Fargues

0   5km
0   3 miles

▶Poppies bring a blaze of colour to this vineyard at Preignac – the largest of the five villages included in the Sauternes AC.

On the Ciron's east bank lie the vineyards of Sauternes and on its west bank those of Barsac. Adjoining Barsac to the north is Cérons, whose speciality is a light sweet white, but increasingly Cérons vineyards are now producing reds and dry whites (which are not allowed the Cérons AC). On the opposite bank of the Garonne are Cadillac, Loupiac and Ste-Croix-du-Mont whose speciality is also sweet white, but whose vineyards rarely produce anything of the concentration of a good Sauternes.

Sauternes and Barsac produce the most exciting sweet wines because their vineyards are regularly attacked by 'noble rot', a form of fungus which settles on the skins of the grapes and feeds off the water in them. This dramatically reduces the amount of juice, but what is left is a sticky concentration of sugar and glycerol. Noble rot occurs only in the autumn, and needs a mixture of humidity and warmth to take root. In warm autumns, fogs rise every morning off the river Ciron, only to be burnt off later in the day by the sun's heat – the perfect combination. Cérons and the ACs on the Garonne's right bank get these conditions to a much lesser degree.

Noble rot usually strikes late in the autumn, if at all, so storms are an ever-present threat since a couple of days' heavy rain can dilute the juice and bloat the grapes. In some years the whole crop can be ruined. Also, noble rot does not strike consistently. On one bunch, some grapes may be totally rotted, some may be partially affected and some untouched. So the top properties have to go through the vines time after time snipping off only the most affected bunches, or sometimes only the most rotted single grapes on a bunch! Very expensive, very time-consuming. When you realize that a single vine may produce as little as one glass of wine, as against the bottle or more that a producer of dry wine could expect it becomes painfully obvious that we've been underestimating – and underpricing – the great sweet wines of Bordeaux for too long.

Somehow the names Sauternes and Barsac have come to mean sweet gooey wines without much discernible character, to be sold off at a fairly low price to anyone who doesn't like dry wines. This implies that they are easy to make, cheap to produce, and incapable of achieving any memorable personality. Nothing could be further from the truth.

The production of fine sweet white wine is an exhausting, risk-laden and extremely expensive affair, requiring nerves of steel, a huge bank balance, and just the right mix of grape varieties, vineyard sites and local climatic conditions. Bordeaux has half-a-dozen localities where, to a greater or lesser extent, the vineyards and the climate get the balance right.

Greatest of these are Barsac and Sauternes. Just north of the town of Langon, the little river Ciron sidles up from the south to join the river Garonne.

MAIN ACs	De Fargues
Barsac	Gilette
Cadillac	Guiraud
Loupiac	Lafaurie-Peyraguey
Ste-Croix-du-Mont	de Malle
Sauternes	Nairac
	Rieussec
MAIN CHÂTEAUX	St-Amand
Bastor-Lamontagne	Suduiraut
Broustet	d'Yquem
Climens	
Coutet	MAIN GRAPES
Doisy-Daëne	Sauvignon Blanc
Doisy-Védrines	Sémillon

SAUTERNES AC
BORDEAUX
Sémillon, Sauvignon Blanc,
Muscadelle

What marks out this small enclave of vineyards inside the larger Graves AC is the particular susceptibility of its grapes to go rotten before they are picked in autumn. That sounds a bit daft, but I'll explain. If you ripen a grape fully during a good summer, it will have enough sugar to convert to a lot of alcohol during fermentation, but the wine will be dry. Even if you stop the fermentation artificially before it has finished and leave some of the sweetness in, it won't be very intense or exciting. What you need to do if you're going to get a really sweet wine is to have so much sugar in the grapes that the yeasts ferment out as much as they can, yet you are still left with masses of unfermented sugar to provide really rich concentration of flavours to the wine.

That's where the 'rot' comes in. There is a particular sort of rot which attacks grapes and instead of ruining the flavour, eats into the skin, then sucks out the water in the grape, leaving behind most of the sugar, which then gets more and more concentrated, and may end up twice as strong as in a normally ripe grape. They call this the 'noble rot', and though it is difficult to feel anything but revulsion when you see these squidgy, messy grapes on the vine, they make great sweet wine. They may contain up to 25 degrees or more of potential alcohol in their sugar, and since the yeasts cannot work at a higher alcoholic strength than 14 to 15 degrees – all the rest remains as sugar. The result is a wine of high alcoholic strength and deep, mouth-coating richness full of flavours like pineapples, peaches, syrup and spice.

For this rot to develop you need special climatic conditions, alternating humidity and heat. The little river Ciron runs along the northern boundary of Sauternes, and in a good autumn, fog rises off the river in the morning, only to be burnt away by the sun later in the day and there you have it – humidity and heat. Sauternes, and its neighbouring AC Barsac, are two of the only areas in France where this happens naturally (the river Layon in the Loire valley can also achieve it). In some vintages the 'rot' doesn't really develop, and then it is not possible to make intensely sweet wine, although it may still be sold as Sauternes, and can be a pleasant adequately sweet drink. It is always expensive, though, because the permitted yield is extremely low at 25 hectolitres per hectare – about half that of a Haut-Médoc red wine. Good vintages should be aged for five to ten years and often twice as long. Best years: 1986, '83, '81, '80, '76, '75, '71, '70. Best producers: Bastor-Lamontagne, de Fargues, Gilette, Guiraud, les Justices, Lafaurie-Peyraguey, Lamothe-Guignard, de Malle, Rabaud-Promis (since 1983), Rayne-Vigneau (since 1983), Rieussec, St-Amand/Chartreuse, Suduiraut, d'Yquem.

SAUVIGNON BLANC

Sauvignon Blanc's strength and weakness are the same – its uncanny suitability to the mood of the '80s. Its wine is sharp, snapping with green, tangy flavours – fresh mown grass, nettles crushed underfoot, blackcurrant leaves – bright, brash, refreshing and ever so easy to understand. Sometimes the wine is riper and deeper – with flavours of gooseberry, of asparagus, a whiff of roasting coffee carried on the wind – but still the effect remains the same. Which is great for how the world feels now. But 20 years ago Sauvignon Blanc was chiefly known as a dull component of boring Bordeaux Blanc – a less fashionable wine would be difficult to find! And 20 years from now? Well, to be absolutely honest – we may have become bored with it, because the one thing Sauvignon hasn't yet revealed is complexity and extra nuances of flavour. While grapes like Chardonnay, Riesling and Sémillon produce wines which mature into exciting styles unrecognizable from their young manifestations, Sauvignon just tastes the same – older, more tired, less fruity, but basically the same.

Right now, though, it is enjoying unprecedented popularity as *the* easy-drinking white grape, along with Chardonnay. Sancerre and Pouilly-Fumé are its two most famous products, but all along the Loire it is planted to soften the tricky Chenin Blanc, and in Touraine it is frequently seen unblended. Its traditional importance in Bordeaux has been to add zip to Sémillon for both sweet and dry wines, but increasingly Bordeaux Blanc is being produced from 100 per cent Sauvignon. The examples from Bergerac and Côtes de Duras are often more successful, and there is no doubt that the most exciting white Graves and Sauternes are those in which Sauvignon blends with Sémillon. Elsewhere, Sauvignon crops up in the centre of France in VDQS wines like Sauvignon de St-Bris and Sauvignon du Haut-Poitou, and is frequently included in new plantations in the far south to add zing to the heavy, dull whites of the Mediterranean basin.

SAUVIGNON DE ST-BRIS VDQS
CHABLIS, BURGUNDY
Sauvignon Blanc

Success seems to be going to the head of Sauvignon de St-Bris, a little outcrop of Loire flavours next to the Chardonnay stronghold of Chablis. A few years ago this tangy, deliciously sharp, gooseberry-tasting white from the village of St-Bris-le-Vineux, just south-west of Chablis, seemed to be a perfect example of Sauvignon, at a price way below Sancerre and Pouilly-Fumé. The last couple of vintages, however, have brought disappointment after disappointment; full, heavy wines, not entirely clean, and woefully short of zip. And at prices not so far short of Sancerre. Did the wine become too popular too fast? It's happened before in France. Still, if the wines don't start to taste better, they'll become unpopular just as fast again – and then maybe they'll take a little more notice of the price-quality ratio which is basic to a successful wine region. Certainly such erratic quality won't help the wine's claim to AC status, so far denied it because Sauvignon is not a permitted grape in the AC Bourgogne area. Best years: 1986, '85. Best producers: Brocard, Sorin, Tapit.

▼ Coulée-de-Serrant, one of the two Savennières *grands crus*. The tiny AC, on the north bank of the Loire, makes the most elegant dry whites in Anjou.

SAVENNIÈRES AC
CENTRAL LOIRE
Chenin Blanc

Savennières is often hailed as the crowning dry wine glory of the Chenin grape – and there are two vineyards designated *grand cru* which further enhance this theory. But as frequently happens with the Chenin, the wine is so rough and unfriendly when young, and the maturation period is so painfully slow – often

occupying 15 years, sometimes more – that it is difficult to embrace Savennières' undoubted quality in an entirely whole-hearted way. Attempts by one or two growers to produce a more immediately soft and fruity wine aren't entirely convincing either, since a good chunk of baby has been thrown out with the bath water.

The AC's 150 acres (60 hectares) are on perilously steep slopes on the north bank of the Loire, opposite the little river Layon, and production veers between 70,000 and 170,000 bottles – the wide variation is caused by a particularly capricious microclimate. Because Savennières used traditionally to be a sweet wine, the AC laws only allow a very low yield of 30 hectolitres per hectare, and demand a very high minimum alcohol of 12 degrees. This results in much wine having to be declassified to Anjou AC in cooler years.

Young Savennières is totally, gum-judderingly dry – the sensation is of feeling rather than tasting, as the steely, ice-bright wine sweeps over your palate. But they do get there in the end. Even if it takes a decade or two, honey begins to soften the steel, and the creaminess of nuts soothes the gaunt herb-harsh dryness. But even at the peak of maturity, there'll still be an acid freshness – part late-winter flowers and their leaves, part the zesty snap of lemon peel.

The two *grand cru* vineyards have their own ACs. They are Savennières-Coulée-de-Serrant, a 15-acre (6-hectare) plot which definitely makes the subtlest and most refined wine; and another similarly sized block of vines, Savennières-la-Roche-aux-Moines, whose wines are a little lighter, but also extremely good. Best years: 1985, '83, '82, '78, '76, '71, '70, '69, '66. Best producers: Baumard, Bizolière, Brincard, Chamboureau, Clos de la Coulée-de-Serrant, Closel, Épiré.

SAVIGNY-LÈS-BEAUNE AC
CÔTE DE BEAUNE, BURGUNDY
Chardonnay, Pinot Blanc

Savigny-lès-Beaune is an important village with almost 1000 acres (400 hectares) of vines running into the Rhoin valley directly north of the town of Beaune. However, almost all of the 1·2 million bottles are red, with only 40–50,000 bottles of white in an average year. Savigny's reds are fairly lean and light, and this quality is evident in the whites, which aren't terribly impressive when they're young but which, after three to four years ageing, do begin to show a bit of dry, nutty class. Best years: 1986, '85. Best producers: Capron-Manieux, Guillemot, Jacob.

SÉMILLON

Sémillon is a bit like a tennis player who can never win at singles, but comes to life brilliantly at doubles and wins title after title. With a couple of exceptions in Bordeaux – the dry Château Rahoul in Graves and the sweet Doisy-Daëne in Barsac (both of which are 100 per cent Sémillon), all France's best Sémillon-based wines are blended with Sauvignon Blanc. They complement each other perfectly.

Sauvignon Blanc is brash, aggressive, acid to taste, and strongly perfumed. Sémillon on the other hand is inclined to be fat and lumpish, often has a rather oily, viscous consistency, is short on acid, short on perfume, short on freshness. But put these two together and the metamorphosis is dramatic. The Sauvignon benefits immeasurably from the weightier Sémillon, while the latter's lumpishness is transformed into a smooth, waxy, lanolin consistency. And its low acid, flabby fruit is woken by the fresh green-grass Sauvignon and broadens out into a lovely flavour of nuts and honey. All the great *crus classés* in Graves and Pessac-Léognan are based on this formula.

Because Sémillon is a high-yielder, experiments have been going on to draw out more personality from Sémillon – cool fermentation in stainless steel can produce a sharp, Sauvignon-style of white, while fermentation and maturation in oak barrels produces a brilliant array of spice, tropical fruits and honey; most leading Graves are now ageing their wine in oak.

Sémillon has another crucial character trait – it has a thin skin and can rot easily. Normally this would be regarded as a serious disadvantage, but in the Sauternes and Barsac regions, the grape is attacked by a particular type of fungus called 'noble rot' which sucks out the water but intensifies the sugar and acid. The result is the greatest range of sweet wines in the world, most of them made from at least 80 per cent Sémillon (the rest being Sauvignon and Muscadelle). And Sémillon's somewhat neutral character comes through in flavours which are not at all grapy, but are rich with pineapple, peach, syrup, butterscotch and barley sugar. Almost all France's Sémillon is in the south-west, and Bordeaux has so much of it that it ranks as France's second most planted white variety with over 49,000 acres (20,000 hectares). The Bordeaux satellites of Bergerac, Buzet and Duras and, to a lesser extent,other south-west wines make up most of the rest. However, it is also being planted experimentally in the far south to add some flavour to France's most widely planted grape – the tasteless Ugni Blanc.

SEYSSEL MOUSSEUX AC
SAVOIE
Molette, Altesse (Roussette)

Seyssel is the best known of the Savoie villages, mainly because it is the headquarters of the region's sparkling wine industry – and we used to see quite a bit of sparkling Seyssel over here. Now, this really was feather-light, water-white fizz and made a fabulous summer Sunday gulper. But the vineyards of Seyssel are extremely limited – less than 250 acres (100 hectares) of chalky limestone slopes on the banks of the Rhône. However, the ambitions of the local fizzers were distinctly beady-eyed and as sales grew and grew, the use of local grapes dropped and dropped. Finally we were left with heavy, sickly fizz of no style whatsoever – a disgrace to the Seyssel tradition.

Luckily, good sense has now prevailed and real Seyssel Mousseux AC – the lovely sharp peppery bite of the Molette and Altesse grapes smoothed out with a creamy yeast – is back on the market and tasting even better than in its previous heyday over a decade ago. The wines are often released with a vintage date and are worth seeking out. There is a little still white Seyssel AC, from the Altesse grape – very light and slightly floral – but it isn't as interesting as the racy, dry, Altesse whites from Chambéry and the Isère valley further south in Savoie. Best producer: Mollex, Varichon & Clerc.

SMITH-HAUT-LAFITTE, CH.
Pessac-Léognan AC
BORDEAUX
Sauvignon Blanc

Smith-Haut-Lafitte stands as a shining example of what investment and commitment can do to a wine. A few years ago if you asked me to describe a boring Graves style white I'd have said it was sulphury, flabby, fruitless, unrefreshing – just like Smith-Haut-Lafitte. Today, if you ask me to describe the brilliant, exciting flavours which are flowing out of the Pessac-Léognan region, I'd say they're packed with apricot and crunchy grapefruit, sharpened up by a nettly bite and a smoky aroma of roasting coffee, and rounded out with a savoury creaminess rather like *fromage blanc* – just like Smith-Haut-Lafitte!

Before 1985, the wine-making here was pedestrian and uninspired; since 1985 it has taken off and – using barrel fermentation and maturation in new oak – has shot Smith to the forefront of modern Bordeaux whites. I was with a wine merchant at Smith-Haut-Lafitte last year and he was saying he didn't think the export market was ready for this type of wine yet. I beg to disagree. This is pure class and as bang up-to-date as it is possible to be. It's also a smack in the eye for the Burgundians because these wines are better than all but the best Côte d'Or whites – and half the price. So far only 15 acres (6 hectares) – out of Smith-Haut-Lafitte's total of 126 acres (51 hectares) in the commune of Martillac – are planted with white grapes – 100 per cent Sauvignon – although a further 15 acres are planned. Interestingly, the white is not 'classified' since there were no white grapes at all when the Classification was decided in 1959, but the white is now easily outstripping the red for quality. Best years: 1988, '87, '86, '85.

SUDUIRAUT, CH.
Sauternes AC, *premier cru classé*
BORDEAUX
Sémillon, Sauvignon Blanc

Although d'Yquem is universally acclaimed as the greatest wine in Sauternes, its neighbour to the north, Château Suduiraut, is probably the smart money's bet for the role of runner-up. Suduiraut has a fresher, more perfumed quality than the other chief contender, d'Yquem's neighbour to the east, Château Rieussec – and if Rieussec is sometimes more blatantly sumptuous, Suduiraut counters this with a viscous ripeness which coats your mouth as if the whole wine were wrapped in melted butter and cream. Add to this a delicious fruit like pineapples and peaches soaked in syrup, and you can get some idea of the expansive, luscious flavours of which Suduirat is capable.

Strangely, although Suduiraut made excellent wine in the two difficult vintages of '79 and '82, in the two super vintages of '83 and '86 the wine, although good, was less thrilling than I expected. The large 175-acre (70-hectare) estate usually produces about 120,000 bottles, and though delicious at only a few years old, the richness and excitement increases enormously after a decade or so. Best years: 1986, '83, '82, '79, '76.

▼Harvest time at Château Suduiraut. On the horizon is its illustrious neighbour, Château d'Yquem.

TAITTINGER
Champagne AC
CHAMPAGNE
Pinot Noir, Chardonnay, Pinot Meunier

This is a company which is on the up. For many years I was infuriated by the fact that their top of the line Comtes de Champagne Blanc de Blancs was one of the most memorable wines produced in Champagne, while their non-vintage Brut – the one I could afford to buy – was dull, lifeless and extremely short on fun, which is what I'm usually after in a simple non-vintage fizz. Well, there's been a very welcome change of direction. The ordinary non-vintage is now soft, honeyed, beautifully balanced between fresh acidity and spice, and showing the relatively high percentage of Chardonnay the company uses. Comtes de Champagne is a real De Luxe – imaginatively packaged, extremely expensive but wonderfully good, full of honeyed spice and round, creamy softness.

I would have thought that producing a wine as good as Comtes de Champagne would satisfy most Champagne houses, but as is increasingly the case, the marketing men have found a way to create another ultra-de-luxe – this one called Vintage Collection – each vintage in a specially-commissioned modern art bottle. The wines are certainly good, but so far I've found the packaging slightly off-putting.

TOURAINE AC
CENTRAL LOIRE
Sauvignon Blanc, Chenin Blanc

Touraine is the most interesting of the Loire's wine provinces. Yet it is by no means one vast vineyard, since Touraine has long been called the 'garden' of France and the grape has to prove its worth against strawberries, plums, wheat, asparagus, sunflowers – whatever the farmer believes will be the most profitable crop for him. The chief white ACs are Vouvray and Montlouis, where the Chenin grape produces the whole gamut of still and sparkling wines, and Jasnières, where the Chenin again produces what is often called the driest wine in France – with justification!

The actual overall Touraine AC covers a relatively small area round the city of Tours, taking in sections of the Loir-et-Cher, Indre-et-Loire and Indre *départements*. Fairly good wines come from the Chenin (often called Pineau de la Loire here), but the best are from Sauvignon. Dry, tangy, with a light apple and gooseberry fruit and a flicker of nettly acidity, Sauvignon de Touraine can be a good Sancerre substitute at half the price. Less ripe grapes are often used to make Touraine Mousseux sparkling wine, which is often fruitier and more relaxing than the more expensive and better known Saumur.

There are three Touraine villages which can add their own names to Touraine AC on the label. Azay-le-Rideau produces fair quality dry and off-dry whites from south-west of Tours. Mesland, on the north bank of the Loire east of Tours, is better known for reds, but is the home of trailblazer François Girault, whose gorgeous dry white, tasting of apricots and nectarines, shows what *can* be achieved with Chenin, by steeping the skins with the wine before fermentation. And Amboise, on the Loire's south bank just east of Tours, makes mostly red and rosé but some good dry Chenin white (for which I have a romantic attachment since a little cave cut into the chalk cliffs at Amboise was the first wine cellar I ever visited!).

Touraine wines should be drunk in the year following the vintage, though Chenin ones can last longer. Best years: 1988, '87, '86, '85. Best producers: Barbou, Baron Briare, Aimé Boucher, Bougrier, Charmoise, Octavie, Oisly & Thésée co-operative; Pavy (Azay-le-Rideau); Brossillon, Girault-Artois (Mesland); Denay, Dutertre (Amboise).

LA TOUR-MARTILLAC, CH.
Péssac-Léognan AC, *cru classé de Graves*
BORDEAUX
Sémillon, Sauvignon Blanc

A Pessac-Léognan Classed Growth which has positively cultivated its old-fashioned image – both in its sturdy, unforthcoming wine styles and in the simple rustic charm of the peaceful little château, hidden away from the hurly-burly at the southern edge of Martillac. Only 10 acres (4 hectares) of the 57 acres (23 hectares) are planted with white grapes, but these are extremely old, some dating back to the 1920s when white grapes were first planted on the estate.

I always found the wine a bit stodgy, but the wind of change which is sweeping through the Graves has at last brushed away the cobwebs and in 1986 new style vinification and the employment of new oak barrels has created a delicious, long-flavoured, apricoty dry wine. Given that the vines are some of the oldest in the region, yielding small amounts of concentrated juice, La Tour-Martillac will be a property to watch from now on. Best years: 1987, '86.

VEUVE CLICQUOT
Champagne AC
CHAMPAGNE
Pinot Noir, Chardonnay, Pinot Meunier

Widows have featured prominently in the affairs of the Champagne houses, usually recovering from the early death of a husband to take charge of the company and propel it to new heights, but when someone talks of 'The Widow' in Champagne, they are sure to be talking of the Widow Clicquot – Veuve Clicquot. Not only was she Champagne's dominant figure in the very difficult years at the beginning of the nineteenth century, but she invented the process of *remuage* – the last factor in the equation needed to get clear Champagne rather than cloudy. The problem is, to make Champagne fizz, a second fermentation is induced inside the bottle – but this produces loads of sludgy dead yeast cells, which stick to the glass and have to be removed. So Veuve

Clicquot invented an A-shaped frame, with holes on both sides. The bottles are put in neck first and over the weeks turned and tapped against the wood, gradually going from 45 degrees to vertical, upside-down. The sludge has been coaxed on to the cork, and it's a comparatively easy job to whip out the cork and its sludge as you turn the bottle upright. It sounds so simple, but until this *remuage* process was invented, between 1814 and 1818, Champagne had to be shipped out with all the gunge still in it.

Luckily, the Veuve Clicquot wine lives up to the widow's standards. The non-vintage is full, toasty, slight honeyed and quite weighty for a sparkling. With a little age it is a most mouth-filling style. There is also a Vintage which resembles the non-vintage but is even fuller, and a De Luxe called Grande Dame after the original widow, which is impressive stuff – but not the kind of wine to drink if you're just after a celebratory splurge.

VIN DE CORSE AC
CORSICA
Vermentino

▼ The Patrimonio area in the north of Corsica produces some of the island's better wines and can add its name to the Vin de Corse AC.

Corsica has been slower than the rest of southern France to catch on to the white wine-making revolution of squeaky-clean, simple, fresh wines – designed solely as thirst-quenchers for the long, sultry Mediterranean days. Yet the advances in wine-making techniques are tailor-made for the blistering climate of Corsica and its fairly flavourless grape varieties.

The greatest enemy during fermentation is overheating of the juice, as all the aroma and fruit flavour are then, quite literally, boiled off. Overheating also creates the conditions for acetic acid – vinegar – to form. The greatest enemy during storage is, again, too much heat, since it can promote bacterial growth, especially in unclean conditions. All over southern France these problems are being combatted by the use of refrigeration, selected yeasts, controlled temperature fermentation and storage – and the employment of stainless steel instead of wood. The result is that even the hopeless Ugni Blanc grape is producing a fair amount of bland but fresh white for immediate consumption.

Well, Corsica is in desperate need of these modern methods, because it is also cursed with a superabundance of Ugni Blanc, planted to blend with the traditional Vermentino grape – which can produce a fat, rather lush, dryish white if carefully used, but which is more likely to turn out flabby and coarse, due to inefficient, outmoded wine-making. Most of the Corsica ACs employ Ugni Blanc and Vermentino (though the best wines are 100 per cent Vermentino), and interesting results are extremely rare, but Vin de Corse Coteaux du Cap Corse AC, in the far north-east, and Vin de Corse Calvi AC, in

the north-west, can produce fair stuff. Otherwise the Vin de Corse Porto Vecchio AC is the most reliable – if that's the word! However, the most interesting wines are the wood-aged Ajaccio AC from Domaine Peraldi, and experiments by the UVAL co-operatives with more classy French grape types. First sightings of both Chenin and Chardonnay under the Vin de Pays de l'Île de Beauté banner are promising. And if you're in this lovely island, do try the sweet Muscats – especially from Cap Corse and Patrimonio – they're deep, rich grapy wines, but they don't have an AC. Daft. Of the 30 million bottles of Corsican wine produced, about 2½ million are white. Best producers: Leccia, Clos Nicrosi, Peraldi, Torraccia, UVAL co-operatives.

VIN DE L'ORLÉANAIS VDQS
UPPER LOIRE
Chardonnay, Pinot Blanc

Orléans is the vinegar capital of France. Situated on the northernmost point of the Loire's long arc across France, and perilously close to the point where grapes just won't ripen at all, it looks to be a very sound location for such an enterprise! Yet, as recently as the last century, Orleans wine was regarded as one of France's outstanding drinks and it was a favourite of the French court for several centuries. Well, the weather must have been a lot better then because most of the 700,000 bottles produced from 370 acres (150 hectares) on both sides of the Loire are a *very* pale rosé of distinctly fragile constitution. But there are about 60,000 bottles of white made from Pinot Blanc and Chardonnay (here called Auvernat) and, astonishingly, the Clos de St-Fiacre somehow manages to produce one of the most delightful, deliciously drinkable Chardonnays in the whole of France. If the medieval kings were supping this sort of wine, I begin to see what all the fuss was about. Drink as young as possible. Best producer: Clos de St-Fiacre.

VIN DE PAYS DES SABLES DU GOLFE DU LION
LANGUEDOC-ROUSSILLON
Ugni Blanc, Clairette, Marsanne and others

This is a surprisingly important *vin de pays*, spreading right across the coastal reaches of the Hérault, Gard and the Bouches-du-Rhône *départements* between Béziers and Marseille. The most important producer of this *vin de pays*, whose name means 'the sands of the gulf of the lion', is the vast Domaines Viticoles des Salins du Midi operation, which sells its wine under the brand name Listel. The Salins du Midi has a virtual monopoly of the country's salt production, extracted from the marshes of the Rhône delta, and also happens to be the largest vineyard owner in France with a staggering 4750 acres (1900 hectares) out on the sandbars of the Camargue at the mouth of the Rhône. Despite the Mediterranean climate, the company produces the best white *vin de pays* in southern France, employing the usual Ugni Blanc and Clairette, but also getting tremendous results out of Marsanne, Muscat, Sauvignon Blanc and Chardonnay. The wines are best drunk very young, but I stumbled over – literally! – a four-year-old Sauvignon the other day and it was actually better than a six-month-old version I'd recently tasted.

VIN DE PAYS D'OC
LANGUEDOC-ROUSSILLON
Ugni Blanc, Macabeo, Bourboulenc

Pays d'Oc is the historic name for most of the south of France. The locals down here said '*oc*' when you asked them if they wanted a glass of wine and further north in France they said '*oui*'. And on that simple difference of how to say 'yes', France came to be divided. Languedoc – the modern name for much of the south of France – means 'Language of Oc'! So the regional Vin de Pays d'Oc covers the Rhône and Provence as well as Languedoc-Roussillon. However, most wines in the region either have AC or VDQS status, or prefer to use more clearly defined departmental *vins de pays*, such as Vin de Pays de l'Aude for wines made throughout the Aude *département*, or zonal *vins de pays* such as Vin de Pays de la Vallée du Paradis for a specific mini-region in the south of the Aude *département*. Only about ten million bottles declare themselves as Vin de Pays d'Oc; only one million of these are white wine and they are unlikely to be very exciting.

VIN DE PAYS DU COMTÉ TOLOSAN
SOUTH-WEST
Sauvignon Blanc, Sémillon, Colombard and others

This *vin de pays régional* covers the enormous area of the entire south-west, but it is a comment on how the traditional ACs and VDQSs are successfully catering for the needs of both traditional and innovative winemakers that the production only totals 2½ million bottles from what is arguably the most important wine area in France. For example, Bordeaux is covered by the regulations, but all quality wines in Bordeaux are *appellation contrôlée*. Even so, there are large numbers of unplanted but suitable vineyard sites in the south-west, and in particular the opportunity for good clean whites from local varieties like Sauvignon, Sémillon and Colombard must be considerable. As yet it's a label we rarely see but I'm sure we'll see more of it in the next few years.

VIN DE PAYS DU JARDIN DE LA FRANCE
LOIRE
Chenin Blanc, Sauvignon Blanc, Chardonnay and others

What a lovely name for a wine – Garden of France. Well, it's a pretty accurate description because Vin de Pays du Jardin de la France is the regional country wine title for the Loire valley, which has for centuries been regarded as France's market garden. Altogether it covers 13 *départements*; although each one is entitled to its own departmental *vin de pays* title, many of them prefer to market their wines under the 'Jardin de la France' umbrella. Production often exceeds 30 million bottles – mostly white and usually very cheap.

The Chenin and the Sauvignon are the most common grapes, but various growers are exploiting the laxness of the regulations to produce Chardonnay wines (not permitted by Loire ACs), often with excellent results – crisp, a little sharp sometimes, but with the crucial Chardonnay creaminess just enough in evidence. (The Jardin de la France title is particularly useful in the Anjou and Muscadet ACs where the Chardonnay has proved it can ripen well.) These are wines to drink young and the Sauvignons and Chardonnays, in particular, can be very attractive.

VIN DE SAVOIE AC
SAVOIE
Altesse, Jacquère, Chardonnay and others

I look back on some of the things I used to write about Savoie wines – that they were light and wispy, feather-frail, you could taste the snow from the mountain streams – all that kind of thing – and I blush. I said they couldn't travel, I said they were only fit for slaking the thirst after an afternoon spent schussing down the nearby pistes, yes, on and on I droned in a blissful state of inaccuracy. I think the problem was that I'd read lots of other writers who'd all said that kind of thing, and I'd wanted the wines to fit this cosy image.

Well, too bad. They don't. Except for the extremely pallid wines of Crépy, Savoie whites have got loads of taste. The main reason is the Altesse grape (also known as Roussette) – a fiery, spicy variety which was brought from Cyprus in the middle ages and which *may* be related to Furmint, the grape which makes the remarkable Hungarian Tokay. Together with the dullish Jacquère, and the lean but tasty Chardonnay and Aligoté, this is grown on various sites down the embryo Rhône valley between Geneva and Lac du Bourget, and on the south-east and south-west-facing curve of mountain slopes below Chambéry. The result is an intensely fruity white – but it isn't soft, easy fruit, it's grapefruit, it's pepper, it's pear and apricot skins, with high, sharp acid and the twirl of tobacco smoke. Those aren't pale, wispy flavours by any means, and as the price of Sancerre heads through the ceiling, a good Altesse-based Savoie makes an ideal alternative at far less money.

Apart from Crépy and Seyssel, most Savoie wines are simply labelled Vin de Savoie, or Vin de Savoie plus the name of a village. The best of these are Abymes, Apremont, Arbin, Chignin, Cruet and Montmélian. There are few large expanses of vineyard since the vines have to contend with holiday housing, ski-lifts, and fairly intense agriculture – so they tend to sprout up all over the region, whenever there's a south-facing slope not yet nabbed for a ski jump. There are 3700 acres (1500 hectares) altogether, producing about 8·3 million bottles, most of it white. You can age the wines for a year or two, especially those with some Chardonnay in them – but they lose their racy, thrilling snap of tangy fruit, so I can't see any point. There is some good sparkling wine made – light and creamy – but most of that comes under its own AC at Seyssel, although Ayze, south-east of Geneva, also has a reputation for it – and its own AC. Best years: 1988, '87, '86. Best producers: Cavaillé, Monin, Monterminod, Neyroud, Ollivier, Perret, Perrier, André Quénard, Raymond Quénard, Rocailles, Tiollier, le Vigneron Savoyard.

VIN DU HAUT-POITOU VDQS
CENTRAL LOIRE
Sauvignon Blanc, Chardonnay, Chenin Blanc

You've got to relish crisp, zingy acidity to like Haut-Poitou whites, because they are austere, squeaky clean demonstrations of the varietal flavour of each grape – the bare essentials, with not an ounce of spare flesh to soften the blow. Your Sauvignon will be as green and nettly and mouthwateringly tart as it knows how to be; your Chardonnay will out-Chablis Chablis – lean, almost lemony, very refreshing but making no attempt to charm. There is also a little Pinot Blanc, and Chenin, but this doesn't surface as a varietal. Not surprisingly, with this high acid, but characterful style they're having a go at sparkling wine, and their Champagne-method Diane de Poitiers is a great success. Haut-Poitou is always vaguely linked with the Loire, but the vineyards, north of Poitiers, are just as near Cognac. The wines' high-tech taste is matched by the co-operative which completely dominates production; its director, virtually single-handed, restored the vineyard area in the '60s and '70s. In general drink the wines young for that 'snap you awake' effect. Best producer: Haut-Poitou co-operative at Neuville.

VIOGNIER

You might question my sanity in including the Viognier grape as one of France's leading varieties when there are less than 75 acres (30 hectares) planted in the whole of the country and less than 10 acres (4 hectares) in the rest of the world put together. Ah, but never mind the quantity, taste the wine – if you can find any! The vine is an incredibly poor yielder of grapes, producing less than any other dry white wine variety, and the two tiny Rhône vineyards – Château Grillet and Condrieu – which make 100 per cent Viognier wines are some of the rarest and most sought-after labels in the world.

Every year or two I manage to get hold of a bottle of Condrieu, I open it, and the room is swamped with a perfume as meadow-fresh as it is autumn-rich. One writer calls that perfume May-blossom – and I sort of know what he means, because it is like that first exhausted gulp of air as you clamber to the top of a steep hill in spring-time, and' the breeze-blown fragrance of the mountain flowers is heady and intoxicating. Taste the wine and you'll swear it's sweet – but it isn't! That rich fruit is like apricot skins and ripe pears all squashed together and smothered with a fatness almost like fresh yoghurt. Strange? Yes. Special? Very. Viognier also occurs in the Côte-Rôtie, just north of Condrieu, where it can be blended in with Syrah to produce one of France's greatest red wines. *Can* be, but few growers have more than five per cent of it today. The Viognier is also planted in minute quantities in the Southern Rhône, and in the Hérault at Mas de Daumas Gassac but is not as yet producing wine with any noticeable Viognier characteristics.

VOUGEOT AC
CÔTE DE NUITS, BURGUNDY
Chardonnay

Vougeot, ever mindful of its world-famous reputation for red Burgundy, doesn't muck about when it comes to labelling white wine – the Chardonnay vines are actually planted in a little *premier cru* vineyard called La Vigne Blanche (the white vine) and the wine is called Clos Blanc de Vougeot. There are only 9000 bottles produced, from vines just outside the walls of the famous Clos de Vougeot, but the wine is quite good – dry and full, and slow to open up. But at five to six years it is attractively nutty – definitely not just a curiosity in this otherwise totally red wine village. Best years: 1986, '85, '83. Best producer: L'Héritier-Guyot.

VINS DE PAYS

The phrase '*vins de pays*' implies that these are the traditional wines of the country districts of France which have been created and enjoyed for centuries by the locals. The reality is a little different. The vast majority of *vins de pays* are impressively modern and forward-looking. The name *vin de pays* was conceived as a dependable category of French wine only in 1968. Until then, in many parts of the country – especially the far south – there was a serious problem of overproduction of very mediocre wine and no incentives available to the grower to improve quality since all the wines were consigned to the anonymity of the blending vats of various shippers and merchants.

The aim was to encourage quality, and to provide a specific guarantee of geographical origin for the wines. In this the *vin de pays* system follows the example set by the two top quality tiers in French wines (see page 8). In effect, *vin de pays* became the third tier of quality, following similar guidelines.

There are three geographically defined categories, each one becoming more specific. *Vins de pays régionaux* cover whole regions, encompassing several *départements*. There are only three of these and any wine grown in the region may qualify, if desired, for this designation. *Vins de pays départementaux* cover the wines of an entire *département*. There are 35 of these. *Vin de pays de zone* is the most specific category, and relates only to the wines of a particular region. In all these account for about 14 per cent of French wine production.

Yield is higher than for ACs since the *vins de pays* are only beginning to create a reputation and cannot as yet command high prices, and minimum alcoholic strength is generally lower.

The grape varieties are specified to eliminate the worst sorts, but the crucial element here is that excellent varieties excluded from a region's ACs but capable of producing high-quality wine are included. Consequently, for example, we are seeing excellent white Chardonnay from the Loire and Languedoc-Roussillon – a grape variety previously unknown there. Increasingly, *vins de pays* are labelled with the grape variety – and these are now the source of some of France's best-value flavours.

▶ The Ardèche is producing some of the most exciting varietal *vins de pays* in the modern style from grapes – like Chardonnay – not traditional to the region.

REGIONAL WINES	l'Hérault
Vin de Pays d'Oc	Pyrénées-Orientales
Vin de Pays du Comté Tolosan	
Vin de Pays du Jardin de la France	ZONAL WINES
	Coteaux de l'Ardèche
DEPARTMENTAL WINES	Coteaux de Peyriac
Bouches-du-Rhône	Côtes de Gascogne
Charentais	l'Yonne
Gard	Vin de Pays des Sables du Golfe du Lion

VOUVRAY AC
CENTRAL LOIRE
Chenin Blanc

Vouvray is a real one-grape town – the exacting and unfriendly Chenin Blanc dominates the vineyards to the exclusion of any other. But good examples demand patience and understanding from the consumer because it may be ten years or more before they start to reveal the exciting flavours which have created the reputation Vouvray has enjoyed since Roman times. This point is rammed home when you pick up a bottle from a supermarket shelf and the label says, 'It is recommended that this bottle be consumed before the year 2000'! That would have made the wine 17 years old. Is there *any* other wine you might find in a supermarket which sports a label like that? I tried the wine – a Domaine des Bidaudières 1983, and although it was an expertly made wine, attempting to be drinkable as young as possible – enjoying it was still something of an academic exercise!

The excruciatingly high acidity of the Chenin grape is both the main problem with young Vouvray, and also the support system which allows the best examples to last 50 years. The grapes grow in 3700 acres (1500 hectares) of picturesque vineyards east of Tours, on a limestone and chalk clay soil – which yields intensely flavoured juice, but, in cool years when the grapes don't ripen, creates even more acidity. Unripe grapes traditionally go to make Vouvray Mousseux AC, produced by the Champagne method and usually of a high standard. However, the still wines are more exciting. They can be dry – in which case they'll be bitingly sharp to start with, but beautifully rounded out into a dry buttermilk and nuts flavour after ten years or so. And they can be sweet (*moelleux*) – the noble rot occasionally infects the grape late in October and the results are wines of peach and honey soft sweetness but ever-present acidity.

Vouvray's greatest role is as a medium-dry wine. Cheap Vouvray has spoilt our appreciation of this style, but when it is properly made from a single domaine, it will start out with the usual rasping acidity, but slowly, perhaps over 20 years, build up an exciting smoky peach, pears and quince fullness – again kept fresh by an acidity as insistent but tongue-tingling as the skin of a green apple. Such wines are classics – and since no-one seems to want them, some of the cheapest classics on the block. Best years: 1985, '83, '82, '78, '76, '75, '70, '69. Best producers: Bidaudières, Brédif, Foreau, Freslier, Huet, Jarry, Poniatowski.

L'YONNE, VIN DE PAYS
CHABLIS, BURGUNDY
Chardonnay, Aligoté, Sacy,
Sauvignon Blanc

The *département* of the Yonne's chief claim to fame is that Chablis, one of the world's most famous white wines, is grown within its borders. Certainly the Chablis vineyards, Burgundy's most northerly, grouped along the banks of the Serein river about 80 miles (130 kilometres) north-west of Dijon and the Côte d'Or, can produce world-class wine from the Chardonnay grape, but there are several other little areas of historic importance in the Yonne, even if their vineyards have now diminished to such an extent that they are looked on as mere oddities.

The village of St-Bris is well-known for good Chardonnay as well as the Sauvignon de St-Bris VDQS. Chardonnay not grown in Chablis AC vineyards can be sold as Bourgogne Blanc, but such wine may also contain some of the local Sacy grape. Vin de Pays de l'Yonne usually applies to wines from young vines in the Chablis region or wines from Chardonnay, Aligoté, Sacy or Sauvignon which don't qualify for any better category. These are normally very light and rather tart, but can be refreshing in a sharp kind of way on a hot summer's day.

D'YQUEM, CH.
Sauternes AC, *grand premier cru*
BORDEAUX
Sémillon, Sauvignon Blanc

Last but not least. In fact, many people would rate Château d'Yquem as the greatest wine in Bordeaux and maybe even the greatest wine in France. Certainly if we're talking about total commitment to quality and a no-compromise approach to wine-making, you simply cannot fault d'Yquem – supreme example of the majestic sweet wines of Sauternes. In 1855, when Bordeaux was busy classifying wine, d'Yquem was accorded a sort of 'first of firsts' position as against the other famous First Growths like Margaux, Latour, and, of course, several other top Sauternes. D'Yquem's title was *grand premier cru* – Great First Growth – the only wine accorded this title. This shows that d'Yquem was regarded as supreme all those years ago – and its position hasn't changed since.

The vineyard is large – 250 acres (100 hectares), planted with Semillon (80 per cent) and Sauvignon (20 per cent) – but production is tiny, rarely reaching 65,000 bottles. When you note that Château La Tour Blanche – another Sauternes First Growth – manages to produce 65,000 bottles from only 75 acres (30 hectares), you begin to understand the sacrifice for quality which takes place. Only fully 'noble-rotted' grapes are picked – often berry by berry! This means that the pickers may have to go through the vineyard as many as eleven times, and that the vintage doesn't finish till the freezing winter days of December – dark, damp and drear.

Noble rot concentrates the juice but radically reduces the volume. Although the Sauternes AC allows a yield of 25 hectolitres per hectare – which is already very low – at d'Yquem the yield is more like eight hectolitres per hectare. This works out at a glass of wine per vine (a great red wine estate might easily produce a bottle of wine per vine). This precious liquid gold is then fermented in new oak barrels – and left to mature in them for three-and-a-half years, before bottling and eventual release. If the wine isn't at the very least outstanding, and preferably incomparable, it isn't released as d'Yquem. In 1964, '72 and '74 the entire crop was declassified; in '79, 60 per cent and in '78, 85 per cent were refused the Château label.

The result is a frantically expensive wine which nonetheless is in constant demand, because for sheer richness, for exotic flavours of vanilla, pineapple, melons, peaches and coconut, wrapped in a cocoon of honey and cream, then enveloped again in a caramel richness so viscous and lush your mouth feels coated with succulence for an eternity after swallowing the wine. . . for all that, and for an ability to age a decade, a generation, a century even, when the wine will be deep dark brown, barely glinting with gold, and will taste of orange chocolate, butterscotch, barley sugar and caramel – for all that. . . no wine in the world can touch d'Yquem. Best years: 1986, '83, '81, '80, '76, '75, '71, '67, '62.

◀ Château d'Yquem, the most prestigious producer in Sauternes, also makes a dry white wine, called 'Y', which can only qualify for the Bordeaux Blanc AC.

BOTTLES, CORKS AND LABELS

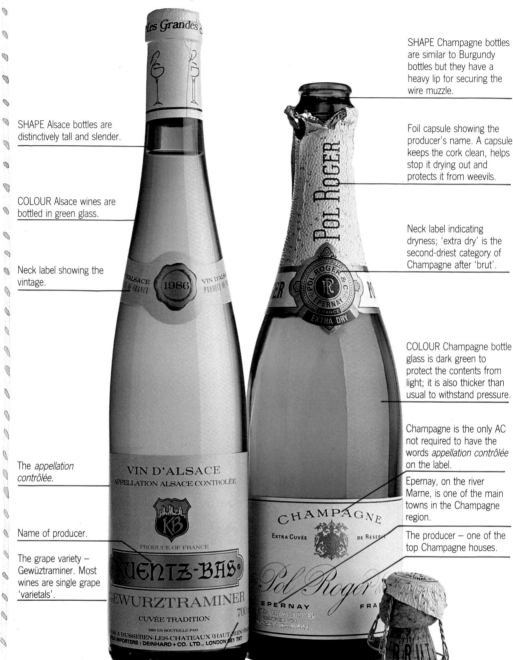

SHAPE Alsace bottles are distinctively tall and slender.

COLOUR Alsace wines are bottled in green glass.

Neck label showing the vintage.

The *appellation contrôlée*.

Name of producer.

The grape variety – Gewüztraminer. Most wines are single grape 'varietals'.

Bottle contents. Although 700ml (70cl) is traditional to Alsace, the EEC is standardizing bottle size to 750ml (75cl).

SHAPE Champagne bottles are similar to Burgundy bottles but they have a heavy lip for securing the wire muzzle.

Foil capsule showing the producer's name. A capsule keeps the cork clean, helps stop it drying out and protects it from weevils.

Neck label indicating dryness; 'extra dry' is the second-driest category of Champagne after 'brut'.

COLOUR Champagne bottle glass is dark green to protect the contents from light; it is also thicker than usual to withstand pressure.

Champagne is the only AC not required to have the words *appellation contrôlée* on the label.

Epernay, on the river Marne, is one of the main towns in the Champagne region.

The producer – one of the top Champagne houses.

The 'mushroom' cork is traditional to Champagne. A metal cap covers the top of the cork to prevent the wire muzzle cutting into it.

120

You can learn something about a wine simply by looking at the bottle – certain regions have traditional shapes and colours (which have often been adopted by similar style wines in other parts of the world). And you can learn a great deal more by understanding the label, which carries a range of essential information, some of it required by law, and some at the discretion of the winemaker or *négociant*.

COLOUR In Bordeaux, clear glass is used for sweet wines such as Sauternes, and also for some dry whites. Green glass always denotes a dry wine.

SHAPE The traditional Bordeaux bottle has high, square shoulders.

The wine-producing estate.

First Growth, as listed in the 1855 classification of Sauternes properties.

Vintage.

Appellation contrôlée.

COLOUR Unusually dark for a Burgundy bottle. A lighter, olive-green is more standard.

SHAPE The classic Burgundy bottle has low, sloping shoulders.

Neck label with vintage and producer's name.

The village name – Puligny-Montrachet is world famous for its *grand cru* wines as well as its own village label.

Bottle contents.

Name of producer.

SERVING
AND STORING
WINE

STORING Wine can stand up to a fair amount of ill-treatment, but there's no doubt we have a better chance of really enjoying it if we treat it with at least a modicum of consideration. After all, a decent wine is a living thing, it is evolving, undergoing physical change in the bottle, both as a reaction to movement, temperature, light, even noise, and as a natural part of the ageing process. Indeed, if there is a general rule it is that the older a bottle of wine the more you must cherish it and involve it in the minimum amount of stress. A really young bottle can bounce about in the car for days, almost bake to death on the back seat, then almost freeze to death in the fridge – and still taste reasonable, not good and not to be recommended, but reasonable.

So. A few guidelines. White wines in general do not benefit from ageing as much as reds, and many light fruity whites from Alsace, the Loire, Entre-Deux-Mers, and the Mâconnais may well lose their freshness if kept for more than a few months. However, the fuller type of Alsace wines, Chablis and Côte d'Or Burgundy, the leading Loire wines from the Chenin grape, and top Graves, Barsac and Sauternes, can all age superbly, and often improve dramatically with a few years' storage.

If you do have a cellar – fantastic, I'm green with envy for a start! If not, let's try to simulate one. A good cellar is dark, quiet, even in temperature and may be very slightly humid. So look for nooks and crannies in the house – a broom cupboard, or an under the stairs space. Put in a few racks, or alternatively store the wine in cardboard boxes – but most important – store the bottles on their *sides*. This will stop the cork drying out, and the air getting in and turning the wine to vinegar.

The *actual* temperature is less important than the stability of temperature, but cool *is* best; 10–12°C is reckoned ideal, and the cooler you store, the slower your wine will mature. But that's cooler than most families would tolerate – so go for a compromise – as *stable* as possible, not in a steamy kitchen and not next to the central heating radiators or hot water tank.

SERVING White wine doesn't need to be decanted – though it can look lovely in cut glass – but the temperature will affect the flavour. One rule of thumb is the cheaper the wine, the colder it should be! For wines that you're actually proud of serving, don't chill them too much, and do it gradually. Half an hour in the deep freeze is not so good as two hours in the refrigerator. Sparkling wines *can* be chilled right down, because it preserves the bubble in the wine. Sauvignon wines from the Loire and Bordeaux can take two–three hours in the fridge because of their green acid edge; Muscadet can take the same kind of treatment. Alsace wine and sweet wines start losing their perfume if you give them more than two hours chilling, and good Burgundies and white Rhônes really shouldn't have more than about an hour or so because they begin to lose their attractive round nuttiness. If you *do* want to chill a wine down in a hurry – fill a jug or bucket with ice *and* water – you'll be amazed at how quickly the wine's temperature drops!

TASTING Well, we're going to drink it rather than swish it round our mouths and spit it out like wine buffs do. But take a moment to look at the colour – some wines have a lovely hue – and do register the smell, which is very often memorable. Then take a decent mouthful, and hold the wine in your mouth for a few moments, breathing through your nose. As the wine warms up in your mouth and the aromas rise into your nasal cavity, you'll get at least ten times the pleasure than if you'd just glugged it back!

FOOD The wonderful thing about white wine is that it's a do-anything, go-anywhere, anytime kind of drink. You can enjoy it with or without food, before, during and after a meal, and, to be honest, it'll go pretty happily with almost any dish you can think of. OK, I suppose a dry, light Muscadet isn't exactly going to titillate the tastebuds parked up against a Black Forest gâteau and a light Bordeaux Blanc is going to get pretty wolloped in a fist-fight with a vindaloo, but, in the main, white wine is wonderfully adaptable.

So let's see what might go best with what. These are a few guidelines based on what I personally find works best – but if you want to drink Beaujolais with

your sea bass, or Muscadet with your mutton – fine! I may well join you.

First, Champagne is the perfect aperitif. It gees you up, makes you feel special and perks up the appetite no end. If you want to drink it right through your meal – and you can afford it – do just that.

Light food is generally better with light wine, because the delicate flavours, say, of seafood can easily be overpowered by a big Meursault. And the salty tang of oysters and mussels *will* clash with a strong-flavoured wine. So a good Muscadet or Entre-Deux-Mers is often the best wine to serve with a starter. If you've got a meaty first course – pâté, charcuterie – I'd go for Alsace whites every time. And I find that salads go best with Sauvignon wines, and for the slighty fatty flavours of eggs and cooked cheese, sparkling wines would again be my choice.

Grilled fish is delicious with Chablis, Sancerre or, again, a good Muscadet. Fish with a rich sauce needs a weightier wine, and Côte d'Or white Burgundies, top-quality Graves or white Châteauneuf-du-Pape are best. Chicken and port *both* go well with white wines - especially Alsace Pinot Gris and Gewürztraminer, and full-bodied wines from the Chardonnay grape. Beef, lamb and game are best with red wines, but big Chardonnays and Alsace wines are pretty good, too.

As for desserts – Sauternes, Muscat de Beaumes-de-Venise or the lovely Clairette de Die Tradition fizz are spot on. And, contrary to the usual belief that red wine is best with cheese, white is usually better, and sweet whites are best of all with the palate-blasting efforts of a Roquefort or a Stilton.

Vintages

ALSACE	88	87	86	85	84	83	82	81	80	79
Alsace Grand Cru	8⌂	6●	5●	10●	4★	10●	5★	7★	4⌄	6⌄
Vendange Tardive	7⌂	5⌂	5⌂	9⌂	3★	10●	-	-	-	-
BORDEAUX	88	87	86	85	84	83	82	81	80	79
Bordeaux Blanc	9●	7★	8★	7⌄	5⌄	8⌄	6⌄	7⌄	4⌄	7⌄
Graves/Pessac-Léognan	9⌂	7●	8●	7★	6★	8★	7★	7★	4⌄	8⌄
Sauternes	7⌂	4⌂	10⌂	6⌂	4★	9⌂	5★	6★	6★	5★
BURGUNDY	88	87	86	85	84	83	82	81	80	79
Bourgogne Blanc	8●	6●	9★	7★	4⌄	7⌄	7⌄	5⌄	4⌄	6⌄
Chablis	7⌂	8●	9●	8★	6★	8★	6⌄	8★	4⌄	5⌄
Côte de Beaune	8⌂	7⌂	10●	8●	6★	7●	7★	5★	4⌄	7⌄
Côte Chalonnaise	7⌂	6⌂	9●	8●	5★	7★	7★	5⌄	4⌄	7⌄
Mâconnais	8●	7★	9★	8★	5⌄	8⌄	6⌄	7⌄	4⌄	6⌄
CHAMPAGNE	88	87	86	85	84	83	82	81	80	79
	8⌂	4⌂	7⌂	9⌂	2●	8⌂	9●	6★	4★	8★
LOIRE	88	87	86	85	84	83	82	81	80	79
Muscadet	8★	9★	8★	7⌄	7⌄	6⌄	6⌄	7⌄	5⌄	6⌄
Sancerre	8●	7★	9★	6★	7★	8⌄	5⌄	8⌄	4⌄	5⌄
Vouvray	8⌂	6⌂	7⌂	9⌂	4⌂	9⌂	7●	6●	4●	6★
Bonnezeaux	7⌂	5⌂	6⌂	10⌂	4⌂	9⌂	7●	5●	4★	6●
RHÔNE	88	87	86	85	84	83	82	81	80	79
Hermitage	9⌂	8⌂	7⌂	8⌂	6●	9⌂	8●	6●	6★	7●
Condrieu	8●	6●	7★	9★	7★	9★	7⌄	7⌄	6⌄	7⌄
Châteauneuf-du-Pape	8●	6★	8★	7⌄	5⌄	7⌄	6⌄	8⌄	7⌄	6⌄

HOW TO READ THE CHART ⌂ = not ready ● = just ready ★ = at peak ⌄ = past its best

The numerals represent an overall rating for each year, bearing in mind that such measures can only ever be broad generalizations. There will be many variations with individual wines and producers.

GLOSSARY

ACIDITY Naturally present in grapes, it gives white wine a refreshing tang.

AGEING Essential process for fine wines. It usually takes place in wooden barrels then often continues in bottles and can last months or years.

ALCOHOLIC CONTENT Alcoholic strength of wine, usually expressed as a percentage of the total volume.

ALCOHOLIC FERMENTATION Process whereby yeasts convert grape sugars into alcohol.

APPELLATION D'ORIGINE CONTRÔLÉE Official designation guaranteeing a wine by geographical origin, grape variety and production method; abbreviated as AC or AOC.

BLANC DE BLANCS White wine, especially Champagne, made only from white grapes. The rarer *blanc de noirs* is white wine made only from black grapes.

CAVE French for 'cellar'.

CHAMPAGNE METHOD Traditional way of making sparkling wine by inducing a second fermentation in the bottle.

CHAPTALIZATION Legal addition of sugar during fermentation to increase alcoholic strength.

CLOS Term for a vineyard that is (or was) wall-enclosed; traditional to Burgundy.

COMMUNE Village. Many French *appellations contrôlées* are based round the produce of a single commune.

CO-OPERATIVE Winery run collectively by growers.

CÔTES, COTEAUX Slopes. Hillside vineyards generally produce better wine than low-lying ones.

CRÉMANT Champagne-method sparkling wine from Alsace, Burgundy and the Loire. In Champagne, applies to wines purposely produced with less bubbles.

CRU French for 'growth'. Used to describe a single vineyard, normally with an additional quality reference as in *grand cru*.

CRU CLASSÉ Literally 'classed growth', indicating that a vineyard is in the top-quality rating system of its region.

CUVE CLOSE Method of making sparkling wine in which the second fermentation takes place in closed tanks.

DOMAINE Estate, especially in Burgundy.

ÉLEVAGE Term covering all wine-making stages between fermentation and bottling.

ESTATE-BOTTLED Wine bottled on the premises where it has been made.

FINING Clarifying wine by adding coagulants, traditionally egg-whites, to the surface. As these drop through the wine they collect all impurities.

LEES Coarse sediment – dead yeasts, etc – thrown by wine in a cask and left behind after racking.

NÉGOCIANT Merchant or shipper who buys in wine from growers, then matures, maybe blends and bottles it.

NOBLE ROT The *botrytis cinerea* fungus which, in warm autumn weather, can attack white grapes, shrivel them and thus concentrate the sugars to produce quality sweet wines such as Sauternes.

OAK Traditional wood for wine casks. During ageing it gives flavours, such as vanillin and tannin, to the wines.

OXIDATION Over-exposure of wine to air causing bacterial decay and loss of fruit.

PÉTILLANT Semi-sparkling wine.

PHYLLOXERA Vine aphid which devastated viticulture worldwide in the late 1800s. Since then, the vulnerable European *vitis vinifera* has been grafted on to phylloxera-resistant American rootstocks.

RACKING Clarification of wine by transferring it from one barrel to another, leaving sediments behind.

SECOND WINE Wine from a designated vineyard sold separately from the main production, under a different name, for a variety of technical reasons. Usually lighter and quicker-maturing than the main wine.

VENDANGE TARDIVE High-quality wine from Alsace, sometimes sweetish, made from late-picked grapes.

VIN DÉLIMITÉ DE QUALITÉ SUPÉRIEURE Second category of French quality control for wines, below AC; abbreviated as VDQS.

VIN DE PAYS French 'country wine'. Third and bottom category for quality, but includes some first-class wines which don't follow local AC regulations.

VIN DOUX NATUREL Sweet wine fortified with grape spirit; abbreviated as VDN. Mostly from the Midi.

INDEX

A page reference in italics indicates main entry.